Who Should Read

D0208082

This book is not just for Jewish people. It is for non-Jews and Jews alike—anyone who is open to healing and to recovery-oriented teachings that can be gleaned from the Bible and the teachings of Jewish tradition.

✓ People who want to enrich their understanding of the Twelve Steps with teachings based on Scripture, as seen through the prism of the Jewish holiday cycle and the calendar.

✓ Everyone facing the struggles of daily living who looks for insight and guidance from the Bible and Jewish tradition as a source of faith, strength, hope, and healing wisdom.

✓ People in Twelve Step recovery programs.

✓ Alcoholics and drug addicts, compulsive gamblers, those with eating disorders and sexual addictions—and the people who care about them.

✓ Individuals who seek an authentic spiritual foundation for holy living based in sacred text and the rhythm of the Hebrew calendar.

✓ Rabbis, priests, and ministers—clergy who want to offer spiritual guidance to congregants and parishioners.

✓ Psychiatrists, psychologists, therapists who seek a religious dimension to the counseling context.

✓ Codependents who now live in or grew up in dysfunctional families.

✓ Jews and non-Jews from all walks of life.

✓ Jews whose spiritual awakening might lead them to take a fresh, mature look at the religion of their birth.

✓ Anyone who read any of the books in the Jewish Lights Publishing Recovery Series including:

  • *Twelve Jewish Steps to Recovery: A Personal Guide for Turning from Alcoholism and Other Addictions*

  • *Renewed Each Day: Daily Twelve Step Recovery Meditations Based on the Bible*

  • *Recovery from Codependence: A Jewish Twelve Steps Guide to Healing Your Soul*

100 Blessings Every Day

Daily Twelve Step Recovery Affirmations, Exercises for Personal Growth & Renewal Reflecting Seasons of the Jewish Year

Rabbi Kerry M. Olitzky

with selected meditations prepared by
RABBI JAMES STONE GOODMAN, DANNY SIEGEL,
& RABBI GORDON TUCKER

Foreword: Are The Twelve Steps Jewish?
by Rabbi Neil Gillman, Associate Professor of Philosophy,
The Jewish Theological Seminary of America

Afterword: Spiritual Renewal in
the Jewish Calendar
by Sir Jay M. Holder, D.C., M.D., Ph.D.
Founder/Medical Director, Exodus Treatment Center

100 Blessings Every Day: Daily Twelve Step Recovery
Affirmations & Exercises for Personal Growth & Renewal
Reflecting Seasons of the Jewish Year
Copyright ©1993 by Kerry M. Olitzky

Library of Congress Cataloging-in-Publication Data
One hundred blessings every day: daily twelve step recovery affirmations
& exercises for personal growth & renewal reflecting seasons of the Jewish
year/by Kerry M. Olitzky; with selected meditations prepared by James
Stone Goodman, Danny Siegel, and Gordon Tucker; foreword by Neil
Gillman; afterword by Jay Holder.

     p.   cm.
ISBN 1-879045-30-3: $14.95
1. Twelve–step programs — Religious aspects — Judaism —
Meditations. 2. Fasts and feasts — Judaism — Meditations.
3. Compulsive behavior — Religious aspects — Judaism. 4. Substance
abuse — Religious aspects — Judaism. I. Goodman, James Stone.
II. Siegel, Danny. III. Tucker, Gordon. IV. Title V. Title: 100 blessings every day.
BM538. T850435 1993
296. 7'2 —dc20   93–9090
                                                                    CIP

First edition
10 9 8 7 6 5 4 3 2 1
Manufactured in the United States of America

Published by JEWISH LIGHTS Publishing
A Division of LongHill Partners, Inc.
P.O. Box 237
Sunset Farm Offices, Route 4
Woodstock, Vermont 05091
Tel: (802) 457-4000 • Fax: (802) 457-4004

For Rabbi Norman J. Cohen,
teacher, colleague, and friend

Contents

How to Use This Book

While this book provides the reader with its own unique blend of inspiration and affirmation, it also serves as a guide to the Jewish calendar, the annual cycle of holiday observances and special Sabbaths. As a result, it provides you with a guide to the rhythm of Jewish living, using the familiar one-day-at-a-time format. Since the Hebrew calendar is soli-lunar, it does not precisely follow the secular calendar which is solar. Different adjustments are made each year according to a traditional rabbinic formula to bring the two in line. This is done through a variation of 29- or 30-day months and an addition of a second month of Adar during leap year.[1]

You might choose to read this book one day at a time, one week at a time, or one month at a time. Whatever you decide, all we ask is that you keep on reading. You might find it helpful to coordinate your reading of this volume with *Renewed Each Day: Daily Twelve Step Recovery Meditations Based on the Bible* (Jewish Lights Publishing, 1992).

Texts generally have been chosen from the liturgical, scriptural, or talmudic material relevant to the particular day, especially when it is a festival or fast. Other sources, including the voices of modern and contemporary texts, have been selected which reflect the themes of the months, as well.

---

1 The basic calendar, to be used in a typical year, may be found on page xxix.

Acknowledgments

Like the other books in the Recovery Series published by Jewish Lights Publishing, the contents reflect the work of many people. To all of them named and anonymous, I express my thanks. As one elderly woman told us when she asked us to send a copy of *Renewed Each Day* to her grandson whom she feared was lost, struggling with his drug addiction, "It is one Jewish soul helping another." I thank God for the opportunity to do such work in this world.

I also thank Aaron Z. with whom I wrote *Renewed Each Day*. Our conversations and his recovery insights are certainly present in many pages of this volume. And to the following people who read page after page, helping me to make sure that I captured the essential message of Jewish life and living on each calendar page: Rabbis David Ellenson, Emily Feigenson, Neil Gillman, Ron Isaacs, Eric Lankin, Steve Rosman, Susan Stone, and Bernard Zlotowitz; and Arlene Chernow, Dr. Robert Deutsch, David Kasakove, and Harriet Rossetto. I also want to thank my editor Jeanne Engelmann for helping me to make sure that I said what I want people to hear. And thanks to the caring people at Hazelden's publishing activity who brought her to us and who work so hard to heal the world.

I have the opportunity to work, study and teach at Hebrew Union College-Jewish Institute of Religion in New York. It is not a privilege which I take lightly. There

I am provided with a sacred environment that allows me the freedom and support to stand on the shoulders on those who came before me and to try to reach higher. I share my ideas with them and they share their strength with me. To Alfred Gottschalk, president; Paul Steinberg, vice president; and Norman Cohen, dean, go my grateful appreciation. Without their constant encouragement, my work would not be possible.

When the publishers at Jewish Lights articulated their vision to me some years ago, they promised that together we could change the direction of Jewish publishing and, in doing so, the Jewish community. And they were right. I am honored to work with them, and to learn from them: Stuart and Antoinette Matlins, colleagues and cherished friends. To the entire staff at Jewish Lights Publishing, I express my abiding admiration, appreciation, and respect. They are makers of dreams, helping to take an abstraction and help make it real. Thanks to Rachel Kahn, whose creative skill as a designer of radiant books draws people to the message, and to Carol Gersten and Jay Rossier, who get the message out so that people can hear it.

More than anything else, I acknowledge the presence of God in my life and the life of my family whose healing made my wife Sheryl's recovery from cancer possible. Praised are You Adonai who heals body and soul—and delivers us all.

Kerry M. Olitzky
New York, New York
Pesach 5753

Preface

The Jewish calendar has a melody, a rhythm of its own. It reflects the soul of the Jewish person and the Jewish people. Called a soli-lunar calendar, it follows the lunar cycle and gets adjusted by the solar seasons. Sometimes it meshes easily and smoothly with the solar calendar. At other times, it feels disjointed—holidays are "late" or "early," never "on time." But it is the way Jewish people divide time and live their lives. The holy days and the events of Jewish history color the calendar with rich hues, throwing lavish blotches of color on each day of the month.

Likewise, the calendar may not always be "in sync" with the seasons of our own life. We have crises, passages, get stuck along the way, even at times when the season says otherwise. Plumb the depths of your life. Find its place now on the calendar and begin there. That's the beauty of the Jewish calendar. We can all find our place in time and then we all can cycle back through it together. It's what helps to anchor us in the world.

In this volume are the thoughts of many people, those who have found their places on the calendar, teachers and students, and those in recovery. For all of us, it is the calendar of the Jewish people wandering through the barren desert, the *midbar*, laboring to find our way home to the Promised Land for ourselves and, symbolically, for all people.

Are the Twelve Steps Jewish?

A Foreword by Rabbi Neil Gillman,
Associate Professor of Jewish Philosophy,
The Jewish Theological Seminary of America
New York, New York

*E*very rabbi is intimately familiar with the sense of despair caused by a certain kind of question, posed in all innocence, usually over a cup of coffee at some synagogue reception. Typically, the question takes this form: "Rabbi, is such-and-such Jewish?" For the "such-and-such," substitute meditation exercises, the resurrection of the dead, transmigration of souls, original sin, the existence of angels and an infinite number of other possibilities. We feel despair because it is nearly impossible to answer such a question in the context of a momentary social interlude. What is required is nothing less than a long lecture on the fundamental nature of the Jewish religion itself.

This "Is it Jewish?" question sees Judaism as a neatly defined system of beliefs and practices. It assumes that Judaism has explicit, agreed-upon boundaries which clearly mark what is in and what is out, what is Jewish and what is not. Nothing is further from the truth. If anything, the more we know about the development of Judaism throughout its history, the more fluid the Jewish system appears. Perhaps our predecessors, only a few decades ago, could speak with some confidence of a core tradition (which they called "normative" or "classical") around which circulated currents that seemed to be more marginal or peripheral. However, that distinction has become highly suspect in our day.

To the question "Are the Twelve Steps Jewish?" then, the only accurate answer is: "Yes. There are certain ancient and authentic Jewish texts and traditions that are reflected in the Twelve Steps. Yet, it is also true that one can find equally ancient and authentic texts and traditions that would call such a statement into question. So it depends on how you understand Judaism, or which variety of historical Judaism you identify with."

Overall, from the broadest possible perspective, there are two striking parallels between the underlying assumptions of the Twelve Steps and Judaism. First, both the Twelve Steps and Judaism emphasize community. Jewish people never confront God alone but always in the context of, and through the medium of, the Jewish community. Our liturgy is formulated in the plural. Our significant ritual moments traditionally require the presence of a *minyan* of ten Jews. The *minyan* functions simply as the entire Jewish people in microcosm. Each of us gains his or her identity within our community. The second parallel: Judaism's emphasis on the need to structure our life experience. The all-encompassing character of *halacha* (Jewish law) and its concern with disciplining the most minute dimensions of our daily lives is probably the most distinctive characteristic of Jewish religion.

This characteristic is also explicit in the Twelve Steps. The addicted person too depends on the group experience. It is within the fellowship that he or she finds the support, understanding and resources to transform his or her life experience. And the Twelve Steps are indeed the addicted person's *halacha*, the carefully delineated discipline that must be attended to, moment by moment, day by day, throughout the rest of one's life—if one is to enjoy an authentic or fully human life experience. They represent the prescriptions through which we bring cosmos out of the chaos that was, in active addiction, the addicted person's characteristic life experience. And if, as some definitions would have it, the primary function of religion in general is precisely to bring cosmos out of chaos, to bring order and structure out of the incipient anarchy that is our typical life experience, then the Twelve Steps accomplish this purpose with astounding success.

Of the many reasons that are advanced for the characterization of the Twelve Step program as intrinsically non-Jewish, most are easily dismissed. A.A. groups do not have to meet in churches. The Lord's Prayer does not have to be recited at the end of a group meeting; the Serenity Prayer or the Twenty-third Psalm can be, and have been, substitutes.

More serious is the charge that the implicit ideology and theology of the Twelve Steps betrays its Christian bias. It is this charge that we must address here.

Our broader claim is that much of what we know today as Christian has solid roots in early Judaism. The formative years of Christianity took place within a thoroughly Jewish communal context. Jesus was a Jew, and so were his apostles and the first generation of his followers. And so was Paul (originally Saul) of Tarsus who is commonly credited with having formulated the essential belief-structure of Christianity. The Twelve Steps may appear to us now to reflect a Christian bias, but this is because they nurse from a strand of Christian thinking which is itself rooted in early Judaism. More specifically, Christianity reflects one of the many strands of Jewish religious expression that were in vogue in the first two centuries of our era.

To allow this charge to go unchallenged, then, simply strengthens the Jewish addicted person's intuitive need to deny his or her addiction and to resist taking the steps necessary to resolve it. It robs the Jewish community of a singularly valuable and effective resource to deal with a problem which, we all now admit, is very much a Jewish problem as well.

We now turn to a distinction elaborated by the late Professor John Herman Randall Jr. with whom I studied philosophy of religion at Columbia University some decades ago. In a seminal footnote in *The Role of Knowledge in Western Religion* (reprinted in 1986 by University Press of America, p.131), Randall distinguishes between what he calls "the temper of humility" and "the temper of humanism" in religion.

In religion, theology and anthropology—our image of God and our image of the human person—are tightly intertwined. Thus, these two tempers can be understood from both of these perspectives. The temper of humility accentuates God's sovereignty and power and our own corresponding nothingness and dependency on God. The temper of humanism accentuates human dignity and strength and God's corresponding vulnerability and dependency on us. In the Bible, the first creation story in Genesis 1 reflects the temper of humility. God is portrayed in terms that accentuate God's majestic and distant sovereignty. God simply speaks, and the world comes into being. In the second creation story (Genesis 2-3), far from being distant, God is portrayed as much more involved in the nitty-gritty of creation, for example, as uncertain about how to find a fitting helper for Adam. We are told how God creates Adam—from the dust of the earth, and Eve—from Adam's rib. None of this detail is present in the earlier story. Later God is portrayed as moving through the garden searching for Adam and Eve. Still later, God makes garments for the two primordial sinners. Both of these images of God are profoundly true, for God is both majestically distant from us and, at the same time, extraordinarily close to us. But each of these texts emphasizes one of these polarities at the expense of the other. So the two images of God could not be more different.

From an anthropological perspective, compare the two verses from Psalms that frequently introduce the *Yizkor* (Memorial) service in our prayerbooks. Psalm 8:5-6 reads: "What is the human that You have been mindful of him, the mortal that You have taken note of her, that you have made the individual little less than divine, and adorned them with glory and majesty." In contrast, Psalm 144:3-4 reads, "Adonai, what is the human that You should care about him, mortals that You should think of her? Humans are like breath; their days are like a passing shadow." Again, both of these images of the human person are profoundly true for we are both extraordinarily fragile creatures and also more powerful, gifted and competent than the rest of creation. Yet the two emphases could not be further apart.

In our theologies of revelation, the temper of humility portrays God as exhaustively communicating, at the outset, every word and letter of the Torah to a passive Israelite community which simply listens and promises to obey. In contrast, the temper of humanism stresses the partial and preliminary nature of that original revelation with the human community assuming the role of determining the shape of God's will from generation to generation. It is epitomized in the postscript to that remarkable story of Achnai's oven (Babylonian Talmud, Bava Metzia 59b) in which God acknowledges being "defeated" by the human court which had ruled contrary to God's explicitly revealed will.

It is in the liturgy of the High Holy days that the interweaving of these two tempers emerges most clearly. The season represents the single most powerful moment in the Jewish liturgical year. It is the season of the great turnabout, the time of repentance from which we emerge as new creations, newly reborn, with all of the possibilities and potentialities inherent in the human situation arrayed before us. That very tension between what we are and what we might be represents precisely the tension between these two tempers.

On one hand, the High Holy day liturgy has us recite: "What are we? What is our life? What is our goodness? What is our virtue? What our help? What our strength? What our might? . . . Indeed all the heros are as nothing in Thy sight, people of renown as though they never existed, the wise as though they were without knowledge, the intelligent as though they lacked insight. . . ." That text is the very embodiment of the temper of humility. But elsewhere, at the climax of the *Unetaneh Tokef* prayer, we are told that we are not at all without resources. Indeed, we are assured that repentance, prayer and acts of lovingkindness have the power to abort God's fateful decree against us. God's decree then depends on our decision. Here is the temper of humanism with a vengeance!

Randall suggests that our goal should be to achieve a balance between these two religious impulses. That resolution is more easily achievable on paper than in life. Another way of looking at it is to suggest that most ancient religious traditions have survived precisely because they provide a multiplicity of anthropological and theological models from which different members of the community can draw upon and emulate at different times in their life experience. Judaism clearly provides such a multiplicity of models; its classical texts reflect both of these tempers.

The Jewishness of the Twelve Steps, then, rests in their nursing from that stream of the tradition that reflects the temper of humility. In this context, the reliance of the Twelve Steps on the temper of humility as it emerges in the Jewish religious tradition is entirely appropriate given the addicted person's sense of utter powerlessness in the face of his or her addiction. More than any other human being, the addicted person has plumbed the depths of the temper of humility.

We return to the High Holy day experience, because it is there that this temper of humility emerges most strikingly. First, the very notion of *teshuvah*, as elaborated by our tradition, captures precisely the type of character transformation that the Twelve Steps strive to achieve. *Teshuvah* is much more than repentance; it is nothing less than an experience of rebirth, the creation of a new human being, the total transformation of a life experience. It represents Judaism's most powerful affirmation of confidence in the potentialities of the human being, its infinite hope in our ability to redirect our lives. At the same time, it reflects a totally hardheaded understanding of human character. *Teshuvah* is not quick and easy, not simply a matter of making an inner decision, but neither is it impossible and beyond reach. It is a day-long, year-long and life-long struggle. We can do effective *teshuvah* on the day of our death, but since we never know which day will be our last, we must do it daily. All of this is part of the implicit ideology of the Twelve Steps.

One of the more detailed elaborations of the process of *teshuvah* has been extracted from Moses Maimonides' *Hilchot Teshuvah* (Laws of Teshuvah) in his compendium of Jewish law called *Mishneh Torah* (chapter two). Here too we speak of "steps" (five in number, although they are not explicitly listed this way), which can easily be matched with some of the Twelve Steps. Maimonides' first step is to recognize, openly and explicitly, that we have sinned (corresponding to Steps One and Four of the Twelve Steps). The second step is to feel regret for our behavior (Step Three). The third is to articulate our sin in words (Steps Five and Ten). Note here that this *vidui* (oral confession) is carried out through our liturgy which, as you recall, is always formulated in the plural. We share both our responsibilities and our resources in our community, as does the addicted person with his or her fellowship. Maimonides' fourth step is to inwardly resolve to act differently in the future (Steps Three and Twelve). But our *teshuvah* is not complete until we have encountered the same situation in which we sinned once again, and this time meet it successfully (Step Twelve).

Note also that Steps Eight and Nine insist that when our sins have led us to injure another person, we must make a direct personal approach to such people and ask for forgiveness, corresponding to the classical Jewish teaching that the fast of the Day of Atonement relieves us only of sins against God. Sins against other human beings must be dealt with by approaching the person we have wronged.

The image of God in the Twelve Steps undergoes a fascinating transformation. At the outset, God emerges as a "Power greater than ourselves"—appropriately for someone who feels totally bereft of power. This Power is " . . . as we understood Him" or open to infinite characterizations. (For some, this "Power greater than ourselves" is precisely A.A.)

But from Step Three on, this Power has become a God who cares, Who listens to our confession, Who removes all our defects, Who listens to prayers and meditations, Who has a will for us, and Who lends us power to carry out God's will for us. This transformation in the image of God is striking. From a "Power," God has emerged as fully personal with infinite "pathos"—to use Abraham Joshua Heschel's term—filled with care and concern for human beings, very much the God of the Bible and of the rabbinic tradition. And the decision "to turn our will and our lives over to the care of God" sounds very much like the biblical characterization of faith as *emunah*—not simply an intellectual "belief that," but something much closer to "belief in," or trust, loyalty and total dependency on God.

The Jewish character of the Twelve Steps, then, is beyond question. That they should appear to some Jews as non-Jewish is as much a commentary on the dimensions of Judaism with which these Jews identify, as it is a commentary on the Twelve Steps themselves. Fortunately for all of us, Judaism is rich and multi-faceted enough to accommodate us all.

How the Jewish Calendar Works

Since Biblical times, the months and years of the Jewish calendar have been established by the cycles of the moon and the sun. Included in Jewish law are guidelines which suggest that the months must follow closely the phases of the moon. These lunar months correspond to the seasons of the year which are determined by the sun.

When the Israelites were liberated from Egypt, the Torah teaches us "This month will be the beginning of the months, the very first of the month" (Exodus 12:2). The season of spring was the beginning of the year, according to the Torah, because it was marked by the rebirth of the nature and the liberation of our people.

The ancient Israelites had no real calendar. They knew of the cycle of the seasons, however, because of its relationship to planting and harvesting. In about the year 350 C.E., Hillel II helped to establish a permanent calendar for the Jewish people that adjusted the lunar year with the solar year. Since that time, this has become our calendar.

The Jewish calendar months are fixed by the cycles of the moon, while the days are fixed by the cycles of the sun. In this way, the Jewish holidays occur in their proper season, as specified in the Bible. However, the dates of Jewish holidays on the secular civil calendar differ from year to year.

There are twelve months in the Jewish calendar. Each of these lunar months has either twenty-nine or thirty days, accounting for a total of three hundred fifty-four days. During Jewish leap years (approximately once every three years), a thirteenth month called Adar II is added.

The Jewish calendar numbers the years from the date of the creation of the world, as determined by ancient Jewish tradition. While many of us believe that the world was created millions of years ago, out of respect for Jewish tradition, we retain this method of numbering the years.

There are several synagogue celebrations directly related to the monthly renewal of the moon. *Rosh Chodesh*, the beginning of every Jewish month, is celebrated as a minor holy day for one day. The day of *Rosh Chodesh* is generally announced at the Sabbath synagogue service of the preceding week. This Sabbath, whenever it occurs, is called *Shabbat Mevarchim*. Although there is no work restriction of *Rosh Chodesh*, Jewish tradition has used it to honor women for their unusual piety by allowing them respite from their work. According to tradition, the Israelite women demonstrated this piety when they did not contribute their jewelry for the making of the golden calf. For many people, men and women, *Rosh Chodesh* serves as time for reflection and personal renewal. It provides us with an opportunity to look at the past month and suggest ways in which we might improve our lives (and our relations with other people) in the new month just ahead.

During the rabbinic period, the beginning of the new month was declared when two witnesses reported to the Sanhedrin that the crescent of a new moon had appeared. The declaration was relayed from city to city by lighting fires on hilltops. Often, fires were lit in error. This caused confusion and a delay in announcing the new month. To make certain that all holidays were celebrated on their proper day, an extra day was added to the prescribed number. Most communities outside of Israel follow this model. However, members of the Reform movement generally observe the holidays according to the original number because of the scientific exactitude with which the calendar is currently determined. The rabbis tell us that when the day of *Rosh Chodesh* was determined by the rabbinical court using the sighting of the new moon, people would assemble for a festive meal. Today, by astronomical calculation, the beginning of the new month takes place at the moment when the moon is exactly between the earth and the sun, and nothing is visible of the moon. It is at that time that the *molad* (or the birth) of the moon takes place.

It takes about twenty-nine and a half days for the moon to circle the earth. Since half days are awkward to count, some months in the Jewish calendar are always twenty-nine days and others are always thirty days. If a month contains thirty days, then the last day of that month and the first day of the next month *both* comprise *Rosh Chodesh*. If a month contains only twenty-nine days, then only the first day of the following month is called *Rosh Chodesh*.

The second celebration of the moon's renewal is called *Kiddush Levanah* or the sanctification of the moon. Several days after the emergence of the new moon, people assembled outside in an open space in order to offer a prayer of thanksgiving for the renewal of life and their hopeful optimism for the future.

The last celebration of the calendar occurs every twenty years. It is called *Birkat Hachamah*, the blessing of the sun. When the cycle of the heavenly bodies completes itself at the spring equinox every twenty-eight years, we give thanks to God for the sun.

Holidays and Festivals at a Glance

FALL

Rosh Hashanah/New Year

Yom Kippur/Day of Atonement

Sukkot/Harvest Festival of Thanksgiving

Shemini Atzeret/Eighth Day of Assembly

Simchat Torah/Rejoicing of the Torah

WINTER

Hanukkah/Festival of Lights

Purim/Festival of Lots

SPRING

Pesach/Passover

Shavuot/Feast of Weeks

A Calendar of Months

	5754 1993-94	5755 1994-95	5756 1995-96	5757 1996-97	5758 1997-98
Tishrei	Sept. 16	Sept. 6	Sept. 25	Sept. 14	Oct. 2
Chesvan	Oct. 16	Oct. 6	Oct. 25	Oct.14	Nov. 1
Kislev	Nov. 15	Nov. 4	Nov. 24	Nov. 12	Nov.30
Tevet	Dec. 15	Dec. 4	Dec. 24	Dec.11	Dec. 30
Shevat	Jan. 13	Jan. 2	Jan. 22	Jan. 9	Jan. 28
Adar	Feb. 12	Feb. 1	Feb. 21	Jan. 8	Feb.27
(Adar II)	—	Mar. 3	—	Mar. 10	—
Nisan	Mar. 13	Apr. 1	Mar. 21	Apr. 8	Mar. 28
Iyar	Apr. 12	May 1	Apr. 20	May 8	Apr. 27
Sivan	May 11	May 30	May 19	June 6	May 26
Tammuz	June 10	June 29	June 18	July 6	June 25
Av	July 9	July 28	July 17	Aug. 4	July 24
Elul	Aug. 8	Aug. 27	Aug. 16	Sept. 3	Aug. 23

In this book, I have provided enough material for use during "full" years (when some months *can* be extended to a full 30 days, rather than 29). However, during leap years, when an additional month of *Adar* (called *Adar II*) is added to the calendar, please repeat the daily meditations for the month of *Adar*. Only leap years include the month of *Adar II*.

The first day of each Hebrew month corresponds to the secular date listed in each column on the calendar. Use this chart to specifically correlate the starting dates of months in the Hebrew calendar with those in the secular calendar. In order to determine the dates for major festivals and fasts, consult page xxxii. However, to check minor days, please consult a current *luach* (Hebrew calendar). This will be particularly important when you want to read material for a special Sabbath.

A Calendar Of

TISHREI	CHESVAN	KISLEV	TEVET	SHEVET	ADAR
1 Rosh Hashanah			1 Hanukkah		
3 Fast of Gedalia			2 ▼		
— Ten Days of Return —					
10 Yom Kippur			10 Fast of 10th of Tevet		
					13 Fast of Esther
					14 Purim
15 Sukkot ➤				15 Tu B'Shevet	15 Shushan Purim
16 [2]					
17					
18 — Hol Ha-Mo'ed —					
19					
20					
21 Hoshana Rabbah					
22 Shemini Atzeret/ Simchat Torah[1]					
23 Simchat Torah					
		25 Hanukkah			
		26			
		27			
		28			
		29			
		30 ▼			

| major holiday | minor holiday | [2] = second day holiday in traditional diaspora congregation only |

➤ Pilgrimage festivals

* Counting of the Omer (Sefirah period begins)

0 Selichot prayers

[1] *Simchat Torah* in Israel only

Festivals and Fasts

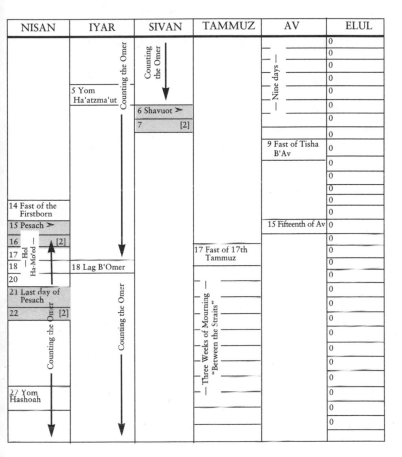

NISAN	IYAR	SIVAN	TAMMUZ	AV	ELUL
					0
		Counting the Omer		— Nine days —	0
					0
					0
	5 Yom Ha'atzma'ut				0
		6 Shavuot ➤			0
	Counting the Omer	7 [2]			0
					0
				9 Fast of Tisha B'Av	0
					0
					0
					0
14 Fast of the Firstborn					0
15 Pesach ➤				15 Fifteenth of Av	0
16 [2]			17 Fast of 17th Tammuz		0
17 Hol Ha-Mo'ed					0
18	18 Lag B'Omer				0
20					0
21 Last day of Pesach			Three Weeks of Mourning "Between the Straits"		0
22 [2]					0
	Counting the Omer				0
					0
					0
27 Yom Hashoah					0
					0
					0

Jewish holidays begin in the evening. The dates listed reflect the day of the holiday — not the previous evening. In some cases (in Reform Judaism and in Israel), the specific date may vary by one day. This calendar reflects the traditional calendar outside of Israel. Only the first day of the holiday is listed in multi-day holidays.

1994-1999

	5754 1994	5755 1995	5756 1996	5757 1997	5758 1998
Rosh Hashanah New Year	Sept. 16	Sept. 6	Sept. 25	Sept. 14	Oct. 2
Yom Kippur Day of Atonement	Sept. 25	Sept. 15	Oct. 4	Sept. 23	Oct. 11
Sukkot Harvest Festival/ Thanksgiving	Sept. 30	Sept. 20	Oct. 9	Sept. 28	Oct. 16
Shemini Atzeret Eighth Day of Assembly	Oct. 7	Sept. 27	Oct. 16	Oct. 5	Oct. 24
Simchat Torah Rejoicing of the Torah	Oct. 8	Sept. 28	Oct. 17	Oct. 6	Oct. 24
Hanukkah Festival of Lights	Nov. 28	Dec. 18	Dec. 6	Dec. 24	Dec. 14

	1995	1996	1997	1998	1999
Purim Festival of Lots	Mar. 15	Mar. 5	Mar. 23	Mar. 11	Mar. 2
Pesach Passover	Mar. 27	Apr. 15	Apr. 4	Apr. 22	Apr. 11
Shavuot Feast of Weeks	May 16	June 4	May 24	June 11	May 31

Since the days on the Hebrew calendar begin in the evening, the holidays listed on this page actually begin the evening before the date listed.

The Twelve Steps
of
Alcoholics Anonymous

The Twelve Steps are reprinted and adapted with permission of Alcoholics Anonymous World Services, Inc. Permission to reprint and adapt the Twelve Steps does not mean that A.A. is affiliated with the program. A.A. is a program of recovery from alcoholism—use of the Twelve Steps in connection with programs and activities which are patterned after A.A. but which address other problems does not imply otherwise.

1. We admitted we were powerless over alcohol—that our lives had become unmanageable.

2. Came to believe that a Power greater than ourselves could restore us to sanity.

3. Made a decision to turn our will and our lives over to the care of God *as we understood Him.*

4. Made a searching and fearless inventory of ourselves.

5. Admitted to God, to ourselves, and to another human being the exact nature of our wrongs.

6. Were entirely ready to have God remove all these defects of character.

7. Humbly asked Him to remove our shortcomings.

8. Made a list of all persons we had harmed, and became willing to make amends to them all.

9. Made direct amends to such people wherever possible, except when to do so would injure them or others.

10. Continued to take personal inventory and when we were wrong promptly admitted it.

11. Sought through prayer and meditation to improve our conscious contact with God *as we understood Him*, praying only for knowledge of His will for us and the power to carry that out.

12. Having had a spiritual awakening as a result of these Steps, we tried to carry this message to alcoholics, and to practice these principles in all our affairs.

(The use of the masculine pronoun in referring to God is the original A.A. language. Like many Twelve Step programs, we have chosen not to use a pronoun at all later in our discussion, but retain the original here.)

Tishrei
A Fresh Start
Early Autumn

It's the beginning of a new year. We have examined our deeds, made amends, and been renewed. But recovery and spiritual renewal do not come quickly or easily. Repentance, *teshuvah*, is hard work. That's really why when we finally—after the long hot summer—get to Rosh Hashanah we call it a *New* Year, because through honest repentance we are given the opportunity to begin life *anew* and get a fresh start on the year—and our lives.

While *Tishrei* is actually the seventh month of the Hebrew calendar, it leads the year nevertheless. The symbol for the month is a scale, reflecting the balance that the month gives our lives. And so with it we begin counting, continuing to keep our lives in balance—one day at a time—from the awe-filled days of Rosh Hashanah and Yom Kippur. Through the harvest of self-searching at Sukkot and the rejoicing of our relationship with God on Simchat Torah.

During the entire month, we are absorbed by the fall holidays. Powerful moods to begin a year, reflections of a life of the spirit. The Gaon of Vilna has taught us: "Each day should be a new experience. Each day we have the opportunity of *a fresh start*. A person who has made *teshuvah* is like a newborn child."

> *Everyone is required to recite at least*
> *one hundred blessings a day.*
>
> —Shulchan Aruch,
> Orach Chaim 46:3

Gratitude is a pure expression of faith. We recognize that we have been blessed with an abundance of good things in our lives. So we take a moment to say "thank you." It shifts our focus from getting, and away from thinking about the things we don't have.

Gratitude does not come easily to most of us. We enjoy complaining and usually have no trouble finding something to complain about. Maybe we should just be grateful to have something to complain about! It has been suggested that we keep a gratitude list of all the things in life to be appreciated—to be used as a little "pick-me-up" on those "poor, poor, pitiful me" days when the calendar beckons us to return.

There is never any shortage of things to be grateful for in our lives. We just don't always see it that way. *Berachot,* blessings, help us to see the world through thankful eyes.

For Growth and Renewal: To reach the level of thanksgiving where we can utter, as the rabbis suggest, one hundred blessings each day may seem a difficult goal. It all begins by being grateful for one thing: Life itself. Today, at the beginning of the year, find something to be grateful for. Then say a prayer of thanks.

May it be your will Adonai our God
and God of our ancestors to renew us
for a good and sweet year.

—on eating an apple
on Rosh Hashanah

There is something so profoundly simple about apples and honey on New Year. It's so basic. For me, it is a prayer of thanksgiving and hope rolled in one. All of my life's aspirations brought into focus. I humbly recognize where I have come from and where I need to go, what I have yet to do to make my life holy. No glitz, no glitter. I simply savor the sweet juices of the fruits of God's world as I prepare myself for the spiritual renewal I yearn for all year long. I know it's possible at any time, but there is something special about the Holy Day season that makes it seem ever the more possible for me.

For me, apples are symbols that I can return. So I get ready for my return with a modest prayer and an unadorned act. According to tradition, when children are born, trees are to be planted—their branches to be used for a *chuppah* (bridal canopy) much later in that person's life. In recovery, through spiritual renewal, we are all as children who take that first breath in the world.

For Growth and Renewal: Share some apples and honey with a friend. Then take a seed and plant it so that you may watch it grow as you do.

> Avinu Malkeinu, *be gracious and answer us,*
> *for we have little merit.*
>
> —from the High Holiday
> Prayer Book

The myth of self-sufficiency has particular appeal for Americans, especially on this fast day of *Tzom Gedaliah*, generally ten to twelve days before the fall equinox, the descent of the sun. The lonesome cowboy hero. Rebels without a cause. Self-made millionaires. The illusion that we did it all ourselves is irresistible.

The false notion that we were—*had* to be—in control was very much a part of the sick thinking that caused us to careen out of control. From a Jewish perspective, ownership is, at best, temporary. There isn't even a Hebrew word to express real ownership. Our very souls are on loan.

The plea of the High Holy Day prayers reveals a humble truth: Even our deeds are not fully our own. We are beneficiaries of Divine assistance in countless ways. This realization helps avert an obsession with self and deepens our faith. The spiritual gifts of true humility and awe are the result. But to receive them, we must get off the "I-way."

For Growth and Renewal: Take your *machzor* (holiday prayerbook) and use the *Avinu Malkeinu* as a Step Four inventory.

> *Today, today, today. Bless us . . .*
> *and help us to grow.*
>
> —from the Rosh Hashanah liturgy

From a prayer that is sung on Rosh Hashanah morning comes the refrain that joyously proclaims God's greatest gift of all: Today is the birthday of the world and our rebirth, as well. No matter how much "clean time" one has, it is often said, one only has today. Today. To return, to renew, to rebuild, to start over.

We can fritter our lives away worrying about things that will never come to pass. Or we can use our past as an escape from the present as effectively—and destructively—as any drug. But if it's happiness or serenity we're looking for, then there truly is no time but the present.

Rabbi Simcha Bunam, the great hasidic rabbi who lived into the early nineteenth century, taught that our real transgression is not that we commit sins—the Holy Blessed One understands that temptation is strong and we are often weak. Rather, our transgression is that at every moment we have an opportunity to turn to God—today—yet we do not turn! The opportunity to do *teshuvah* is here for us today, always.

For Growth and Renewal: Learning to live today, one day at a time, is perhaps the greatest blessing of recovery. Do something *today* that makes you realize that you are alive.

> *If a person uses broken vessels, it is considered
> an embarrassment. But God seeks out broken
> vessels for Divine use, as it says: "God is
> the healer of shattered hearts."*

—Leviticus Rabbah 7:2

Each series of the shofar blasts that are sounded on Rosh Hashanah begins and ends with a *tekiah*—a whole note. In between are *shevarim* and *teruah*—shorter broken notes. Reflecting on the moving tones of the shofar, Rabbi Isaac Horowitz, a 17th century rabbi, considered the theme of Rosh Hashanah this way: "We begin whole. Along the path of life we become broken [through pain, mistakes, loss, failure, illness, weakness]. The end is whole—we will be whole again. There is hope."

A friend told me that he once decided to break his anonymity and shared some of his thoughts on Torah and recovery to a business client with whom he felt a certain spiritual affinity. He had some doubts as to whether he was doing the right thing. After all, the other person was not in recovery. Would she understand? How would she react? She was genuinely delighted and appreciated that he trusted her enough to share some of his recovery thoughts with her. Then she said something simple yet exquisitely profound: "The way I see it, we're all recovering from something."

For Growth and Renewal: Seek out a friend and share your spiritual recovery with them. It's (advanced) Step Five work.

---

*Where penitents stand, the wholly righteous
cannot stand.*

—Babylonian Talmud,
Berachot 34b

The Jewish tradition has always accorded the highest of status to those who have turned their lives around through *teshuvah*, repentance. They are considered even more pious than the ones who had never sinned. As the noted Talmudist Rabbi Adin Steinsaltz puts it, "The penitent has at his disposal not only the forces of good in his soul and in his world, but also those of evil, which he transforms into essences of holiness." Beyond the person, *teshuvah* is seen as an act of cosmic significance. This is perhaps the essential message of *Shabbat Shuvah*, the Sabbath of Return, between Rosh Hashanah and Yom Kippur. You can always return; the power to do so is in your hands.

Recovery gives us a chance to transform bad into good, suffering into joy. It may be much more difficult to get back on track than to have been rolling smoothly all along, but it is certainly is a more memorable ride. Sometimes you have to walk down into the valley to get to the mountaintop. Perhaps, for us, there was no other way.

For Growth and Renewal: Is there something that you have been meaning to fix for a while, but you just haven't gotten around to it? Fix something that is broken. Remember, it's possible to repair.

7

> *The truly pious are inscribed for good at
> the very beginning of the penitential season.
> Courtesy demands that we regard our neighbor
> as truly pious: God merely needs to put the
> Divine seal of approval on the decision.*

—Babylonian Talmud,
Rosh Hashanah 16b

A circuit preacher came to the town of Tiktin on *Shabbat Shuvah*, the Sabbath of Return, and urged the community to repent. Afterwards, the local rabbi said to him, "Why couldn't you reprove me in private instead of shaming me in public?" The preacher replied, "I referred to no individual in particular. I only spoke in general terms." "No," said the rabbi. "All my congregants are good folk. You could have had in mind only me."

Keep the focus on yourself. It's difficult not to criticize, to paint the canvas of another's life as you would live it. As I tell my own children, "Remember, they [the folks that wronged them] have to live with themselves so don't you worry about it." It's easy to find faults in others; it's one of the ways we avoid finding fault with ourselves. We are all looking for more meaning in our lives, to come closer to God. Look inside and remember what you find so that you can learn from it. One of the things we'll learn is that our neighbor can also be our friend.

For Growth and Renewal: Do something nice for a neighbor you who feel has wronged you. Make "direct amends" and repair yourself as you contribute to the repair of the world.

> *Deliver him from going down in the pit.*
> *I have found a ransom.*
>
> —Job 33:23-24

The old Yom Kippur custom of *kapparot* is a form of scapegoat ceremony that involved taking a rooster or hen—or even some money—and twirling it around your head while reciting a prayer. In the prayer, we ask that the chicken be killed in our place. Or, more constructively, the money is then given for *tzedakah*. This is a transforming ritual that moves the focus from hatred to healing.

Sooner or later in recovery, at a certain level, some of us begin to sense that we have a certain sick need to punish ourselves. We feel guilt-ridden and ashamed of who we are. Even if we are done with the drugs, gambling, the compulsive sex or eating habits, we may yet look for new way to abuse ourselves. It's a restless, no-good feeling that is sure to sabotage our progress, unless we are willing to look at and deal with it. We don't have to be our own scapegoats anymore.

For Growth and Renewal: Think back over the past year. Did you blame yourself for something that was out of your control? Seize it. Rid yourself of it. Then go out and give *tzedakah* in exchange.

> *No matter how much you stir mud,*
> *it remains mud.*
>
> —Rabbi Menachem Mendl of Kotzk,
> early nineteenth century hasidic leader

Leave it to the Kotzker Rebbe to find meaning in every-day mud. As we sift through the wreckage of our past, there may be a tendency to despair. It's not constructive to dwell on what can't be changed. No amount of analysis, regret, or guilt is going to undo the past. Mud remains mud. Our past is over. Thank God. We have learned some hard lessons. So don't ask, "Why did I do it?" Instead, ask yourself: "What am I going to do about it?"

True change, what we call *teshuvah*, comes when, faced with the same temptation to sin, we do not fall prey to it again. That's how we know that we have succeeded in our struggle toward recovery. Can we go out with friends and not end up gambling the night away? The *Kol Nidre* vow does not release us from these "second sins." It allows us to see them before they get here, to know they are coming, to prepare to meet them head-on. As my friend Aaron Z. once told me, "The mud remains mud . . . but I have stopped stirring." We can all be free of mud—clean. We have survived our past, unashamed of what we no longer are.

For Growth and Renewal: There are always things left to reconcile. Choose one "muddy" thing that you want to clean up and get yourself cleaner.

> *Two are better off than one. They have*
> *a greater reward for their labor.*
>
> —Ecclesiastes 9:9

We would like to think that we can do it on our own, but we can't. How many times have we said, "I don't need you. I don't need anyone"—to those we have pushed away? For what? An extra boost? Another drink? Then we find ourselves alone, to face who we are, what we have done. Broken, shattered—like the first set of Ten Commandment tablets. According to Jewish tradition, the second set was given on Yom Kippur. This time, Moses carved and God wrote, the result of human interaction with the Divine.

During Yom Kippur, we stand as a community to confess our shortcomings. The confessional prayer is said as "we." As we have found in recovery, there is spiritual strength in numbers. People healing together is itself a powerful form of atonement: To rebuild our lives, we begin with ourselves. But we can't go it alone. There are others who will help us find our way, if we let them. When relationships are built on a firm foundation of sacred trust between people, they can't be broken. In community, in the shadow of the protective care of the *Shechinah,* God's mystical presence on earth, there is enough strength to carry us all.

For Growth and Renewal: Make the local morning *minyan* (prayer quorum). Help someone bear the burden of saying *Kaddish.*

When one must, one can.

—Yiddish folk saying

At times, all of us feel weary. Too many demands. It seems like it would be easier to run, to leave it all behind. Then we might find the rest we need, the personal strength to face our compulsions. The prophet Jonah tried it. God called out to him, "Go to Nineveh, go where I send you. Face the task that I have set before you." Thinking that he could actually escape his life, Jonah ran to a place called Tarshish. Finally, only after he bottomed out, feeling like he had been swallowed up, did he face up to his life's challenge. Only then was he ready to listen to God.

Unlike Jonah, we don't have to wind up in the belly of an ocean beast before we come to our senses. Our "beast" is in our bellies! The sooner we realize that, the sooner we can grow.

Sometimes, as the *Besht*, the founder of the Hasidic movement, said: "We must lose ourselves to find God—or even ourselves." Addiction taught us that no matter how hard we try to run away from ourselves, we are still there. Recovery teaches us we don't have to run.

For Growth and Renewal: Stop running. "Lose yourself" in prayer and see what you have found.

> *Light is sown for the righteous,*
> *and gladness for the upright in heart.*
>
> —Psalm 97:11

Rabbi Shlomo Riskin, well-known rabbi of New York's Lincoln Square Synagogue and now chief rabbi of the city of Efrat, Israel, once made the astounding assertion that Yom Kippur was not a sad day. A day of fasting and breast-beating hardly seems like a walk in the park, but Rabbi Riskin insisted: Yom Kippur is the happiest day on the Jewish calendar, because it is the day on which we *atone* and are forgiven, becoming *"at-one"* once again.

You don't have to be an addict of any kind to suffer spiritually. We all endure emotional bumps and bruises in the course of our lives. We hurt so much, for so long. It becomes normal. That's the worst kind of sickness—the one you don't even know is there.

God wants us to be joyful in our return. This is how the Baal Shem Tov, founder of the Hasidic movement, put it: "It is the aim and essence of my pilgrimage on earth to show my brethren by living demonstration how one may serve God with merriment and rejoicing. For one who is full of joy is full of love for people and one's fellow creatures." Approach your atonement joyfully.

For Growth and Renewal: Be an example that others might follow. Happily share your story of recovery.

Do not fight against God . . . for
you will not succeed.

—II Chronicles 13:12

This notion would seem obvious—but our ego, when left unchecked, is usually more driven to dominate than to defer. So, on we struggle, even against our own best interests, stubbornly asserting our will ahead of our Higher Power's—or worse, acting as if the latter simply does not exist. And that's when we really do ourselves harm. The brick walls we run into simply because we don't want them to be there can hurt us worst of all.

This becomes really focused for us on Yom Kippur. Rabbi Levi Yitzchak of Berditchev often tried to assert his will. And quite honestly, he did it well. He would stand on the *bimah* on Yom Kippur with ultimate chutzpah and challenge God to join him in his struggle. In a prayerful dialogue, they came to terms with one another. Once while leading the congregation in prayer, he abruptly stopped. Levi Yitzchak said, "I no longer have the strength to speak for you. Speak for Yourself and proclaim our pardon." Levi Yitzchak wanted God to be God. And God wanted Levi Yitzchak to be Levi Yitzchak. And the Higher Power wants you to be you.

For Growth and Renewal: Find your place in prayer with God and then remember it. But continue the dialogue.

For I know that you are a compassionate
and gracious God, slow to anger, abounding
in kindness, renouncing punishment.

—Jonah 4:2

It's ironic. Sometimes we fear success even more than we fear failure. Jonah did. He had the unique honor of being the only prophet in the Bible to whom the people really listened. Yet he ran! He was angry. He wanted the people to be punished. Why? Because he lacked compassion for others. And himself. Fearing change in others, he also feared change in himself.

Jonah's bottom is about as low as you can go—the deep, dark depths of what seems to be a whale's belly. But Jonah's problem really is the fear in his own gut. Bachya ibn Pakuda, the eleventh century Spanish moralist, wrote: "I'd be ashamed were God to see me fear anyone but God."

If God can make compassionate changes, so can we. It sounds presumptuous, but not when we remember we were made in the Divine image, just a little lower than the angels.

For Growth and Renewal: Self-change comes hard, but it can come if you work at it. Break up the change you want to make into parts, then take it one part at a time. God will help you on the way.

*A bundle of reeds cannot be broken by an adult;
but, taken separately, even a child
can break them.*

—Tanhuma Nitzavim

On the holiday of Sukkot, we take the *lulav* and *etrog*, the myrtle and the willow. We shake them all together after saying a special blessing. The Talmud emphasizes the importance of holding these four different species together: They represent various individual human attributes.

The symbolism: Not only does it take all kinds to make this *mitzvah* work, it also takes a certain all-togetherness, a unity. The same applies to synagogue communities. And to fellowships. We are different people who come from different traditions and different walks of life—but what brings us together is a common purpose that transcends all that.

The unity of synagogue fellowship is vitally important to our own well-being. We can learn something from everybody. In fact, our differences probably help contribute to the vitality of the message of recovery. Maybe the recovery message of the *lulav* is this: To learn how to survive life's inevitable shakes without getting all bent out of shape.

For Growth and Renewal: Place your hands together with others and shake the *lulav*. And enjoy the harvest of unity.

> *No human is expendable. If one is slighted or*
> *excluded, the whole of society is* pasul, *unfit.*
> —based on Vayikra Rabbah Emor 30:12

If an *etrog* or any other ritual object is *pasul*, it is unfit for use. That remains a fair moral test for our community as well. How well do we treat our weakest, disabled, and otherwise afflicted members? As recovering people, we may empathize more with the downtrodden than others. We have seen "the dregs" of society—and it is us! We too have been shunned, excluded. Doors have been closed to us—even slammed on us, but it may have been us doing the closing. As a result, we have also come to a better understanding of the fact that, rich or poor, black or white, Jew or Christian, there is more that we have in common than our disease.

The prophet Nehemiah put well what Judaism has always affirmed: "One human being is worth as much as the whole creation." We are all part of God's world. Our job is to make it whole (*shalom*) once again.

For Growth and Renewal: Reach out to someone in your fellowship—beyond her recovery. Through the study of Torah and the practice of the Twelve Steps, help her to feel whole again.

> *Who causes the winds to blow*
> *and the rain to fall . . .*

—inserted in the Amidah prayer,
between Sukkot and Pesach

Sukkot reminds us of how really fragile is the life we too often take for granted. We leave our comfortable homes to dwell—if only for little more than a week—in flimsy structures. Temporary dwellings that offer little protection from the wilderness with thatched roofs that allow us to be constantly reminded that we are surrounded *and* protected by God, the Creator of all we see—the One who indeed causes the winds to blow and the rain to fall. For each who dwell in them, they become *sukkot shalom*, sukkahs of peace, of tranquility, of serenity. Just as these rickety little huts protected our ancestors during their journey through their desert, they protect us through ours as well.

And so at the same time that we celebrate Sukkot—and the winds and rains truly pound against these modest structures—we pray for the inspirational winds to blow against, and the saving rains to fall on us, fully acknowledging God as the Author of all creation, recognizing the central role of the Higher Power in our recovery.

For Growth and Renewal: Build a sukkah, recite the blessing. Let it be a protective shelter, a sukkah of peace for you, as it has been for generations who have come before you.

> *The one who has not witnessed the joy of*
> *drawing the water has never experienced real joy.*
>
> —Sukkah 5:1

In Jewish folk culture, the origins of some ceremonies are elusive. They are part of who we are although we are not sure how they developed. They help to make our lives holy. We stick with them. We don't fully know why the Twelve Steps work either, but they do. So we continue to work the program.

Imagine the scene for a moment. Thousands of people have made their journey, a pilgrimage, to ancient Jerusalem for Sukkot to watch water being poured into large earthenware jugs. In the midst of the festival of Sukkot, the people acknowledged that they had survived the wilderness and had come home. And there were expressions of joy everywhere. Dancing, singing, special celebration. "Therefore, with joy," taught the prophet Isaiah (12:3), "will you draw water from the wells of redemption." The journey to Jerusalem alone is always worth it: To breathe its air, to gaze at its mountainside, to walk among its people. With community, there is healing. We have learned all that in the rooms. During Sukkot, we are given the chance to remember it.

For Growth and Renewal: As you bathe or shower today, imagine these waters flowing from those collected in ancient days and be healed by them.

> *God took dust from the four corners of the earth*
> *so that humans might be at home everywhere.*
>
> —Rashi based on Babylonian
> Talmud, Sanhedrin 38a-b

That "at home" feeling is a funny emotion, truly hard to explain. More than an address or a location on the map. Much more than a zip code—even plus four. No decorator can help us get there. Feeling at home, especially in a sukkah, is real serenity, *shelemut*, that sense of being at peace, comfortable, with self—and others. It's a cozy, uncomplicated feeling. What's odd about it is that as much as we search for it, trying to create it externally, it eludes us. Life always seems better as it is lived by others—who seem richer or even wiser, who have more things, more status, more influence in the community. Stop searching elsewhere.

Home is not only where you make it—but also what you make it. Home is when you make peace with who you were as much as who you are. Home is wherever and whenever you let God transform your lives. Menachem Mendl of Kotzk has taught us that God dwells wherever individuals invite God to dwell. Make God feel at home in your life and you'll feel at home in it—anywhere.

For Growth and Renewal: Invite God to dwell in your home. Put up a new *mezuzzah* and rededicate your life.

> *At first, the Evil Inclination becomes a guest, and afterwards, it becomes proprietor of the house.*
>
> —Babylonian Talmud, Sukkah 52a

During Sukkot, it is customary to invite guests to celebrate in our Sukkah. We learned it from Moses whom the rabbis teach us kept the four flaps of his tent open so that he might run and greet visitors regardless of which direction they were traveling. We call this tradition *ushpizin* and we even imagine inviting guests from the Jewish historical past to join us. According to the Talmud, the practice of hospitality is even greater than the reception of God (Shabbat 127a). But we have to be careful who we invite. In the excitement of the festival, we might forget how fragile the sukkah really is—and so still are we.

When we're speaking of alcohol and drugs and gambling, we just never invite those guests into our sukkah or back into our lives. They are just not welcome. With eating and sex and codependent relationships, it's not that simple. We have to eat; loving sex is part of mature living. And we live with various kinds of relationships with people. Just make sure these "guests" know how to behave.

For Growth and Renewal: Invite people into your sukkah in order to celebrate your sobriety with you.

*Open the door of repentance only the width of
the eye of a needle and God will open it wide
enough for carriages and wagons to pass through.*

—Song of Songs Rabbah 5.2

The whole month of *Elul* is devoted to the soul-searching
and the self-scrutiny necessary to mend our ways. Then
comes *Tishrei:* Rosh Hashanah, the Ten Days of Penitence
. . . culminating in Yom Kippur, when the final prayers of
the *Neilah* service reflect the closing Gates of Judgment.
But wait. According to tradition, the seventh day of the
Sukkot festival (the twenty-first of *Tishrei*) is known as
Hoshana Rabbah—"the great saving." So great is God's
compassion that this day was set aside to forgive any sins
that were insufficiently atoned for during the High Holy
Days.

When it comes to turning our lives around, it is never too
late. It never takes much to start—just the width of the
eye of a needle. Just the desire to stop abusing and a commitment to keep coming back. Recovery, like *teshuvah*,
means never having to be resigned to the despair and
depravity of your condition. The deeper the bottom, the
more miraculous the return. And every meeting is filled
with walking, talking miracles . . . those who have been
"greatly saved" indeed.

For Growth and Renewal: Go to a meeting and save
yourself by nurturing your on-going recovery. Then do
Twelve Step work to help someone else.

---

*I charge you: Be strong and resolute. Do not be
terrified or dismayed for Adonai your God
is with you wherever you go.*

—Joshua 1:9, from the Haftarah
for Shemini Atzeret in Eretz Israel

Just when you think that the fall holiday season is finally over—enough of a good thing already—there is more to come. And so on the eighth day, we are asked once again to assemble as a community. We are about to leave our desert dwellings and enter our homes once again. But we are worried. Just as we got settled into one routine, we have to get a fresh start on a new one.

That's the way our addiction seemed. It was routine and comfortable. We were terrifed to leave it in order to enter recovery. But we did—we had to. We may still be terrified and will be for a long time to come. But listen to the words of the book of Joshua: "*Chazak v'ematz*. Be strong and resolute." Simple words with a profound message. Look how far we have come to get to this place. Look at where you are now. There's new life ahead and only slavery behind you. These words follow us throughout our journey. New territory, challenges and struggles. As you move from today (Shemini Atzeret) to tomorrow (Simchat Torah), rely on your inner strength and rely on God. Neither will let you down.

For Growth and Renewal: When you are faced with a new challenge or an old struggle, speak these words to yourself and be strengthened: Be strong and resolute.

Contrition on a fast day does not bring you any closer to God than a devout heart's joy on a Sabbath or festival.

—Judah Halevi,
medieval poet

*T*wo weeks after the solemnity of the High Holy Days is the celebration of Simchat Torah, a joyous festival marking the yearly completion (according to most calendars)—and the simultaneous beginning anew—of the weekly Torah readings. It is one of the happiest days in the calendar, marked by singing and dancing with the Torah, and, yes, even a drink or two for those who can.

It is important to note that observing this upbeat festival is every bit as religious as attending worship services on Rosh Hashanah and Yom Kippur. Torah provides us with *the* way to celebrate life—without using the old methods of drink, drugs, food, sex and gambling. Echoing the sentiment of the biblical poet, we shout, I will exult and jubilantly rejoice with the Torah; it is our strength and our light.

For Growth and Renewal: Take the time to see what *should* be celebrated. Then take the Torah and the Twelve Step Program in your hands and dance with it. When you forget that you are dancing, then you know you really are.

24

> *A small coin before the eyes*
> *will hide the biggest mountain.*
>
> —Rabbi Nachman of Bratzlav,
> late eighteenth century hasidic rebbe

One of the things recovery teaches is that we do not have to rely exclusively on our thinking. It's a relief to say: "I don't know." Ask for help. Seek the advice of sponsor, friends and rabbi. Leave the burden of knowing where it belongs—with God!

A big part of learning to live life on life's terms during the month of *Tishrei* is to keep things in perspective. We're all guilty of over-reacting to minor inconveniences—traffic lights that turn too soon, having to wait to be seated in a restaurant, phone calls at inconvenient times. Our emotional equilibrium tilts and serenity becomes little more than an eight-letter word.

Particularly on Simchat Torah, I see how Torah can open my eyes. Learning Torah not only helps me see the world more clearly, it also helps me to better see myself. When the scroll is rolled from end to beginning again, I get a chance to look at my life struggles one more time! And if I don't get it right, I know that I will get the opportunity again—next year.

For Growth and Renewal: Practice saying "I don't know." When it comes time to speak the words, they will flow easily from your lips. Don't ask me when it will happen. I just don't know.

> *On the seventh day God completed the work*
> *which God had been doing . . . then God blessed*
> *the seventh day and called it holy, because on it*
> *God ceased from all the work of Creation.*
>
> —Genesis 1:32-33

When it came to creating the world, God chose to do it one day at a time! Then God rested. It wasn't divine fatigue. God established the Sabbath as a basic pattern for spiritually healthy living for us to follow.

We may feel like doing everything at once. On some days, we may even feel everything at once. No matter how overwhelming a project may appear, we get there only by making steady, consistent progress. Homes are built one brick at a time.

The final part of this Genesis verse reveals this spiritual lesson: Taking a break can be holy. To stand back and let it all be separates us from our work as an artist is separate from her painting. In our addictive society, we can easily get caught up in our doing at the expense of our being. As recovery provides us with a better way to live, so can Shabbat, the climax of creation, renew us spiritually. Thank God for this wonderful island of time when we do not have to change a thing!

For Growth and Renewal: This Shabbat, take time out for yourself. Then carry some of these Sabbath moments into the week ahead.

> *If you can't have what you want,*
> *want what you can have.*
>
> —Solomon Ibn Gabirol,
> eleventh century Spanish
> poet philosopher

People are about as happy as they make up their minds to be. This month of *Tishrei* helps us to frame that point-of-view. In a similar sense, people make recovery and spiritual renewal about as easy or difficult as they want it to be. If one focuses on feeling deprived, if one views going to meetings or synagogue as a burdensome time commitment, recovery will become no less necessary—just more miserable. And, as any addict knows, there are better ways to be miserable.

Recovery with a smile works better. As it says in Leviticus Rabbah (34.9), "When one performs a good deed, she should do so with a cheerful heart." And make no mistake: Being in recovery is one of the best deeds of all—we are saving our lives. A cheerful heart is a more willing one. The part of us that resists becoming better, the part that prefers the negative—that is our sick part.

There is so much that we can have, so much that we do have. And the option to smile joyfully is one of them.

For Growth and Renewal: If your day goes wrong, remember that you can save it—and you—with a smile. So start smiling.

*As far as the East is from the West, so far has
God removed our transgressions from us.*

—Psalm 103:12

So much work to do, so much damage to fix! It can feel
quite overwhelming . . . until we realize that we don't
have to do it all at once. One day, one week, one month
at a time. In fact, we can take some comfort in knowing
that in committing ourselves to recovery, we have already
done the main thing. One Hasidic rabbi, Nathan David
Sidlovtzer, asked "How far is it from east to west?" After
his students had barraged him with several answers, he
replied, "It is only one step to turn from east to west.
Likewise a sinner needs but a slight mental turning-about
to be far removed from his transgressions, east to west."

Just because a task seems daunting does not mean we can
avoid it. Easy does it . . . but do it. The midrash provides
some very relevant guidance: "What does the unwise person say? 'Who can learn Torah? The Talmud is too long.'
What does the wise person say? 'I will study two laws
today and another two tomorrow until I have learned the
entire Torah'" (Leviticus Rabbah 19:2).

For Growth and Renewal: It's a lot to learn and a lot to
do so we better get going, one Torah text at a time, one
Twelve Step idea at a time. Use a *mizrach* (a wall plaque
facing Jerusalem), or a recovery Step, to focus your prayer
and your heart.

It's good to talk about troubles that are over.

—Yiddish folk saying

When we listen to others tell their stories at a meeting, it is hard not to feel very grateful. We are fortunate enough to survive our self-inflicted insanity and have been renewed for the new year. So many have not. Nevertheless, those "troubles that are over" are what brought us here. They are important to remember, but continually rehashing "war stories" from the bad old days may not be enough to win the battles of today. The troubles of the present may be more difficult to share—but they are also more necessary. We need to dare to share whatever is on our minds and in our hearts—the good, the bad, and the ugly. Remember, we don't just share at meetings to sound or feel good—we share to keep our recovery going for another day.

After the holidays are over, and the hustle and bustle and the excitement that goes with them, there is a certain feeling of let down. And so we return to the routine of everyday living, of everyday recovery. But that's what gives us stability. And that's what gives us a sense of our place in the universe and the God who guides it everyday and every way.

For Growth and Renewal: Concentrate on your new routine and raise it to holy levels. Living a holy life is what helps you keep clean.

> *Did God not know where Adam was*
> *[in the garden]? God asked in order to open*
> *the way to repentance.*
>
> —Tanhuma, Tazria 1:9

Of course, God knew where Adam was in the garden. But God understood the human mind—better than we do. Often, someone else has to frame the question before we begin to understand—even when the answers seem so obvious from the outside looking in. God asked Adam the same question that God is constantly asking us, even now—"Do you know where you are?" In other words, "Are you really aware of where your actions have taken you?" But there's more; God asked Adam (and continues to ask us) this question in order to help us move elsewhere, to do *teshuvah*, to get a fresh start on the road home.

It's ironic but true that through Adam's errant action in the garden, his path for repentance was sown. And so it is with us. Without rebellion, there can be no repentance.

For Growth and Renewal: Ask yourself what God asked Adam: "*Ayeka?* Where are you?" Where has my life taken me? Continue to take your Step Nine inventory and admit where you went wrong. Then go right. All it takes is a slight turning.

> *Humans without* mitzvot *are truly naked.*
> —Pirke de Rabbi Eliezer 14

What a powerful image! Like Adam in the garden, before he ate from the tree, he had no conscience, no real sense of self. Some may consider this bliss. I know that I would not have liked the feeling. Ignorance is not bliss. Of course, I probably would not have known any better.

But I think that I know what Adam felt when he recognized that he was naked. It is like living a life without *mitzvot,* a life without the presence of God constantly in one's midst.

Mitzvot are both holy instructions and our response to them. In a sense, they become holy when we do them. Without our response, they seem somewhat meaningless. With our response, they are a dialogue with God, each one bringing us closer and closer together.

For Growth and Renewal: Consider which *mitzvot* help to clothe your soul. Begin by "clothing the naked," the homeless, in your community. Such actions help us to remember and renew God's creation.

Cheshvan
Making Ready
Mid-Autumn

The crunch of the fall holidays is behind us. In *Marcheshvan*, as the month is also known, we take the opportunity to regain a sense of order and routine in our lives. Sometimes that's the most difficult. It's what one friend calls "getting ready for the long haul."

As soon as fall has changed the foliage into a wide range of rainbow hues—and we accustom ourselves to its beauty—winter threatens to cast its shadow on us. Thus, *Cheshvan* is colored in its own way by blessings for rain. Our ancestors knew how important winter rain would be to insure a spring harvest. And so they prayed that God would rain divine blessing on them.

In the synagogue, the cycle of Torah reading moves us from Noah—who was charged by God to preserve the world even as God was prepared to wash it clean—to the faith struggles of our ancestors, Abraham and Sarah. As we walk with these forebears, our own journeys seem more surefooted.

It is gratefulness which makes the soul great.

—Abraham Joshua Heschel,
contemporary theologian

Gratitude is one key which unlocks the spiritual treasure of faith. Instead of complaining about what we don't have, we can instead appreciate our gifts of life. Taking things for granted is a spiritual acid that can corrode our faith. But gratitude is not so much about what to be grateful for as it is to Whom. If we are truly thankful in our hearts, our souls instinctively know to Whom our thanks are due. That's the "conscious contact" that Step Eleven is talking about. Maybe that's why our sages instruct us to say one hundred blessings every day.

Sometimes we feel that the world is filled with our pain and everyone else is oblivious to it. So we are instructed to thank God for the good and the bad. It is a difficult task to transcend our pain in order to rebuild our faith, but pain can lead us to a spiritual life. We are constantly reminded that the world was created in an orderly fashion by God for us. So following the fall harvest, we plant again. We don't always have the vision to see it, but remembering Whom to thank can better help us realize that there is a world of good that we have already been given.

For Growth and Renewal: Focus on something in your life for which you are ready to utter a prayer of thanksgiving.

> *When I die and stand in the court of justice, they*
> *will ask me if I had been as just as I should have.*
> *I will answer, "No." Then they will ask me if I*
> *had been as charitable as I should have. I will*
> *answer, "No." Did I study as much as I should*
> *have? Again, I will answer, "No." Did I pray as*
> *much as I should have? And this time, too, I will*
> *have to give the same answer. Then the Supreme*
> *Judge will smile and say: "Elimelech, you spoke*
> *the truth. For this alone you will have a share in*
> *the world to come."*

—Rabbi Elimelech of Lizensk,
eighteenth century Hasidic rabbi

Recovery is a program of progress, not perfection. Honesty, openness, and a willingness to heal provide us with a foundation. Elimelech comforts us by reminding us that we don't have to be perfect to win God's acceptance. Just a simple, succinct, honest admission of the limits of one human being. As the Yiddish proverb put it, "With truth, one reaches God." In recovery, as in life, honesty brings great rewards. It makes it possible for others to know who we are and for us to get to know ourselves.

Falling short and experiencing setbacks are all a part of daily living. By being open and honest about life, we keep our recovery going, even when we feel that we are standing still.

For Growth and Renewal: Be truthful about how you want to better your recovery. Then seize the moment.

> *When I come to the next world, no one will ask*
> *me why I wasn't like Moses. Instead, they will*
> *ask me why wasn't I like Zusya? Why didn't I*
> *live up to what I was capable of?*

—Rabbi Zusya of Hanipol,
late eighteenth century hero
of hasidic folk tales

I once heard a comedian remark, "I always wanted to be somebody—but I guess I should have been more specific." Who we are is just fine. The challenge is to live up to what we *can* be. We have learned the hard way that we cannot run from ourselves. And we certainly can't run from God. Twelve Step programs have taught us: "No matter where you go, there you are again."

Recovery teaches us to accept who we are, to work within that reality. We can better accept who we are if we know that we are trying to be the person that we can be. It is as possible to change for the better as it is to yield to temptation. The choice is always ours. If we cheat and try to be anything less, we are cheating ourselves. There will be mistakes, setbacks. The wilderness in the year ahead is full of hills and valleys. Our margin for error is at least as great as our margin for achievement. The only real failure is when we stop trying. Ask yourself: What can I do today to make me more like me?

For Growth and Renewal: When you have trouble finding yourself, say a prayer. Thank God that you are alive. And then do something simple like doing the dishes or mowing the lawn. Such activities help us to feel human again.

Act while you can; while you have the chance,
the means, and the strength.

—Babylonian Talmud,
Shabbat 151a

Now is always here. Tomorrow never really gets here. It is an illusion caught between time and space. It's too easy to put off our recovery 'til tomorrow, to avoid the potential for healing. It's second nature for us to avoid. But avoiding, as we have learned, has its own consequences.

Maybe we are just afraid. When it comes to confronting a problem, fear can get in the way. Replace it with faith. Things *can* get better. Stop trying to figure everything out all at once. Doing the right thing, even though we haven't figured it all out, has a positive spiritual value of its own—consider Step Three!

It took Moses forty days and nights up on the mountain to receive revelation, after he had prepared himself for weeks. When he finally came down, thinking his task complete then seeing the golden calf, he gathered his strength to ascend the mountain once again. Sometimes we have to be ready to climb the mountain when we least expect it.

For Growth and Renewal: It is okay to proceed calmly. Remember, putting things off until tomorrow does not get it done today. Recovery is not a race—but it's no rest either.

Offer the sacrifices of righteousness.

—Psalm 4:6

Every worthwhile endeavor requires some sacrifice. But not of animals or money. Just self. To reach any goal may mean letting go of a part of ourselves. We can have anything we want. We just can't have *everything* we want.

Society makes doing and getting too easy. Instant gratification. But the results are usually as fleeting as a drug or gambling high. Our spiritual imperative should be to place principles ahead of pleasure. When we make the pursuit of pleasure our goal in life, we wind up sacrificing a piece of our souls.

Through recovery, we learn to forego doing what we think we want to do in order to doing what we have to do. Making meetings and honoring service commitments may interfere with our living a "normal life," but so did addictions and compulsive behaviors. Nothing says so much about what is important in life than how much we are willing to set aside to achieve it. Putting recovery first is what will make us last.

For Growth and Renewal: Doing the right thing might not always be easy, but it is always the right thing. But first, we have to be ready. Get ready by placing your spiritual priorities today ahead of everything else.

One who stiffens one's neck in stubbornness
will suddenly be broken beyond repair.

—Proverbs 29:1

Addicted persons are stubborn. Prior to entering recovery, we refused to acknowledge any other viewpoint but our own. Addictions help distort reality to the point where even our own viewpoint is besides the point. That's the appeal. For a time, addictions make it easier for some of us to dismiss any viewpoints contrary to our own. The text from Proverbs seems to suggest that our compulsions push us beyond repair. Nonsense. It is the *potential* for repair that seems to be just "beyond" our reach.

For some of us, it is only after it *seems* that we are "broken beyond repair," that we can begin to admit the truth: Our stubborn denial of our problem only aggravated our problem. But the worst victims of our stubbornness is ourselves.

Staying open and honest will help us recuperate from the spiritual arthritis of stubbornness. In the bitterness of *Marcheshvan*, we are ready for change.

For Growth and Renewal: Admit to yourself something that you are still being stubborn about. Then take the bitterness and make it sweet.

Rabbi Gamliel taught, "Do God's will as if it were your own, so that God may do your will as God's own will. Adapt your will to God's will, so that God may change the will of others instead of yours."

—*Pirke Avot 2:4*

A friend advised me: If you are really working Step Three, your life isn't your business anymore. Doing things our own way is what got us here. We thought we had all the answers. We didn't even know the right questions. Instead of wanting to *do* good, we only wanted to *feel* good. Recovery works by opening us up to receive guidance from others and help from a Higher Power. What is wanted from us is more important than what we want.

This does not mean that we dismiss all of our desires. Even if this were possible, Jewish tradition does not advocate it. Drives are normal. It is merely a question of priorities, perspective, and limitations. Get ready to change your life. Recognize that what you want is not all-important to the well-being of the universe. Learn how to accept outcomes that are contrary to personal wishes. As our faith deepens, we will come to believe that we are all part of a plan that we may not always understand.

A condensed version of the third Step: Ours won't, God's *will*.

For Growth and Renewal: How do we discover what God wants for us? We pray. We ask. And we listen.

The one who can't endure the bad
will not live to see the good.

—Jewish folk saying

What other sentiment would you expect from a people that has survived so much adversity? It's a prescription for living life on life's terms—not our own—without the sugar-coating. No one says that we have to enjoy adversity. And, although it is only human nature to seek every reasonable means for avoiding pain, many of us went to extremely unreasonable lengths to avoid our pain—until the escape hole we dug for ourselves became nearly inescapable—and intolerably painful. In recovery, we learn to face adversity. Not without fear, not without flinching. But at least we no longer run. We know that whatever we're going through will eventually pass, that we don't have to go through everything alone.

Some say that adversity builds character. In our long cultural journey, the Jewish people have known the pain of persecution and social alienation. Forget "dysfunctional"—we have survived tyrants who were deadly demons. And yet, for the most part, we have chosen joy over bitterness, and pursued peace ahead of revenge. Every bad time that has ever been cannot erase today.

For Growth and Renewal: Consider what you may have been running away from. Then run toward it. Remember, the distance between east and west is only one step. Go ahead. Make the turn.

> *When you dwell in darkness for a long period of time and then emerge in the light, you must get accustomed to it gradually.*

—Zohar i, 170a

Spiritual darkness and addiction go hand in hand. As a result, we really can't see anything. With spiritual renewal comes light. Recovery is slow and gradual, but we can get there—as long as we accustom ourselves to that light. At first our recovery may feel a bit overwhelming. After all, we were numb to our feelings for so long. But once we get focused we are able to see all the colors of God's creation in their radiant brilliance. Like the canvas of creation, God has taken paintbrush in hand and colored our recovery.

Bill W., the co-founder of A.A., often said that alcoholics were "all-or-nothing" people. What are tiny emotional hurts for others become heart-rending crises for us. A minor fender-bender can throw us into a dizzying tailspin. As one Twelve Step saying puts it, "Time takes time."

It is tempting to grab more of this good thing called recovery and stuff it into our famished souls, but it doesn't work that way. Recovery is a slow fix. Get ready for it one day at a time.

For Growth and Renewal: As you light Shabbat candles, allow Shabbat serenity to enter your life and set your soul on fire.

One should pray to be safeguarded against misfortune before it is at hand.

—Babylonian Talmud,
Sanhedrin 44b

This talmudic text explains why Step Three encourages us to turn our will to God. In that turning, we are indeed protected from the clutches of our own addiction. We may not be protected from everything, but without our relationship with God, we are not protected from anything. Often prayer is difficult. The words get stuck in our throats. We can begin simply: Thank you for keeping us alive. Together we'll work to keep it that way.

We don't have to wait for a crisis to become full-blown before doing something about it either. We can pray proactively. And we can live proactively instead of reacting to every dark cloud that blows our way.

Living on purpose begins when we come to believe that our lives have a purpose. The Talmud says, "The Holy Blessed One did not create anything without a purpose" (Shabbat 77b).

For Growth and Renewal: Don't wait until you're sinking to try to figure out your purpose in life. Ask God. Ask again and again. God is big enough to listen.

---

*The evil impulse is sweet in the beginning
and bitter in the end.*

—Jerusalem Talmud, 14:3

As soon as you think that you have finally learned all you need to know about your recovery, your addiction has a way of teaching you even more about yourself. Autumn evolves into winter. The seasons change and so do you. You can never escape your *yetzer harah*, your evil impulse. It is part of being human, always there to tempt and tease you, always scheming to try to trap you. It's a special way to get you ready for daily living. Get used to it. The evil impulse will always be there, right at your side.

And so too will be the Twelve Step recovery program. You can "drop a dime on your disease" by sharing your dark, dirty secrets with others at a meeting—or wallow in the pit of your own terminal uniqueness. You can call your bookie or call a recovery friend. You can "move a muscle" until your evil impulse gets tired of waiting for you.

The choice is always yours. If at times it's a hard one to make (and there are days when it will surely be), you can at least be grateful that recovery gives you that choice.

For Growth and Renewal: Ask for help. What seems so terrifying in the beginning is simply your disease sweet-talking you to a bitter end.

> *People do not keep things in mind*
> *unless they have stumbled in them.*
>
> —Babylonian Talmud,
> Shabbat 120a

You are the only one who truly knows what it is like to be a slave to *your* addiction. Always keep it in mind. Perhaps that is why we are all instructed to look upon ourselves as if we had been delivered from Egyptian servitude. From that shared experience of slavery, we come to understand one another's pain. Then when we stumble, and we certainly will, we can recall what it was like to lose our footing in the first place.

Few people I know decided to enter recovery on their own—even when they realized they had a problem. They thought they could stop all by themselves. To their horror, they discovered they couldn't. You know you are an addict when your disease whispers to you: "No you're not. You just haven't yet found the way to drink (or drug, gamble, or eat) that works for you."

Only when we have fallen often enough—or far enough— do we receive the gift of desperation—with its focus on the message of recovery. It is as if our lives depended on it. Indeed they do.

For Growth and Renewal: Go out for a walk. With each step, leave your slavery and addiction behind.

> *The Sabbath is scented with the perfume of Paradise. As it reaches earth, sorrow and sighing flee away. Peace and joy reign supreme.*
>
> —Zohar

Shabbat can open us up to encounters that are beyond this world. At the end of the week, I can feel my body shut down. My mind begins to free itself of weekday clutter even as the sun descends. And I am able to concentrate on one thing: Nothing. It's a special kind of nothing, the kind I get ready for all week. It's the kind of nothing that was heard when Torah was revealed on Mt. Sinai. This holy silence allows us to hear what is important, eclipsing the noises of the world. And in the distance, if you listen carefully, a sweet Shabbat melody can be heard. It warms my soul, slowly lifting it heavenward. Shabbat is the best antidote to addiction you could hope for.

Talk about putting first things first! Although God had rested after creating the world, the world was created for the Sabbath. Shabbat is not only a day which helps us recharge for the days ahead. The work week is for doing what is necessary to clear some space out of our lives for Shabbat. *Not* creating, setting aside our desire for *busyness*, helps us maintain our perspective and our ability to give ourselves a break.

For Growth and Renewal: Make room in your life, this week, for Shabbat. Just don't do anything and keep "easy doing" it.

The one who walks in integrity honors God.

—Bereishit Rabbah 8

Addiction has taken us *down* many roads. All of them eventually dead end. Only one road can lead us anywhere we want to go. That one road, of spiritual renewal, is the one which leads us to God. After you have entered recovery and God has helped to restore order to your life, remember that you still have the rest of your life to live. Make sure that you honor your Creator with a life worthy of Divine creation.

There is a certain kind of misery and despair that I think all addicts know: When we actually become so lost in our own maze of lies, half-truths, distortions, and even denials, we no longer know, or even care, what's true anymore. It is very apt that cocaine is called "the big lie." But you don't have to be an addict to have your life marred by dishonesty.

The Lizensker Rebbe, Elimelech, said, "When a person becomes dissatisfied with one's work, it is a sure sign that he is not conducting it honestly." It's the same with one's life. The bottom line: Dishonest living not only dishonors God, it *dis-integrates* our souls.

For Growth and Renewal: What lie did you tell today? Big or small, fix it with truth.

> *The one who ponders one's conduct*
> *brings much good to oneself.*
>
> —Leviticus Rabbah 9:3

We really are what we do. Too many people forget that notion and just act on impulse, the *evil* impulse, the *yetzer harah*! Take this advice: Think about what you are about to do, what harm it may bring to yourself or to others. After all, that's probably what brought you into recovery in the first place.

One of the tools that recovery offers to combat urges is the option to "think it through." When you do, the consequences always outweigh the initial thrill of getting high. The notion that we can avoid our impulses and that our actions matter are the pillars of moral behavior.

The rabbis define wisdom as being able to foresee the consequence of our acts. If we did, who would ever sin? We'd realize, right up front, how lousy we'd eventually feel and refrain from doing it.

The sharper our foresight, the better we will be. We don't have to be prophets. When it comes to temptation, "seeing" a few hours down the road is usually sufficient.

For Growth and Renewal: What are you planning on doing tonight? Think it through before you decide. Then do something else.

> *The Divine test of a person's worth*
> *is not theology but life.*
>
> —Babylonian Talmud,
> Baba Kamma 38a

In other words, no one is particularly concerned about the construct of the "God of your understanding." I only suggest that you believe, because I have experienced the healing power of that belief. It has transformed me. I know that God can heal you too—but you have to be willing to let God into your life.

So don't worry about what to believe. As Step Two indicates, "We came to believe." It's a process. But the process begins with admitting that help *is* possible. "We can be restored to sanity." Many people feel that their group is their Higher Power, helping them to do what they couldn't do alone. And there's nothing wrong with that at all. God works through people. Hope is an excellent stepping stone to faith.

So is unity. The *Shema* [Hear O Israel, Adonai is our God. Adonai is One.] is the essential Jewish affirmation of the unity of God. "When a person is at one, God is one." In other words, we need to put ourselves back together to regain a sense of God. Getting connected to people in recovery is a vital part of that process.

For Growth and Renewal: Repeat the words of *Shema* over and over. Let them become a *kavannah* (literally, the intention of prayer), a Jewish mantra of sorts, to start your day.

> *Envy, lust, and vanity are nothing*
> *but three taverns.*

—Menachem Mendl of Kotzk,
early nineteenth Hasidic leader

*L*eave it to the Kotzker rebbe to say something so piercing that its truth scorches our souls. Envy, lust, and vanity are no less addictive than are our chemicals or addictions of choice. As behaviors, they may even be more compelling. And they all lead us to the same place: Nowhere. So even though you have managed to stay away from bars that serve alcohol and from gambling tables with unlimited credit, make sure you stay away from these other taverns too.

Taverns or caverns? We can hide out and wallow in each of the three, but they are all bottomless pits. We can nurse our envy like a cold drink but to keep sipping from that cup is to keep thirsting. Lust never sleeps. No matter whom you're with, it's all the "shame." As for vanity, the midrash puts it well: "When the Evil Will sees a person walking aimlessly, preening his garments and curling his hair, it says, 'This one is mine'" (Genesis Rabbah 22.6).

Taverns all—on a dead end street. Steer clear. Happy Hour is someplace else, perhaps at a synagogue or meeting near you.

For Growth and Renewal: What other compulsive behaviors accompany your addictions? Then stop visiting them, one tavern at a time.

The one who is truly rich is the one
who is happy with one's portion.

—*Pirke Avot* 4:1

Recovery will take a long time, the rest of your life. But it will also save it. If you ever think that you are finished with recovery, your addiction will likely finish you. Sure, you may feel angry, cheated. Others may seem to have it easier. When you begin to see how fortunate you are, how truly full your life is, you will begin to realize how rich with blessings your life really is.

It always moves me when I hear people express their gratitude for the program, despite the adversity in their lives. A compulsive gambler says that he is grateful to be alive today. You know, deep in your heart, that he means it. A woman has just ended an unhealthy relationship, but she is grateful. She comes to meetings to talk about it.

Our ability to want is limitless; our capacity for gratitude, appreciably less. The key to contentment, however, has more to do with how we feel about what we have than how much we have. Feeling deprived deprives us of the opportunity to feel content.

For Growth and Renewal: Be grateful with what you have by sharing it with someone who has less.

> *Rabbi Simeon ben Lakish said, "A person*
> *should always rouse the good impulse against*
> *the inclination to do evil so that one may succeed*
> *in overcoming it. But if not, more potent means*
> *are at her command, such as immersing oneself*
> *in the study of Torah."*
>
> —Babylonian Talmud, Berachot 5a

It all sounds pretty easy, doesn't it? If you study Torah, you will be dissuaded from the desire to do evil. But listen to the language of the Talmud. If you *immerse* yourself in it. If it fills your pores, courses through your blood, explodes in your soul. If your study leads to action. Creed and deed together; that's the Jewish way. Why not give it a try? Take out a *sefer* (sacred Jewish book) and begin to study, one word at a time. It's better to do it with a friend, a *chaver*, a study partner. I promise you—it will lift your soul and warm your heart!

Torah as the antidote for evil? Makes perfect sense, at least according to Jewish belief. People want to taste forbidden fruit, but God's will is otherwise. The Torah is not just a morally instructive collection of Bible stories. It is a God-given blueprint for living. Said the wise King Solomon, "Wisdom's true beginning is desire of instruction . . . and that brings us near to God." To grow, in any area, we need to remain teachable.

For Growth and Renewal: Spend a day immersed in Torah. And try it with a friend. You'll both grow closer, and closer to God, as well.

---

*Even the evil which God brings down on
the world, God brings down with wisdom.*

—Jerusalem Talmud,
Yevamot 8:3

Look at it this way. If it weren't for your addiction, you would not have entered recovery. Without recovery, you may not have begun the road to spiritual renewal. Yes, God's wisdom is beyond our understanding. I guess that's why we work so hard to get there. Go out and get wise!

One rabbi told me, "In a way, every addict is fortunate to have been given kind of a wake up call. Were it not for hitting bottom, you might still be asleep." Certainly no one wants pain, sorrow or evil fortune, but they are inevitable in any life. We can try to run. Many of us do. But hiding has a pain of its own.

Better to look at life's difficulties right in the eye and blink back a tear or two. The hasidic rabbi, Yehiel Michael of Zlotchov, said, "The fact that evil confronts good gives humans the possibility of victory." Maybe that's why we say "Stick with the winners." In unity there is strength.

For Growth and Renewal: Focus on one of the major difficulties you are still facing. Then let yourself cry. They are cleansing tears. Now face the challenge head-on— with a friend. It goes easier.

People can only learn what their heart desires.

—Babylonian Talmud,
Avodah Zarah 19a

What you *say* about your desire to make *teshuvah* doesn't matter. What matters is whether the desire to return to God is imprinted on your heart. Lip service will not do. Good intentions won't get you there. Only a soul-wrenching drive to get on the path to recovery and stay there will get you there. The prophet Jeremiah instructed the Israelites to circumcise their hearts, not their bodies. That's where the covenant with God truly belongs.

There are times when you may have sat through meetings that seemed like they were ten hours long. But you sat. There are days when the compulsive temptation to use or abuse stays perched on your shoulder. And you literally have to talk to yourself out of drinking or drugging or eating or gambling.

Those are the times when actions teach us about our true desire: To be renewed. It's hard to admit, but our actions speak more loudly than our words. If we are truly willing to recover, then we are ready to take certain Steps, One through Twelve.

For Growth and Renewal: Develop a conversation with yourself that keeps you straight. Make it a dialogue with God.

If I am not for myself, who will be for me? But if
I am only for myself, what am I? And [if I do]
not [act] now, when [will I]?

　　　　　　　　　　　　　　　　—*Pirke Avot* 1:14

You've probably read these famous lines by Rabbi Hillel a hundred times. They provide such a perfect framework for renewal. Perhaps that is why this sage advice speaks to so many people. Think about it for a moment. Only you can recover for yourself. But there is more to recovery than looking out for yourself. Step Twelve encourages us to take what we have learned and help others as well. Sponsors, mentors—two different names for essentially the same holy people. And finally, there is the notion of time. *Now* is always the best time to get ready for spiritual renewal.

"If not now, when?" What a marvelously succinct way of staying focused on the moment and the task at hand. Yesterday is over. Tomorrow, who knows what will happen? It's always about today. And about the balance and tension between fulfilling our own needs and the needs of others. We need to learn to care enough about ourselves, not just so we can glow with self-esteem, but so that we can love others as we have been loved. Attending exclusively to our own needs diminishes us spiritually. In community, *we* are for each other.

For Growth and Renewal: Tape this text to your refrigerator door or your daily calendar. Let it guide you through the day.

Adonai upholds all who fall and raises up the ones who are bowed down.

—Psalm 145:14

As you make your way through the winding path of recovery, keep reminding yourself of this fundamental religious truth. Regardless of why we sought out spiritual renewal—whether it be an addiction to food or chemical substances or compulsive behaviors or simply because we lost our way in the world—we still count on God for the same support.

One doesn't have to be an addict to stumble or fall. Any human being can. But there is a spiritual principle that transcends the law of gravity: What falls down can be raised up again. The key to this ascent may well be our own ability to get humble and bow our heads and bend the knee in prayer.

Being in recovery or believing deeply in God is certainly no guarantee that all will always be well—simply that we will somehow find the inner strength to cope. Raise us up, God, whenever we fall. And strengthen us when our burdens of life bend us.

For Growth and Renewal: As you say your daily prayers, be conscious of your humility as you bend the knee and lower your head in God's presence.

*For a person to be Godlike, that person must be
a partner in the act of creation.*

—adapted from Babylonian Talmud,
Shabbat 10a, 119b

Spiritual renewal is a partnership. We depend on God for lots of help—but we have to rely on ourselves as well. Recovery is much like birth. That's why the rabbis teach that we are reborn each day. Daily, we have the chance to start over. What we do with that opportunity is up to us. It makes us partners with God.

In this context it is interesting to note that, of all God's creations, Man and Woman are not accorded the "and God saw that it was good" Divine seal of approval because whether we are good has been left to us. We are the "wild card" in God's plan. Rabbi Harold Kushner put it well when he said that "Feeding the hungry, supporting the poor, comforting the sick and lonely. These are not things that God does; they are things that we do, and when we do them, God is present in our lives."

Perhaps turning our lives over to the care of God means nothing less than committing ourselves to those principles and purposes that God cares about, but chooses not to do all by Godself.

For Growth and Renewal: Do something today to turn your will over to God by "feeding the hungry, supporting the poor, or comforting the sick and lonely."

If a person repents out of love for God, he needs no cure. If from fear, she must be healed.

—Babylonian Talmud,
Yoma 87a

Fear and pain can be great motivators, but love is even better. What kept us running was fear or guilt or shame. But I've noticed that, sooner or later, people with time in the program are no longer as motivated by fear of drinking as they are by a desire to drink—to keep growing spiritually.

When we react out of fear, even to something as fearful as the misery of compulsive behaviors, we are, in a sense, running scared. It is better to stand still. Better yet, to stand for. The Twelve Steps and our conscious contact with God gives us purpose. Fellowship and community helps cure our sense of alienation. And our belief that God really does love us is probably the most spiritually healing balm of all.

For Growth and Renewal: Run for your life. With each step, run toward your recovery and away from your addictions and compulsions. And take someone else along for the jog of his or her life.

> *Noah drank of the wine and got drunk!*
> *(As a result), he was uncovered in his tent.*
>
> —Genesis 9:21

There is a first time for everything and a last. With the world barely dry from the Flood and the rainbow just faded, the world's most righteous human gets naked drunk. In Noah's defense, one commentator explains that he learned to cultivate the vine but was ignorant of the fruit's intoxicating effects. Great excuse, but you can only use it once.

Human beings are not angels. Temptation, curiosity, pleasure and excitement constantly drive us. Whether the fruit is forbidden by God, or one that should be may be, an important distinction. The latter shows more growth. Outside the gates of Eden, we must make ready to stand on our own two feet.

The behavior of Noah's sons is also quite instructive. One son makes fun of his father. The others respectfully cover him. They reflect the essential human challenge: Do we help or do we hurt? Do we fall down or do we pick ourselves up? Do we make our lives holy or profane? God has promised not to destroy the world again, but we are left free to destroy our own. The choice is ours.

For Growth and Renewal: When we pick others up, we pick ourselves up as well. Help others—and help yourself.

One should live so that at the end of the day a person may say, "I have not wasted my day."

—Zohar

While the essence of this teaching is nearly impossible to achieve on a regular basis, let it stand as a goal, a standard toward which to strive. For each day *is* a blessing, a hope-filled venture into the unknown. Sure you can stay home, protected by a familiar environment. But where can you go when you have closed the door to the world?

There is a Hebrew term for wasted time, *bitul zeman*, literally "voided time." And it is considered wrongful. Because if life is sacred, then time is the most precious resource of all.

As addicted persons, we wasted major portions of our lives getting "wasted." We wasted time, money, relationships, and our own self-worth, but now we are living on purpose. One of my fellowship friends always asks, "What have you done today for your recovery?" It's a good question.

For Growth and Renewal: Make a meeting. Go to *shul.* Call on a friend. Recite a blessing. Do something good for somebody and yourself. Every day in active recovery is a day not wasted.

> *You can't dance at two weddings.*
>
> —Yiddish folk saying

Earlier in his recovery, my friend used to try to do two things on Friday night. He would have a traditional Shabbat meal and then go to a meeting which was in walking distance to his home. It didn't work. He felt too rushed at the meal and "Shabbat deprived" at the meeting. It eventually occurred to him that he wasn't being fair to either experience and was shortchanging both. So he decided to stay at home on Friday evening, and has never regretted his decision. Observing Shabbat contributes to spiritual growth and to recovery. There is room in life for both.

Sometimes, when we feel overwhelmed by our commitments, we may be attempting too much. Instead of feeling burdened, we can ask: What are our priorities? What can we do to regain a sense of balance, of *shelemut* (wholeness)?

The message of recovery and Shabbat share a common theme: Give yourself a break. Easy does it. It doesn't take much to make us feel overwhelmed. We don't always know our limits until we bump into them. When things get hectic, it is a good idea to simplify, set priorities, cut back and then ease into Shabbat.

For Growth and Renewal: Don't do anything this Shabbat. Spend it at home and in the synagogue. That's where you can just be.

---

*The love of people is at the same time a love
for God, for when we love one, we necessarily
love one's handiwork.*

—Rabbi Judah Loew of Prague,
the MaHaRaL sixteenth century
talmudist, moralist and mathematician

When a learned but miserly man asked Rabbi Abraham of Stretyn for a way to attain the fear of God, Rabbi Abraham offered him instead a way to gain the love of God. "That's even better," exulted the man, "Give it to me!"

"It is the love of people," replied the rabbi.

Loving other people can get us out of the maze of our endless self-absorption. It may be the most potent form of *teshuvah.* The love of others leads to a renewed love of self. It's hard to love everyone, especially those who have seemingly wronged you. And so, it is probably one of the most difficult tasks in recovery. That's why it's important to continue working at it.

For Growth and Renewal: Beyond making amends to those whom you have wronged, start loving those around you—including those who may have, during your active addiction, done harm to you. Start with a flower, a note, or a simple hello. It's never easy, just easier. Keep at it. And remember, "Easy does it" becomes easier.

*The greater the person, the greater
the evil inclination.*

—Babylonian Talmud,
Sukkah 52a

*O*nce some disciples of Rabbi Pinchas stopped talking when he entered the House of Study. They were embarrassed. When he questioned their sudden silence, they said, "Rabbi, we were discussing how afraid we were that the Evil Inclination will pursue us." "Don't worry," the rabbi replied. "You are not significant enough for it to pursue you. For the time being, you are still pursuing it."

Inclinations, both good and evil, are normal. They drive us to eat, to seek shelter, and have children. Yet, it's a funny thing how we actually pursue our drives, sometimes running after them, claiming that they are simple human chemistry. The need to eat becomes transformed into an eating disorder. The desire to bear children becomes confused with a sexual obsession. Unchecked, some of even the most "normal" drives can drive us straight into a brick wall. That's when we crash. Knowing how to drive and when to be driven is the key to middle ground that addicted people often find difficult to find. Giving control to the "driver" outside of ourselves gets us going in the right direction.

For Growth and Renewal: Through working Steps One, Two, and Three, you may learn that *not* being in the driver's seat is the only way to get yourself going.

Kislev
Freedom
Late Autumn

*L*eaves are gone from the trees, pushed out to make room for future blossoms. The days are getting longer. Winter looms large even where the winter's clime is not so abrupt. Heavy darkness envelops us like the night, more each day. Yearning to hold on to the diminishing light, we kindle candles to dispel the gloom. But we have learned that real light comes from the soul's reflection of the Divine. We hunger for this holy light to illumine our paths as we venture out into life with renewed strength.

Hopeful, we know what lies beyond. We are able to anticipate the future as daylight begins to gain its strength once again and overtake the sullen darkness.

A taste of freedom comes during the end of the month in the form of Hanukkah. Eight full days of radiant light. And the spin of a dreidle reminds us that even in this topsy world there are many miracles to behold. And we are free to enjoy them. "A great miracle happened here" to us. Renewed, feeling truly free, we are filled with life.

---

*If your impulse to do evil begins to tempt and
mock you, push it aside with words of Torah and
God will consider you as having created peace,
for serenity will be your achievement.*

—Bereishit Rabbah 22:6

Like the crafty serpent in the Garden of Eden, our disease truly speaks to us with a forked tongue—always whispering to us of enticing short-term comforts with no mention of the long-term cost and pain. It gives us rationalization, denial, and self-serving sweet-talk. In short, our addiction lies.

But the good news is that we don't have to listen. As a popular Twelve Step slogan puts it, "Move a muscle, change a thought." We don't ever have to do what we're thinking of doing. Indeed, if merely having an urge to once again sample our "forbidden fruit" disqualified one from recovery, we don't know too many people who would be left to recover. "Minds are shaped by deeds," wrote the author of *Sefer Hahinuch.* The next time an urge or any unhealthy thought enters your head, push it aside by doing some mental push-ups or talk it over with a friend—but don't let it bring you down.

For Growth and Renewal: Share your struggle with a friend. Any burden, when shared with a friend, is lighter. It's what we call "spiritual physics."

When a person has learned to subdue his chief enemy, yetzer harah, *the evil impulse, that person finds it easier to subdue other foes.*

—Tikkune Zohar 178a

Regardless of your addiction, whether it is to alcohol or drugs, or you compulsively gamble or eat, or look for acceptance by purging yourself or giving sexually of your body freely, one thing is for sure. You can deal with *anything* else once you have learned how to deal with your disease. Life itself will continue to be hard. In recovery, you may see the difficulties of life clearly for the first time in many years. Life has been blurred by chemicals and compulsive behaviors for so long. But through spiritual renewal, everything else will seem easier. It is a matter of fact and the experience of thousands of others: It is your recovery that will give you the strength to confront the challenges of everyday living head on.

The first step the Maccabees took was rejecting Roman domination. That step was followed by many battles, but none quite as difficult as the first. Step One is always the most difficult. But with God as our ally, we can brave its many challenges.

For Growth and Renewal: Make a list of the difficulties in life that you seem to be facing right this minute. Consider how your addiction made them worse, not better. Now choose one that you are willing and able to face. Save the next one for tomorrow.

The phoenix grows for a thousand years, then passes through flame and emerges new-born.

—Bereishit Rabbah, 19:5

The phoenix is one of the mysteries of the ancient world that intrigues us even when we don't fully understand its message. It's okay to say "I don't know" what it means. Saying "I don't know" is something that recovery has taught us. It's a message that we are constantly confronted with opportunities to learn again and again. But what we do understand is the insight for recovery that the rabbis of the Talmud offer us in their understanding of the mystery of the phoenix. Like the phoenix, we know what it is like to pass through fire and become reborn. And we are grateful beyond words. Too many of our friends have passed through the fires of active addiction and died.

Whether we understand the ancient myth—even believe it—really doesn't matter. What does matter is that we do acknowledge that the growth of the phoenix reflects the life of the human spirit. Regardless of what has happened to us, we all still have the potential to grow. That's what Twelve Step recovery is all about.

For Growth and Renewal: Try not to focus on what you *don't* know. Instead, take hold of what you *do* know. Use this knowledge as a path for your continuing recovery. Then take what you have learned and teach it to someone else.

The tongue of the wise uses knowledge correctly
But the mouth of fools pours out foolishness.

—Proverbs 15:2

Work the steps in your recovery, all twelve of them. Then work them again. Confide in your sponsor. Share your story in fellowship meetings. Go to your rabbi. Invite your rabbi to join you on your journey. Be not critical of yourself or others, but remember the insight of this proverb. Listen and learn. Talk to walk. Remember, when all you want to do is talk, no one will want to listen and you won't be able to hear yourself either.

Torah knowledge is not like science or math. Neither is it simply remembering who said what and where. For real insight into Torah—the kind that sets you free—you have to turn on a different level of understanding. But it offers us the potential for real wisdom, real healing. Like those things you have learned from the Torah, you are free to use what you have learned in recovery to keep yourself there and help others get there. Use this knowledge and your freedom wisely. Otherwise, you may not be in recovery anymore.

For Growth and Renewal: You too have Torah to share. Sharing your story helps people struggle with their own recovery and understand that renewal is possible. Think before you speak. Then go with your heart.

> *It is better to hear the rebuke of the wise*
> *than for a person to hear the song of fools.*
>
> —Kohelet 7:6

In this post-modern "touchy-feely" world, we may have lost our appreciation for loving rebuke, that kind of criticism that is possible only in a loving, supportive environment. God insists on it. Loving rebuke is our obligation, say the rabbis. Tough love. The prophets used it, even with kings. Do you remember when King David sinned with Batsheva and Nathan called him to task for it? Even kings have to be chastised sometimes.

Sure, we may think that we would rather hear empty rhetoric, hollow compliments, seductive ego strokes. We used to think that we liked the feeling of a quick fix or a quickie in bed—but we soon realized, even as the high quickly dissipated, that we never *really* liked it. We simply couldn't get free of it. Now's the chance. Confront your neighbor. Tell her that you love her—and get her to a meeting, and to a house of worship. Then work Step Nine—it's all part of the same program: Helping people to help themselves.

For Growth and Renewal: Tell the truth. No more "enabling behavior" for you or your codependent. But remember the wisdom of Step Nine. Don't hurt; just help people to help themselves.

If you walk straight, you will not stumble.

—Yiddish folk saying

It's such simple advice whose profound insight is probably the foundation of most Jewish wisdom. If you walk straight, according to the path that God has chosen for you, you will not stumble and fall. Go ahead. Turn it over. Make your will meet God's will.

As terrific and down-to-earth as Yiddish folk sayings are (and even biting sometimes), in translation—especially in the English of the native-born—they miss the mark just a bit. So I close my eyes, trying to conjure up the image of my bubbe, my grandmother, of blessed memory, the last of our family from Russia, and hear her speak these words of advice to me in her own inimitable way. She was less than five feet of pure wisdom, made even more potent by the unforgiving weather of time. Her insights came from a life that was lived beyond the sacred text; she was living Torah. How many times did she tell me things like this that went in and out of my youthful ears only to recall them long after she was gone! Recovery wisdom should make sense to everyone whether we are in recovery or not. Perhaps it is because we are all in recovery from something!

For Growth and Renewal: Work Step Three and put this Yiddish text in a place where you will see it often. And follow the advice of my bubbe. It helped me. It can help you too.

> *A sigh breaks the body of a person.*
>
> —Babylonian Talmud,
> Berachot 58b

*N*ow that's insight. Whether in recovery or just struggling with the challenges of everyday living, everyone has felt *that* sigh. It begins in your toes and quickly moves through your body until it gains its strength, issuing full force from your lips. It's overwhelming. Fleeting desperation. Temporary paralysis. All in a split second.

And yet somehow, when that sigh is gone—we are able to move forward. The chemicals have poisoned our body and yet it is a sigh that threatens to break us. After all that we have gone through, even when we feel totally destroyed, God lifts up our broken bodies and joins them with our broken souls. And in the process, we are renewed.

Such renewal does not seem possible. Honest prayer—with words and feelings that comes straight from the heart—is also required. Just open up your heart, your mind, and your mouth; and let the words of your prayers bring you back to God.

For Growth and Renewal: Even after exhausting physical exercise, we seem less tired. Prayer works the same way. Morning prayers shape our entire day. And somehow *those* sighs just disappear, one by one. Have you prayed this morning?

> *To avoid prayer constantly is to forge a gap*
> *between man and God which can*
> *widen into an abyss.*
>
> —Abraham Joshua Heschel,
> contemporary theologian

For the record, Heschel surely would have included women had he lived a little longer into this generation. Nevertheless, the sentiment is clear. Prayer brings us closer to God. It's a theologian's understanding of Step Eleven.

Each day of our lives, we are presented with the freedom to choose between good and evil, a life of blessing or iniquity. While God's knowledge is certainly different than our own and God's perspective on time beyond our comprehension (for in the Divine mind past and future converge on the present), our choice coexists with God's knowledge of it. To make the right choice, we have to be in touch and in tune with God. Prayerful communication, regardless of method, is the only way.

When you don't pray, you don't enter into any kind of a dialogue with the Holy One of Blessing. Instead, you distance yourself. It's your responsibility to enter into dialogue with God. You are free to choose, of course. I did.

For Growth and Renewal: Open up your heart to prayer. Words will come. Dance. Sing. Pray. Or be silent. But direct your thoughts heavenward.

The truly humble person is unable to feel anger.

—Isaac Kalish of Warka,
the Vorker Rebbe,
early nineteenth century hasidic rabbi

Sure, we get angry. Who doesn't? But anger gets in the way of recovery and renewal. It's all-consuming, a kind of undifferentiated negative energy that gets in our way. Anger colors everything. It immobilizes us. We get stuck in it. Anger is one of the many things that led us to our addiction. If we can root out each of our addictions, one at a time, we might be able to find out how we got here in the first place. Not only will such a process of self-inquiry help, but without anger, it may no longer hurt.

In recovery, we transform our anger into humility—and bow our heads before God. Stop blaming yourself or those you love. Without humility, we can't do Step Seven. What's humility anyway? Simply a recognition that we're no so great and that God is greater. That's why we ask God help us in the process of removing our shortcomings. In working our Twelve Step Program, we are partners with God, only God is a little more so.

For Growth and Renewal: When you feel yourself getting angry, look at yourself in a mirror. Think over why others may be angry at you. It's a humbling experience.

> *I abhor my words*
> *seeing that I am dust and ashes.*
>
> —Job 42:6

A sobering thought and excellent advice for those of us who often find it difficult to hear ourselves (or anyone else for that matter). Such a statement requires real humility. After what we have been through, we feel like Job and understand his sense of self. Or lack of it. We even think that Job's story was written about us. Raise yourself above such self-pity. Remember, somehow Job never lost his faith—amid circumstances that were truly unfair. He was caught in a game of cosmic proportions. We're lucky—those games are over.

Understanding all this helps put Job's experience into context. Our lives are filled with ups and downs. Drugs brought us down; recovery keeps us up. Recall the advice of Rabbi Simcha Bunam, a wonderfully instructive hasidic rabbi. He taught that we should keep two scraps of paper, one in each pocket. On the first crumpled page, gently write: "I am only dust and ashes." On the second, boldly write: "The world was created for me." And remember the difference between the two.

For Growth and Renewal: When you feel the need, select one of the little *pintelach*, these scraps of paper, as my Bubbe would call them, and let it guide you throughout your day. The trick is to know when to pick which piece of paper.

*The knowledge that whatever occurs to you
is for your good raises you to the heights
of living in Paradise.*

—Rabbi Nachman of Bratzlav,
late eighteenth century hasidic rebbe

As my mother would say, "Everything always works out." As a child I thought this advice was rather naive, but it was not a cliche. It was a statement of faith. You just have to believe Rabbi Nachman and keep believing him. I do.

Whatever the day, we can get to Paradise when we are indeed content with what we have: "*Ashreinu. Mah tov chelkeinu u'mah nayim goraleinu. U'mah yafah yerushteinu.* We are filled with happiness. Our portion in life is good. Our lot is pleasant. The legacy we have inherited is exquisite." It's a catchy text in Hebrew and very soothing. I like to hum it to myself.

Dare I suggest that Paradise is therefore only a state of mind? Perhaps. Shabbat takes us there every week—when we let it. For one full day, we get a glimpse of how truly serene our world can be. On Shabbat, all we have to do is nothing. That's the beauty of Shabbat nothingness: It leads us to Paradise and we don't even have to leave the neighborhood.

For Growth and Renewal: Mull the words of "ashreinu" over in your mind. Then wear them on your heart.

> *Exile contains redemption within itself as a seed contains the fruit. Hard work and real diligence will bring out the hidden reward.*

> —Rabbi Yehudah Aryeh Leib of Ger,
> the Sefat Emet, late nineteenth century
> founder of Ger hasidism

In our addiction is our recovery. Whoa! That's quite a statement. But that's what the Gerer rebbe, Aryeh Leib, is saying. Could we have gotten to renewal without our compulsive behaviors and codependency? Maybe. Perhaps. It doesn't really matter. What matters is that you examine yourself in order to recognize that you are empty and that God can fill you up. That goes for all of us: Whether you are in recovery or are just spiritually hungry. Or both.

Now that you are in recovery and struggling to stay there, search for renewal and work the steps. Work them hard. Just like with strenuous physical exercise, let the spiritual sweat pour out of you. The exhaustion is exhilarating. It reminds us how alive we really are.

For Growth and Renewal: This is a good time to remember that the goal of Twelve Step recovery is not to work the step to completion, but rather to keep working the step. One does not simply finish working one step and then go on to the next. Keep working the steps. They are good spiritual exercises to help you stay in shape.

Eat your honey for it is good.

—Proverbs 24:13

Down to earth Jewish folk wisdom, the kind I really like. A simple truth. Traditionally, honey was dripped on a Jewish child's first book so that he might remember that learning Torah is sweet. Of course, the honey is good. We just forgot how sweet it tasted, that's all. We were so busy trying to use alcohol to fill our emptiness, drugs to expand our mind or sex to help ease our sense of loneliness that we missed out on simple joys in life. No more. With God's help, we are ready to taste life's sweetness once again.

When Moses sent scouts into Canaan before the settlement of the land, most brought back reports of its dangers. They were afraid to cross into the Promised Land, afraid of the new challenges that they would have to face. Only Joshua and Caleb saw a land flowing with milk and *honey* and urged Moses to take them across. It was the same place. The other scouts were just looking for the wrong things. Yes, the honey is good; it's sweet too.

For Growth and Renewal: Start studying again. Take a drop of honey and place it on a *sefer* (book). Savor its sweetness. Then keep reading.

Sleep on the bare ground but grow in belief.

—Menachem Mendl of Kotzk,
early nineteenth century
hasidic leader

The Kotzker rebbe, Menachem Mendl, is known for his most unusual insights, so piercing, so enigmatic, that they grab your soul and capture your spirit. Each time I read his teachings, I feel spiritually stretched by them. For Menachem Mendl, belief in God may not only be the most important thing in life, it may be the only thing in life.

When belief in God continues to grow, everything else becomes less important. Through this belief, all else is enriched. We can even sleep on the bare ground; we don't have to worry, because we won't even know the difference.

If you enter into covenant with God—the same kind that was established with Moses on Mt. Sinai—perhaps without the thunder and lightning—your recovery from addiction, too, will grow. And everything else—including yourself—will grow along with it.

For Growth and Renewal: Try sleeping on the floor tonight. Rest calmly and invite the *shechinah*, God's divine presence, to join you. In God's presence, you can indeed continue to grow.

Adonai is your shade.

—Psalm 121:5

An odd, but gently powerful expression. We don't usually think of God as a shelter from the heat or light. But you know the feeling. Think of driving in the winter sun. It's cold outside. Yet the radiant sun is beating down on you. You can't get any relief, no matter which direction you go. The sun is blinding, glaring—hard to see the road that unfolds in front of you. The road melts into the horizon.

Then suddenly, a cloud passes over and a sense of moderation seems to return. You're actually relieved by the lack of intense light. You realize that it's not dark. It's not the end of the day. It's respite: Relief and release.

One could say that this is a Step Three expression, when God's will provides shade for our own.

For Growth and Renewal: At the height of the day's sun, close all the shades in your home. Sheltered from the sun and heat, embrace the stillness and the calm.

> *The one who loves Torah*
> *is never satisfied with Torah.*
>
> —Devarim Rabbah 2:23

Torah is a guide for living and a map for life. As we unfurl its ancient scrolls, it tells us how to get from one place to another. Torah shows us how far we can really go. We may have had no idea that this kind of travel was even possible before recovery. As you journey in sobriety, you realize perhaps more than ever before how, just like with the study of Torah, the journey gets longer even as you travel further in it.

That's the way Torah is. You can never get enough of it, because there is no end to it. There is always more to learn. More to see. More to feel. More to hope. Even as it quenches our desire for truth, it makes us thirst for more. Likewise, the more we learn in recovery and the better we get at it, the more we want it.

For Growth and Renewal: Go into the synagogue and (with the help of your rabbi, if you need it), roll the Torah to this week's Torah portion. Pay close attention to the way the *etz chayim* (Torah rollers) feel in your hands, the smell of the parchment. Consider how many people have done this before. You are part of all those who have come before. Read the words of Torah aloud. Study its ancient message; it will quiet your soul.

*The fear of Adonai is
the beginning of knowledge.*

—Proverbs 1:7

This is an expression with which lots of people have difficulty. Many don't understand how we can have a loving relationship with a God whom we fear. Perhaps a better translation of the Hebrew would be respect—or even reverence. The important notion is to remember that you are you (recovery helps us realize this part) and that *God is God* (spiritual renewal helps us realize this part).

We each have our job to do in this world—God included. It's more of a partnership than anything else, a sacred union, a covenant. Just remember your place in the agreement and then you'll be able to figure out the rest. It is not that knowledge begins when we realize how little we know. Sure, that's true. But more than that, knowledge begins when we realize how much God knows!

For Growth and Renewal: Go to a dictionary and look up the word respect. Then compare it with fear. Determine which word most reflects your understanding of your Higher Power.

The joy of the heart begets song.

—Zohar ii, 93a

Everyone has a song to sing. Somewhere inside of you the words are yearning to come out. It is addiction that has been robbing you of your voice. No more. In recovery, you can learn how to sing again. Perhaps softly, more cautiously at first. Then, through recovery, as you gain confidence, the words will be released from their protective prison inside your soul. Gentle melodies to mend a broken spirit.

People think that you have to have a good voice in order to sing. That's ridiculous. Good voices belong on the stage, in the theater. But real song is felt in the heart. When joy overtakes you, you have no choice but to sing. It just spills out.

When you hurt, it's hard to sing. The pain saps your strength, the desire of even to speak. The words seem stuck in your throat. Until you are ready, listen to the voices of others. Let them calm you, raise you up.

For Growth and Renewal: Don't worry about what other people think. Sing out loud. Sing out strong. "*Shiru lAdonai shir chadash*. Sing unto God a new song." You'll be glad you did.

Jacob struggled with a stranger all night.
Then the stranger said, "Let me go, for dawn is
breaking." But Jacob answered, "I will not
let you go, unless you bless me."

—Genesis 32:25-27

Some teachers see the stranger as an angel. Others see him as the stranger within, the part of us that says it's okay to deceive others, to cut corners, to taste forbidden fruits. Jacob and the stranger struggle wordlessly through the night. It is only when dawn is breaking that the stranger says, "Let me go." It is as if he cannot tolerate the light of day. The dark side never can.

You have spent many a night battling your stranger. Despite the insanity of it all, we know how hard it is to let go. Perhaps, like Jacob, we need to know that something good will come from it all. Recovery is that blessing. Through it, we are helped to choose life and return to the Source of all blessing. As his blessing, Jacob's name is changed to Israel. In recovery, we gain a new identity too: My name is _____ and I am an overeater. The road to recovery begins when we acknowledge who we are. It is easier for us to make this admission now, because we are finally doing something about it. For us, the struggle of "eating to live and living to eat" is over. We didn't just quit, we freely surrendered. Thank God!

For Growth and Renewal: Never let go without a blessing! Let go of someone you had been holding too tight and bless her.

The greatest sinner is the one who regrets
his previous goodness.

—Zohar iii, 101a

When in the throes of active addiction, we don't care about our previous goodness. We don't really care about anything. Perhaps that's among one of its greatest sins. But in recovery, as we begin to regain a sense of self through the Twelve Steps and through spiritual renewal, we begin to ask ourselves exactly what we are or—better yet—what we have become. When we recognize all of the wrongs we have done, the people whom we love most and hurt the deepest, we develop a sense of shame, perceive a lack of self worth. We hit the bottom and we know it.

But recovery teaches us that we must not forget that we are essentially good folks, that our addiction dragged us down. But it did not destroy the goodness that God created within us. Through spiritual renewal, we can reclaim that goodness, hold it close to us, and make it our own once again.

For Growth and Renewal: Reach deep down inside of you and grab hold of some of the goodness that your addiction had camouflaged. Then share it with others.

> *Do not join the scoffers so that
> you don't learn to imitate them.*

—Avot d'Rabbi Natan 26:2

The way to stay clean is to stay away from people who drink, use drugs, overeat, gamble, or are sexually addicted. Sounds like good advice. But it's more than that. It's also the unholy behavior—the eating, the sex, and the gambling—that often accompanies or replaces the booze and coke. When you are in active addiction, nothing else matters. But when you are in recovery, everything matters.

The ancient Israelites were instructed to stay away from foreign nations, because God was afraid that the Israelites would go astray as a result of mingling with them. God was right. Each time they got too close, they got themselves in trouble. Sensitive to the same challenge, the rabbis built what they called "fences around the Torah"—protective laws that would prevent people from violating the essentials.

When you are an active addict, out of control, behaving compulsively, it is your essence that risks getting defiled. Just stay away. Get close to God instead.

For Growth and Renewal: Build a fence around the behaviors that drew you away from God. Change the way you had been "living." Fence out those activities that violate your essential goodness.

*The one truly called a human being
is the one who subdues his impulses.*

—Zohar ii, 128a

What does it truly take to make one a human being—and not an animal? It is an age-old question. We know what it takes to make us animals—addictions have shown us that. Like pigs, they have encouraged us to wallow in the filth. No wonder pork isn't kosher! To be truly human, we have to control—better, perhaps, to channel—our impulses toward productive means.

The rabbis have taught us that the impulse to do evil, what they call the *yetzer harah*, drives us to develop careers, start families, and build homes for ourselves. But these drives should only be considered evil when they get out of control. For when they are indeed out of control, they fuel our addictions and compulsive behaviors.

Intimate strangers beating within the same soul. Another one of those paradoxes of life but an opportunity to reach toward balance and serenity.

For Growth and Renewal: Stay clean. Stay sober. Stop gambling. Balance your eating. No more compulsive sex. Become human once again.

> *Everyday a good person will seek to realize*
> *his moral position; his whole life will be*
> *a penitent endeavor.*

—Babylonian Talmud,
Shabbat 153a

People are basically good. That's how God made us. We are free to choose to live our lives according to that goodness or we can—as our addiction has shown us—just screw it all up. *Teshuvah*, repentance, and spiritual renewal, have taught us that we can change, that we can return to the goodness that is essentially us. It really is up to us.

The wonderful thing about recovery through *teshuvah* is that once we are in it, it frames our entire perspective on life. Everything becomes colored by it. And the colors are brilliant, rainbow-like. But what our disease has taught us is that recovery is a life-long process. So is spiritual renewal. We live our lives trying to be better, to do better, to reach closer toward God. It's a life worth living and a journey worth taking. And it brings us back to ourselves. And that's pretty good.

For Growth and Renewal: Do something today to change your life. Consider one immorality, however slight, and just stop doing it. Use the energy elsewhere—to keep straight.

Before you pray that words of Torah enter your
very being, pray that your sins be forgiven.

—Eliyahu Rabbah 13

The slate has to be washed clean before you can start writing on it again. Soulful confession, *cheshbon hanefesh*, is contained in Steps Four and Five. You don't need to wait for Yom Kippur. It only comes once a year. In order to work Steps Four and Five, confession is as necessary as it is with Step Ten. When we see what we have done wrong, we admit it.

Some people think that after Yom Kippur, they are released from the obligation to come clean. It's simply not true. There is even a tradition that suggests that you have until Hanukkah to do what you didn't *finish* doing on Yom Kippur. The fact is that we never really finish doing it, *teshuvah* that is.

Pray for forgiveness when the calendar seems to want it, but doesn't call for it—when the nights are long and the days are short. This time of year gives a great deal of time to think and to study—to purge our souls—and live holy lives once again.

For Growth and Renewal: Let the brightness of the Hanukkah lights illumine your soul so that you may see yourself more clearly. Then decide what and how you will change, making your life a little brighter.

> *The prayer of a sick person for his own recovery*
> *avails more than the prayer of another.*
>
> —Bereishit Rabbah 53:14

There were lots of people along the way that thought that they were helping us. They called in sick for us when we didn't show up for work. They made up excuses for our missing family gatherings. They sat with us while we were totally out of it. In their own way, they tried to get us sober. But none of it worked—until we were ready to get clean on our own. We have to do it ourselves. Others will help us, but they can't do it for us.

When the Israelites wanted their freedom from the Assyrian-Greeks, they waited to be redeemed. Mattathias knew that they could wait no longer. And so with his sons and daughters, with Judah the Maccabee at the lead, and with those who stood with them, they defeated the mighty armies. This was not only a military victory, a turning to action, as some would have it— this was also a victory of the spirit. Voting with their feet, their action taught us an important spiritual lesson: "I will surrender, but only to God."

For Growth and Renewal: Spin the dreidle. Let *it* spin out of control and be thankful that you have stopped spinning.

> *Whoever is zealous for the Law and would*
> *maintain the covenant, let that person follow me.*
>
> —1 Maccabees 27

These are the classic words of Mattathias, the unyielding force behind the rebellion that led to the victory of the Maccabees over the Assyrian-Greeks. These words became his touchstone. He refused to allow any but God to guide him. Let his words be our standard for recovery, as well.

All who would struggle for recovery and spiritual renewal under the guidance of God: Let us walk together. Among those who honestly try to help are those who are not with us—who are not in favor of our recovery, who unknowingly "enable" us and may be unwittingly against us. Those who tempt us, who supply us, who foster our compulsive behaviors and deny us our self, are against us. Freedom from addiction is ours if we but strive toward it.

Let us walk together in recovery and continue the work of Mattathias, keeping our part of the real bargain—our covenant with God.

For Growth and Renewal: Consider what you can do today to maintain the covenant so that others will want to follow your example. Pick one thing special. Go ahead: "Walk the talk."

For the redeeming wonders and mighty deeds
which you performed for our ancestors
in this season in days of old . . .

—from Al Hanissim prayer,
added to the Amidah
during Hanukkah

Al Hanissim: God, we know what you did for those who came before us. In treatment centers and fellowship meeting rooms, we have seen the results of your Divine labor. And we are grateful for it all. Please, therefore, help us as well. For our sake and for the sake of all those who support our effort to return to You. Redeem us from these foreign forces, alien to us. We humbly ask you to work with us that we might carry your message forward into the world and help others who struggle as we do for insight and truth. We long to draw close to You.

For the miracle of recovery, for the wonderment of spiritual renewal, we thank you. Bless us as you have blessed others who have wrestled free from the throes of active addiction and codependency. And may those who come after us come to you in joy, thankful for the lives of blessing which You have bestowed on them.

For Growth and Renewal: Now that you have recognized the real freedom that recovery has given you—what is possible with God's help—say a prayer of thanksgiving. You are free to do so.

> *Not by might and not by power,*
> *but by My spirit, says Adonai.*

> —Zechariah 4:6,
> from the Haftarah
> on Shabbat Hanukkah

When I gaze into the flames of the Hanukkah candles, watching them burn, the simple beauty overwhelms me. No glitz, no glitter. Just a flickering flame struggling to illumine the world. To make the world holy isn't really so complicated. All it takes is a little light. One candle and then two—desperately fighting the darkness—carrying the light, one to the other. My soul is set on fire.

Next year, we don't start with nine candles; we start over again with one. Enriched, we bring one more year's worth of living to the festival and our celebration of it.

Through my mind, over and over again, I hear these prophetic words of Zechariah. And I know that they are true. I feel it in my bones. I wear it on my heart. It is inscribed on my soul. And I feel wonderfully free.

For Growth and Renewal: As you prepare to light the Hanukkah candles, remember the role of the *shamash* candle, the one which lights the others. It "sponsors" the Hanukkah experience and the sets the hearts of the world on fire. What can you do today to be the *shamash* for another?

Nes gadol hayah poh.
A great miracle happened here.

—words inscribed on
an Israeli dreidle

Israeli dreidles differ only slightly from the ones made in other places. Those little spinning tops proclaim to the world that the miracle happened *here* rather than *there* (*sham,* the Hebrew word you find on dreidles made elsewhere). Here or there. When we're talking miracles, the world's too small for such a distinction. The miracle of recovery and spiritual renewal takes place here *and* there and constantly.

Such miracles don't happen on their own. It took the courage of a Maccabee, one individual, to forge the path for freedom. This person became living Torah for others to follow. He had the spark, the zeal, to break out of the chains of potential bondage. It was slavery of a different sort but slavery just the same. Menachem Mendl of Kotzk has taught us, "One does not acquire the least spark of holiness without effort." It takes work to achieve the miracle of freedom from active addiction, but such work leads us to the miracle of recovery.

For Growth and Renewal: Play the game of dreidle with your friends. It doesn't matter on which side the dreidle falls. You've already won.

One must light the Hanukkah candle
so its flame rises by itself.

—RASHI, Rabbi Solomon ben Isaac,
leading commentator
from the eleventh century

Is it not strange that Hanukkah began with revolt, war, all the bloodshed we associate with the battlefield? Is it not an act of genius on the part of the Talmudic rabbis that what was—in terms of color—the red of battle, has become the brightness of candles pushing back the black of darkness? Our Rabbis realized there was too much darkness in the winter. Rather than succumb to its sadness, they engaged it in battle, much as the Maccabees did when they took on the Syrian-Greeks. They defied the darkness and proclaimed, "Eight nights you shall light candles, one more each night, and blessing God at each moment the light increases." At first, even for them, it was no easy task. They disagreed in the schools of learning nearly two thousand years ago. One said, "Begin with all the candles, and light one less each night," the other— by which we now live each year—declared, "No, no, more light. Always more light." And so we begin with a little light against the huge darkness. On that first night, the enemy still seems so mighty. But then we add another candle, and another, and another, until the menorah is full. There is no doubt that the light—hope against despair—wins out.   —Danny Siegel

For Growth and Renewal: The light is always victorious. So go light your candles.

95

Tevet
Self-Reliance
Early Winter

*T*he lingering final days of Hanukkah which usher in *Tevet* are soon over. Flickering candles return to darkness—having proven that simple illumination can brighten the world. With *Tevet* come the unrelenting winter rains in Israel. They pound the ancient hills, pour down the mountainside. The streets of Jerusalem run cold with mud, drenching the earth, eroding the planted fields and smothering the valleys with fresh soil. The mountains in the north are snow-covered, storing up winter water for spring. As a result, therefore, the month has come to be called *Tevet*, the muddy month.

But *Tevet* does not reflect the familiar mud of the Dead Sea with its immediately soothing, healing qualities. Instead, it reminds us how harsh winter can be. Yet, we have learned that it must be so if spring is to bring forth renewed growth. As fierce as the winter rains seem, we pray for these saving waters of winter.

The tenth of the month is given over to daytime fasting; it was on this day that Nebuchadnezzar lay siege to Jerusalem and eventually took her from our midst. Yes, the outside world can be cold, so people rely more on themselves—and one another—for warmth.

We must enhance the light,
not fight the darkness.

—Aharon David Gordon,
Hebrew writer, spiritual
mentor of Labor Zionism

There's no point in fighting the darkness. Darkness has no substance. It's simply nothing. Darkness will disappear in the presence of God's light. The only way we can see the obstacles in front of us is with Divine light. Without this light, we'll trip over ourselves. Divine light allows us to see ourselves more clearly. It will fully illuminate our path and guide us on our journey home. See for yourself.

Perhaps more than anything else, candles—light of all kinds—help us to focus in Judaism, to center us. Regardless of the season, the holiday, the festival, we are constantly reminded that the light of Torah—God's light—as reflected throughout creation, is the only sure way to dispel our personal darkness. We celebrate new months and new moons, sunlight and sunset. Blessings all.

For Growth and Renewal: The rabbis teach us that we should arise early in the morning in order to do a *mitzvah*. Get up early in the morning and watch the sun rise. Let God's light illumine your life just as the sun brings brightness to the earth.

Blessed is the match consumed in kindling flame.

—Hannah Senesh,
poet, Hagganah fighter
who perished in Nazi Europe

How many times did we turn off all the lights in our house and just sit in the dark? Or raid the refrigerator in the gloom of night? Or in our drunken stupor, not even realize that day had passed into night because we had passed out? Without light, we cannot see the ugliness of our addiction.

To make light, something has to be burned, transformed in the process. That fuel, that source of spiritual energy, too, is holy, because without it we would have no light. "We kindle these [Hanukkah] lights . . . because they are holy" suggests the *Hanerot Hallalu* prayer. Light is particularly holy when it leads us to rely on ourselves, toward the goal of personal renewal and redemption. Without light, there is darkness. We have spent too much of our lives in the dark already. No more.

For Growth and Renewal: We are taught to add candles, one for each night, to increase light (rather than diminish it). Place your menorah in the window. Let it increase the light for those who walk in the darkness and tell of the miracle of your recovery to others.

A righteous person may fall seven times,
yet rise again.

—Proverbs 24:16

Someone once said that you're successful if you get up one more time than you've been knocked down. Our sages tell us that success is not about accumulating things, but about overcoming our inclination toward evil.

Success comes in persisting past setbacks, in getting up again. Nobody is perfect and no sane person enjoys pain. Nevertheless, because of fear of failure, many people stop trying. And there is no way to succeed without really trying.

We took a great many risks during our active addiction— perhaps unwittingly—but we took them. Now, we should take healthy risks in recovery. Calling someone for the first time, reaching out to someone, letting our guard down, coming back after a slip—these are all examples of taking a chance on recovery, and that's the one bet that can pay off beyond your wildest dreams.

You only fail in recovery once you stop trying. The winners in the program are the ones who keep trying even on the days they don't feel like trying.

For Growth and Renewal: Take a chance on someone's recovery. Reach out and make a friend. But not before you work on your own.

---

*Pious people think that they are unworthy of
God's gifts while others think they are deserving
of such gifts and more.*

—Rabbi Yehudah Aryeh Leib of Ger, the Sefat Emet,
late nineteenth century founder of Ger hasidism

The human heart has such a limitless appetite. We want even more than our eyes can see, thinking that we deserve it all. To focus on what we don't have is a sure way to fuel envy, jealousy and greed—and to blind us to the blessings of what we do have. And to focus on what we *can't* have is an effective way to keep us frustrated and feeling perpetually deprived. When the angels complained that God had given the Torah to humans instead of to the angels, God replied, "Were you slaves in Egypt?" (Babylonian Talmud, Shabbat 88b). Strike a balance in your life. Be worthy of the blessing of recovery and renewal.

Shifting our attention to what we can have—the joy of Judaism and recovery—is a good antidote to the self-inflicted despair of feeling terminally deprived. Recovery doesn't keep us from having anything worthwhile. Instead, it greatly enhances our potential to enjoy and appreciate life. It is only the disease that whispers to us otherwise. Let us learn *not* to listen. Be worthy.

For Growth and Renewal: The Twelve Step Program gives us a number of options we can use to defuse an urge. Call someone to talk about it. "Tell on your disease" at a meeting. Move a muscle to change a thought.

*The Torah's ways are pleasant and all who grasp
hold of her [teachings] find peace.*

—Proverbs 3:17

Shalom. Has it ever occurred to you that the traditional Jewish greeting is just another word for serenity? Peace, serenity, balance. A fundamental Jewish ideal. We pray for it. We honor those who pursue it. And, ideally, we work toward it. The Sabbath itself is a day of peace, a glimpse in a future world filled with it.

This sense of wholeness, of completeness, is indispensable to recovery: By being grateful for what we have and what we *can* change—and by accepting what we don't have and can't change—we feel complete, whole, as we are. No additional ingredients are necessary. A sense of *shalom* provides us with the stable foundation necessary for continued spiritual growth. We may not always be serene. In fact, we won't be! But we can always choose to pray and accept it.

For Growth and Renewal: Say a prayer for peace. Then give God a hand; remove an obstacle to personal peace, *shalom,* in your life.

First become a blessing to yourself so that you
may be a blessing to others.

—Rabbi Samson Raphael Hirsch,
foremost exponent of Orthodox Judaism,
nineteenth century Germany

In the heady first blush of "getting the program," we may feel immediately inspired to become a Twelve Step prophet. Our compulsions just won't stop! Before we convert the world, however, we would do better to focus on the message of recovery for ourselves.

It's like that old story about the boy scout who got pretty scuffed up from helping the older woman cross the street—because that's not where she wanted to go! Just think how resistant you would have been—or were—to your friends' and family efforts to "save" you, before you became willing to admit that you had a drinking or drug use or eating or gambling problem and needed to do something about it.

The power of example can reach into another's heart more deeply than anything else. In simpler terms, we have to clean up our own back yard before we can put a rake to our neighbor's.

For Growth and Renewal: Teach others about recovery by being an example to others. "Walk the talk."

> *If your entire body is in pain,*
> *occupy yourself with Torah.*
>
> —Babylonian Talmud,
> Eruvin 54a

Addicted persons are unable to differentiate pain. All we know is that we hurt. Everything gets lumped together in the mind. As a result, we can only focus on feeding the addiction. At the same time, we are depriving the soul. We think that it is our bodies that ache when it is our souls which really suffer. That's why trying to change the way our bodies feel will *never* help. The pain only gets worse. There is an alternative: Torah. There is nothing better. Not the high from alcohol or drugs, food or gambling.

Yet, the first few times you engage yourself with Torah, you may have to force yourself. Some say it is an acquired taste. Good habits are often as difficult to develop as bad ones are to break. But the occupation of Torah is more than just prayer or study. It is total immersion. That's why the rabbis liken it to a soothing balm, one that calms the soul as it cradles the body.

For Growth and Renewal: Torah is God's love letter to you. Read it over the way you would any love letter. Caress its edges. Savor its lingering fragrance. Let it delight you.

> *When a person does not see others or want to see*
> *them, there is darkness in the world.*
>
> —Abraham Samuel Benjamin Wolf Sofer,
> the Ketav Sofer, rabbi, rosh yeshivah
> in Pressburg, nineteenth century

Loneliness is one of the darkest feelings we know. Maybe that's why we feel it so intensely at night. It can sap our strength and render us virtually paralyzed. And, as a result, we don't want to be with anyone, especially ourselves. But God did not want us to be alone. God made Adam *and* Eve. Companions. Friends. Even lovers. But those that see the creation story as the world's first romance novel may be missing the point. Adam was never really alone. Nor was Eve. Both had God as their companions.

Recovery opens us up to that revelation. In program, with others, we learn that we were and are never really alone. In our despair, we only think that way. It seems pretty obvious. Think about it. One friend told me, "If I didn't feel alone all of the time, would I sleep with nearly every person I meet, soon after I have met them? Or would alcohol be my most constant companion?" Even when the world seems to crowd us out, and we feel isolated and estranged, the light is always there. Just open your eyes to it.

For Growth and Renewal: When you are ready ("Easy does it"), spend some time alone. Listen to the sounds around you—the sounds of God's world. You're not really alone. We are all there right by your side.

> *. . . the fast of the tenth [month] shall be to the house of Judah joy and gladness and cheerful seasons. Therefore, you should love truth and peace.*
>
> —Zechariah 8:19

While we usually think of fasting on Yom Kippur, there are other fast days on the Jewish calendar. Just as Step Four is not something that you work once and then go on to the next step, the introspection that takes place on Yom Kippur is never really complete either. It helps us to establish a pattern for the entire year. So on the day when Nebuchadnezzar began to lay siege to Jerusalem, the tenth of *Tevet*, we fast—ever mindful of our own deeds as well. Such daylight fasting allows us to focus our thoughts. It's one of the peculiarities of historical Jewish tradition that when an enemy takes hold of us, it is we who must reconsider our deeds.

But our text takes us even further. In the midst of remembering the agony of Jerusalem, we should be joyful. Maybe it's because we are alive to remember. It's certainly a lesson worth learning. Regardless of what happens, always be joyful and, as Zechariah has taught us, love peace and truth.

For Growth and Renewal: Carry the image of Jerusalem in your mind. When you feel threatened, let her walls surround you and be comforted.

Adonai, Adonai, merciful and gracious, long-suffering, abundant in goodness and truth, merciful unto the thousandth generation, forgiving iniquity, transgression and sin.

—Exodus 34:6b-7a

What more could you ask for from a Higher Power? These familiar attributes of God are part of the Torah reading for the observance of the tenth of Tevet. (They are read at other times during the year, as well). This Torah text reminds us that while we may have led unworthy lives, undeserving of much recognition, God is patient and forgiving and deems us all worthy. All we have to do is turn toward God and keep turning. Don't look back or worry about tomorrow. Just move forward *today*. The midrash reminds us, "God always judges humans on their present circumstances, not where they are or will be" (Genesis Rabbah 53:14).

But these are virtues for us to follow, as well. "As God is merciful, you too must be merciful. As God is forgiving, so too should you be forgiving" (Babylonian Talmud, Shabbat 133). We always have the opportunity to redirect our lives and follow God's example. And God is always there ready to help us. So what are you waiting for?

For Growth and Renewal: Do one thing today—*right now*—to redirect your life. Start relying on yourself.

> *The one who is truly wise*
> *sees the consequences of his actions.*

> —Babylonian Talmud,
> Tamid 32a

You've probably heard the expression that hindsight is always perfect or, at least, nearly so. Had we known where a life of addiction might have led us, perhaps we wouldn't have gone in that direction. But our lives were out of our control. We've admitted that. Better insight might have helped us out, had we taken the trouble to look. Real *vision*, the wisdom to see self and the consequences of our actions, certainly would have. In recovery, we have learned that lesson. But the past is over. It is behind us. Let's just leave it there. It helps us not to dwell on it, because then we can't move forward at all. But now, with renewed vision, and the ability to rely on self once again—the self we had previously not trusted—we can finally go the distance and look forward, a future *is* ahead of us.

Some thought that drugs would offer vision. Others thought that alcohol might color all that we would see. Both simply blurred reality so that we didn't even see the brick wall we had built around us. Spiritual renewal provides us with tools to tear down that wall and use the raw materials to build a bridge instead.

For Growth and Renewal: Forge a path for yourself into the future. Don't worry about the years ahead—or the years behind. Just put one step in front of the other.

One person's life is equal to all creation.
—Avot d'Rabbi Natan 31

Are you willing to take Rabbi Natan's advice and save the world? Such heroic acts do not take place overseas in far-flung lands, limited to the activities of Nobel Peace Prize recipients. They begin with the self.

Your life *is* equal to all creation. How do you come to appreciate this wisdom? Perhaps when you pick yourself up after you fall. When you admit to being "powerless over alcohol [drugs and other addictions and compulsive behaviors]." When you recognize—even when the world seems so cold, dark and gloomy—that your unique potential is yours alone to shape, under the loving guidance of a Higher Power. The hasidic teacher the Tzaddok Ha-kohen of Lublin teaches, "Sometimes a person has a sense of despair and has no desire to study Torah or do *mitzvot,* but these days often mark a prologue to a great ascent in one's spiritual development. At such a time of despair, the person may engage in an examination of one's deeds and this may lead that person to greater heights." Keep counting your days in sobriety. Know how far you have come from your active addiction, and look forward to what spiritual growth is ahead.

For Growth and Renewal: Examine your deeds today. Keep working Step Ten; when you examine yourself, you see all creation.

The one who avoids evil is a fool.

—Babylonian Talmud,
Sanhedrin 97a

Did you really think that once you entered recovery, and "turned it over," that evil and temptation would simply give up on you, fall by the wayside or turn to its next victim? Not so fast. The potential for evil is part of the fabric of the world. Our obligation to our recovery and to ourselves is to recognize its many guises, to see evil for what it is and what it can do—has done—to us and not to be seduced by it. It's not easy either. Even the strongest, most faithful among us must be on our guard—beyond the alcohol and the drugs, the compulsive behaviors of gambling, eating, and sex, no matter how many years of sobriety we have celebrated.

The rabbis teach that Abraham was taunted by evil each step along the way as he made the journey to Mt. Moriah to ostensibly sacrifice Isaac. He quickly learned that evil lurks where you least expect it. Better to confront it than pretend it doesn't exist.

We confront evil with positive behaviors, by working the program, by creating holy time and space in which to live.

For Growth and Renewal: Come face to face with the evil. Transform it and make it holy, one challenge at a time.

---

*The more a person submits to God, the louder
that person can raise one's voice and be heard.*

— Rabbi Yechezkel of Kuzmir,
head of hasidic dynasty in
Kuzmir, nineteenth century

This certainly sounds like a paradoxical statement. But
it's really a recovery insight: Step Three wisdom. We can't
fully understand it unless we are committed to the path of
spiritual renewal. We call it "turning it over." Judaism
calls it covenant. Both really say the same thing. This is
another example of how the Twelve Steps and Judaism
are indeed compatible. When we live our lives allied with
God, our journey in life is flooded with meaning. We *can*
raise our voices above the pain of our addiction.

Like recovery, spiritual renewal is a process, not a goal.
We are always en route. Thus, we must remain on our
guard, making sure that we don't exchange one self-effac-
ing behavior for another. Once a student came to Rabbi
Hanoch of Alexander and said to him, "I have finally
overcome my evil inclination and now I would like to act
with piety." Rabbi Hanoch chuckled, "Had you the
strength, you would have sinned. Your evil inclination has
simply been transformed from lust to haughtiness, for the
evil inclination for pride remains with a person until his
last dying breath."

For Growth and Renewal: As you raise your voice above
others in prayer, be mindful of the evil inclination for
pride that constantly challenges all of us, ever cognizant
of God above.

---

*Rabbi Illai said, "A person is known by three
things: One's cup (koso), one's pocket (kiso),
and one's anger (keso)."*

—Babylonian Talmud,
Eruvin 65b

At first glance, this might seem like another example of rabbinic wordplay. Yet, this simple statement provides us with real insight for our Step Four work. And it's not quite as threatening as other techniques. Instead, in a gentle, down-to-earth manner that we have come to appreciate as the clever wisdom of the rabbis of the Talmud, we are told to look at just three things. But in examining those three perspectives on self, we can come to better understand who we are.

As you are looking, don't be disappointed. No matter how many times you work Step Four, there will always be more work to do. You will *never* find perfection. It was that flawed search for perfection that led many into active addiction and codependence. Listen to the words of the teacher whom tradition calls the Sefat Emet: "Ever since Adam sinned, good and evil have been mixed together. There is nothing of a holy nature which is not accompanied by a certain degree of shadow." We will always have a dark side. May it drive us to do good and overcome the evil.

For Growth and Renewal: Make a list of your good traits, including those which emanate from a dark side. Then concentrate on the light they give, not the shadow they create.

We hope you will enjoy this book and that you will find it useful and use it to enrich your life.

Book title: _____

Your comments: _____

How you learned of this book: _____

Reasons why you bought this book: (check all that apply)
□ Subject   □ Author   □ Attractive Cover   □ Attractive Inside
□ Recommendation of Friend   □ Recommendation of Reviewer   □ Gift

If purchased: Bookseller _____ City _____ State _____

Please send me a JEWISH LIGHTS Publishing catalog. I am particularly interested in: (check all that apply)

1. □ Spirituality
2. □ Mysticism
3. □ Philosophy/Theology
4. □ History/Politics
5. □ Women's Issues
6. □ Environmental Issues
7. □ Recovery/Self-help
8. □ Children's Books
9. □ Limited Edition Books
10. □ Haggadahs
11. □ Audio Tapes of Books
12. □ Audio Tapes of Author Lectures

Name _____
Street _____
City _____ State _____ Zip _____ Phone _____

JEWISH LIGHTS Publishing
P.O. Box 237, Woodstock, Vermont 05091   Tel: (802) 457-4000 Fax: (802) 457-4004
JEWISH LIGHTS Publishing titles are available at better booksellers

JEWISH LIGHTS Publishing

Sunset Farm Offices / Route 4

P.O. Box 237

Woodstock, Vermont 05091

> *Knowledge by itself is insufficient.*
> *It must also penetrate the heart.*
>
> —Rabbi Israel Salanter,
> nineteenth century founder
> of the Musar movement

In this modern age of instant information with today's faster, more efficient computers making yesterday's electronic marvels immediately obsolete, our apparent quest for knowledge knows no bounds. And neither do we. We want things faster and faster and only what is current so we often disregard the wisdom that has been handed down to us. This information age has transformed us into people who feel with our heads instead of our hearts. As a result, we talk about things instead of feeling them, experiencing them. Intellectual discussions may warm our minds but our souls remain out in the cold.

For knowledge to penetrate the heart, to set our souls on fire, we have to use our whole bodies and literally "walk the talk." Consider what one teacher, Rabbi Nachman of Bratzlav, wants to teach us: "There is a faith which is only in the heart and that is not enough. It must pervade the whole body."

For Growth and Renewal: Be aware of when you are avoiding your feelings by playing mind games instead. Then stop playing them. Express instead what is on your heart and in your soul.

Sin is difficult only the first time.

—Yiddish proverb

Can you remember the first time you purged yourself of
the food you had just eaten? Initially, it was probably difficult, but you quickly got used to it. Then it became routine—you probably didn't think much about it. One
friend suggested to me: "I was so blind to what I was
doing that I began to brag to my friends about it. I'd tell
them that it was a great way to lose weight. I didn't realize that I was losing *myself* in the process."

The rabbis suggest that God decided to deliver the
Israelites from Egypt when God realized that they had
gotten used to Egyptian slavery. For addicted persons,
that's not hard to understand. There is a certain point
when living without the addiction, the slavery, is such a
distant memory that it gets put out of your mind entirely.
But just as sin is difficult only the first time, getting on the
road to recovery, and relying on yourself once again, is
only hard at the beginning. Once you get used to recovery, it too will become easier. But don't think that recovery will get too easy; recovery doesn't work that way.

For Growth and Renewal: There are many things that
get overshadowed by our addictions. What things do you
still do—that you shouldn't be doing—that have become
part of your routine? Rely on yourself to shake loose of
these addictions, as well.

If I am not for myself, I am nobody.
But to be somebody, I must be there for others.
And I must act now.

—*Pirke Avot* 1:14,
adapted by Rabbi Alfred Wolf

This is a flawless formula for recovery from codependence. Balance, moderation, middle ground. What we strive for in recovery through the Twelve Steps can be found in this rabbi's interpretation of Hillel's classic statement from *Pirke Avot.* Our vain attempt to live solely for other people—our codependence—came at the expense of self. It helped to get us into this mess in the first place. When we live for others, we have no life left for ourselves. We may have forgotten about it in our active addiction, but recovery reminds us of that we do want to live.

Yet, as Step Twelve teaches us, when the time comes, we must also be there for others—in the same way our sponsor, our fellowship friends, our spiritual guide is there for us.

And we must act now. For ourselves, for those we love, for friends in our community. Tomorrow is always too late.

For Growth and Renewal: Are there still parts of your recovery that you have been putting off? *Now* is the time to deal with those behaviors.

> *The one who walks with humility*
> *has clear thoughts.*
>
> —Rabbi Nachman of Bratzlav,
> late eighteenth century hasidic rebbe

Humility is such a misunderstood concept. Some people are so busy trying to be humble that their "pious arrogance" gets in the way. Our ancestor Jacob knew about humility, for as *Toledot Yaacov Yosef* teaches us, "Because he lay down on the ground submissively, the Divine Presence immediately appeared to him." That's why the Program talks about getting down on your knees to pray. It may seem contrived, but there is no better way to feel the presence of a Higher Power. Think back to the Holy Days when the High Priest (now the rabbi and cantor) lay prone on the ground during the Grand Aleynu prayer. What better model do we need?

Nevertheless, bowing down is really tough for some Jews. They see it as Christian behavior. So Nachman of Bratzlav, echoing the wisdom of the prophets, suggests that one should walk with humility. It's his suggestion as a way to clear your head. It's a balancing act once again. I know what those walks are like, especially at night in the cold of winter. It's a time for self-reflection and inner-searching. Twelve Steps on the move.

For Growth and Renewal: Walk upright. Rely on self. And be aware of the presence of God above and beyond you.

> *One cannot understand the present*
> *unless one understands the past.*
>
> —Yehudah Leib Eiger of Lublin,
> nineteenth century hasidic rabbi

This is something that the Jewish people learned a long time ago. It's one of the many reasons that Judaism and the Twelve Steps fit together so neatly. For those in recovery, seeking spiritual renewal, each breathes life into the other. We probe the past—even simulate it—in order to learn from it. We've made it part of our calendar. One need not dwell on the past. That keeps us there. Instead, we grow beyond it.

Sure, it's easier to stay in the past where it was comfortable because it was so familiar. That way, the uncertainty of the future never has to be faced. But that's not reality and it is certainly not living. Stop being slave to the past, addicted to alcohol and drugs and behaving compulsively. If we understand how we got into Egyptian slavery in the first place, we may be able to avoid it the next time.

For Growth and Renewal: Each time the Torah is read in public, we are re-enacting the revelation of Torah at Sinai, between the journey from Egyptian slavery to the Promised Land. As you retrace the footsteps of our ancestors, retrace your own as well. Take time to understand your past so that you can avoid what enslaves you as you live today and tomorrow.

> *An antidote for the Evil Inclination is*
> *to remind oneself of the day of death.*
>
> —Babylonian Talmud,
> Berachot 5a

"**H**ow does that help?" we wonder. Not only does such advice remind us of who we really are—merely mortal—but it also encourages us to "repent on the day of our death." Eventually, there will be an ultimate end to our driving, the fueling of our addiction. Death will control it. But recovery gives us the chance to direct our lives right now.

Moses Maimonides, the twelfth century Jewish philosopher, reminds us: "Do not imagine that character is determined at birth. We have been given free will. Any person can become as righteous as Moses or as wicked as Jeroboam. We ourselves decide whether to make ourselves learned or ignorant, compassionate or cruel, generous or miserly. No one forces us, no one decides for us, no one drags us along the path of another; we ourselves, by our own volition, choose our way." We have chosen a way. It may have taken us some time to get here, with some detours along the way. But the important thing is that we, indeed, are here.

For Growth and Renewal: Take the advice of the Talmud. Today, when you are tempted—and you surely will be—remind yourself that each day you used, you nearly died. Set aside this day of death for you to repent.

> *In life, you discover that people are called by*
> *three names: One is the name that person is*
> *called by father and mother. One is the name*
> *people call the person and one is the name*
> *one acquires for oneself.*
>
> —Tanchuma, Vayachel 1

The text concludes—as we would—"The best one is the name one acquires for oneself." What a name we acquired for ourselves! Step Nine instructs us to try to repair the damage we have done in active addiction. And as colleague Rabbi Larry Kushner always reminds us, "If you can't fix what is broken, go fix something else."

Whatever name we might have been known by in active addiction, recovery gives us the opportunity to gain a new name for ourselves. And indeed, we will, through the process of spiritual renewal, acquire a new name for ourselves. When Jacob struggled through the night with the stranger, he refused to let this stranger-angel go before he was blessed. And so the stranger-angel blessed him by giving him a new name: Israel. This new name was a blessing. And so it is for us, as well. After we struggle with the many nights—and days—of active addiction, we are blessed with a new name and a renewed life.

For Growth and Renewal: Some people find that in recovery they indeed like to use a new name. Often in recovery, some will use their Hebrew names. Try on your new identity, your new self.

One can reach God anywhere.

—Rabbi Menachem Mendl of Kotzk,
early nineteenth century hasidic leader

The Kotzker Rebbe goes on to teach: "The difference is which gate one uses to approach God. If one goes through the gate of heaven—one finds God immediately. But if one uses the other gates, one also finds other things along the way." It took many of us a long time to find God in our lives. There were many other things that we encountered along the way. For those in recovery, we found alcohol and drugs and eating disorders, compulsive sex and gambling along the way. But for others, we simply found hedonism, a material world, the distractions of contemporary society.

The truth is, whether we are in recovery or not, we all need to be healed. Regardless of how we got here in the first place, our souls yearn for it. Without healing, we cannot reach God. There's just too much anger, too much pain for God to find a place in our hearts. We're all afraid. The world in which we live is often terrifying. No matter how big we feel, we are so very small. With God's help, we can be healed. Believe it. I do.

For Growth and Renewal: Reach out to God and be healed. Reach out to others and be a channel for God's healing.

When a person has faith, that person can see.

—Rabbi Nachman of Bratzlav,
late eighteenth century
hasidic rebbe

Another word that scares some people off: Faith. It sets off alarms, sounds too Christian, too fundamentalist. "How can we teach self-reliance and faith at the same time?" some ask. "They seem to contradict one another." And then they wonder why the walls of denial keep getting bigger and stronger! Faith in oneself and in God are branches on the same tree of life. With faith in ourselves, we are able to reach God. With faith in God, we see ourselves more clearly.

Look what the Seer of Lublin had to say: "If you think that you have no blemish, that you are perfect [and do not need God], it shows that you have not truly accepted the yoke of the heavenly reign and that is surely why you do not know about your own blemishes."

We all have blemishes, "shortcomings," and "defects of character." Through repentance (*teshuvah*), in recovery, we can see and grow beyond them.

For Growth and Renewal: Do your Step Seven work. Consider your shortcomings—not those of others—and what God can help you do to overcome them. Then follow your own advice.

---

*As a face sees its reflection in the water, so does
one person's heart reflect another's feelings.*

—Proverbs 27:19

Empathy. Feeling another's pain. Supporting another's spiritual journey. That's one of the many ways the program works. And it does work. There are thousands alive today to prove it. But there's a big disparity between creating supportive environments for recovery, "enabling behaviors," and codependence. Get to know the difference between them. Separate yourself from another's compulsive behaviors. That knowledge can help save your life.

It may not seem so right away, but knowing the difference—and acting on that knowledge—may also help save the life of others that you love. Some like to call it "tough love." And it is tough. Very difficult. You will have to make some very hard decisions in the days to come. Life and death decisions. Make no mistake about it. But no more excuses. No more empty apologies. Just recovery and renewal. It's the only acceptable behavior. We all know how it feels. Many among us were in the very same place. The reflections in the water cited above in Proverbs are our own.

For Growth and Renewal: As the rabbis suggest, there is something redemptive about water. Go to the nearest lake or river. Consider your own reflection. Then cast your codependence into the water.

---

*Only when one is barefoot can one feel
the stones underfoot.*

—Hasidic teaching

I imagine that it is the profound simplicity of Hasidic wisdom that engages and captivates us. This particular image, from the desert wanderings of our people, speaks to all of us. Whether we live in urban centers or the sprawl of suburbia, this Hasidic teaching reflects our own desert journey. It is not merely a journey through recovery for those who are leaving a life of active addiction from chemicals or compulsive behaviors. Rather, it is the journey of all of our lives, the journey of life itself.

Regardless of our relationship with our Higher Power, it is we who ultimately must place one foot in front of the other. Tired, feeling the pain of each step along the way, we also know that we must move forward nonetheless. To not move is to be paralyzed, to be swept backwards by the blinding desert winds. And with each step, we are closer to our destination of a promised land: Calm, serene, flowing with milk and honey.

For Growth and Renewal: When one gets up from the first seven days of mourning, one symbolically walks around the block as a re-entry to life. Now in recovery, out of the *midbar* (desert), take a walk around your neighborhood. Now you can feel at home.

---

*For every deficiency in the body, there is
a corresponding deficiency in the soul.*

—Dov Baer, the Maggid of Mezritch,
eighteenth century hasidic leader

While we think of chemical addiction as a disease—which it is—like other diseases that afflict the body, it reflects a sickness that lies deeply embedded in the soul. One friend told me, "Inside I felt empty. I tried to fill the emptiness with all kinds of chemicals. I started with pot, then cocaine, and finally, pharmaceuticals of all kinds. And when they didn't help, I tried getting closer to people with my body. But nothing worked. I only felt emptier." No! Chemicals—drugs or alcohol—will not work. Neither will food nor gambling nor compulsive sex. Nothing foreign can heal the soul.

Only through a relationship with God can you begin to identify ways which will help heal your soul. Reading these meditations is a good start. Studying Torah with a friend is an even better one.

For Growth and Renewal: When you do a mitzvah—and studying Torah is a mitzvah—and when you follow the Twelve Step Program, remember that you do so to bring you closer to God, making your life holy, helping to heal your soul at the same time.

*A person does not commit a sin
unless the spirit of folly enters him.*

—Babylonian Talmud,
Sotah 3a

What really motivated you to purge yourself of food the first time? Was it something spontaneous or had you been trying for a while, trying to get up the "courage"? What part of you were you trying to get rid of? Maybe it was just one of a long list of ways you were trying to control the foods you put into your body. Simply another attempt at compulsive dieting. Until you realized that it was you who was out of control.

Can you recapture the moment of your first high, so that you might learn from it? The rabbis of the Talmud have called it "folly." Now you certainly realize that it truly was folly, but then you thought you weren't doing anything wrong. Maybe you were simply trying to be what you thought others wanted you to be.

Sure, trying to recall the beginning of any addiction is painful. You want to forget. But remembering can be part of the cleansing process of recovery, leading us on the way to spiritual renewal.

For Growth and Renewal: Memory is a powerful tool in recovery. That's why lists are important to Twelve Step programs. Make a list of all the things that you want to remember not to repeat. And be redeemed and renewed by the memory.

Those who sow in tears will reap in joy.

—Psalm 126:5

This ancient song of the returning exiles from Babylonia to ancient Israel has become an almost inseparable part of Jewish liturgy and ritual. For me, it reflects *the* lesson of the individual Jewish soul. As part of our taste of what the world can be like, we sing these words on Shabbat before Birkat Hamazon, the so-called Grace After Meals. Spoken by Prime Minister Menachem Begin, this psalm was even part of the ceremony at the signing of the Camp David peace accords.

Each life will have its fill of tears. Like it or not, we accept it, acknowledge it, even embrace it. Our responsibility, therefore, is to plant those tears so that we might joyously reap the fruits of these painful labors. To choose any other way is to choose death. But God has told us—even though we have been given the choice—"Therefore, choose life." Refuse to accept death as an alternative. And as testimony, stay alive—stay sober and keep clean.

For Growth and Renewal: Sing this Psalm of Ascent (Psalm 126). As you consider each word, remember that recovery has given you the chance to ascend into holy life. Let your tears of sorrow be transformed into tears of joy.

Shevat
Rebirth
Mid-Winter

*I*t often doesn't look like spring will ever come during mid-winter. With snow still blanketing much of the earth in the north and the world looking so serene, of one thing we can be certain. Nature again prepares itself anew. There is more light each day. Sap is just beginning to flow deep inside the trees. Life is renewed and hope is restored. Consequently, we feel reborn.

This month, whose name is related to the term for the beating or striking of instruments, can come as early as January 1 or end as late as March 1. This is both a month of historical feasting and fasting as we recall the events of our past. And on the fifteenth of the month Tu Bishevat is celebrated. While this is the day that marks the separation of tithes from one year to the next, it also reflects the revival and redemption of the land and our firm belief in the "Author of all creation who renews that creation daily."

It is also the time of the year when people expressed their support of the community with a contribution of funds to the ancient Temple and an accounting of self. This Shabbat Shekalim, the first of five special sabbaths which anticipate Pesach when these funds were collected, frames the end of the month.

> *O that I had wings like a dove!*
> *I would fly off and find rest.*

—Psalms 55:7

The urge to escape, quickly, instantly, and without strings, is as old as Adam trying to hide from God after he ate the apple. And that's not really bad in and of itself. We all need a break now and then from the stresses of our lives, our relationships—even from ourselves. Unfortunately, that's just the delicious little self-forgetting thrill that our "escape of choice" gave us. A wise recovery counselor once suggested that addiction may be a painful but perhaps necessary detour along the spiritual growth path leading to self-transcendence: That we were not so much running away as, albeit unwittingly, we were limping *towards*.

But where are you going? Adam didn't know, so he hid. Then he was expelled from the garden. Don't hide. In recovery, you feel reborn. So decide where you want to go and get going. But don't forget the advice of the rabbis, "Make God your travelling companion."

For Growth and Renewal: Discover new ways in which you can make God your travelling companion throughout your recovery. Recite the *Tefillat Haderech* (the traveller's prayer) and be on your way.

When you have eaten your fill, give thanks
to Adonai, your God, for the good land
which God has given you.

—Deuteronomy 8:10

Whenever we eat, whether it is part of our normal daily living or in celebration of one event or another, we give thanks to God who constantly provides us with food for body and soul. Gratitude for what we have eaten, gratitude for being alive. By expressing our thanks to God whenever we eat, we are able to frequently acknowledge God's presence in our lives. This historical feast day, the second of *Shevat*, which is no longer really part of the calendar of mainstream Jewish observance, marks the anniversary of the death of Alexander Yannai, one of the Hasmonean kings of Judea and a high priest during the years 103-76 B.C.E.

Whenever we have the opportunity to express our thanks to God, we do so, over all that we see and do. Some people say that the constant repetition of all these prayers and blessings is overdoing it. But the saying of prayers and blessings helps us to establish a *holy* routine in our lives and feel *whole* as a result. Anyhow, how can we overdo our gratitude for being in recovery? Nothing comes close to it. Through it, we have the chance to get close to God.

For Growth and Renewal: When you eat, trace the source of your food, each step along the path. Then say a prayer of thanks.

*A person's deeds are used by Adonai as seeds for
the planting in the Garden of Eden; thus, each
person creates one's own Paradise. The reverse is
true when that person commits transgressions.*

—Dov Baer, the Maggid of Mezritch,
eighteenth century hasidic leader

We can't always have Paradise, but we can find serenity,
fully reborn in recovery, as long as our deeds are firmly
planted and gently nourished. What does it take to create
Paradise in our own midst? Is it even possible or are we
kidding ourselves, after the life we have lived, the pain we
have caused? With the guarantee of Shabbat every week,
Paradise is always possible.

It is said that the Messiah can't come on Shabbat, because
the Messiah is already present on Shabbat. We get a little
taste of Paradise during Shabbat. Then some hours later,
it slips away from us and we have to return to the reality
of living. We can wait for a few days to make *Havdalah*,
separating secular from the holy, but we eventually have
to make it. There is no getting around it. As an alternative, we take with us "Sabbath moments," sacred fragments of holy time. They carry us through the vagaries of
the world. Eventually, we have to let go of Shabbat
Paradise in order to have enough time to prepare for it
again.

For Growth and Renewal: Plant your own seeds of
Paradise by giving to someone in need. Then nurture them
as you both grow.

> *Prayer begins where our power ends.*
>
> —Abraham Joshua Heschel,
> contemporary theologian

A well-known expression puts it this way, "There are no atheists in foxholes." Maybe we had to reach the end of our rope to get to the point where God's rope begins. If so, that was our spiritual turning point, where we can start over, and once reborn, actually begin our lives again—our *teshuvah* moment. And the only way to get there is through prayer.

Some people in the program see ego as a smug little acronym that stands for "Easing God Out." The Hasidim teach that it is the "I" of individuals, self-centeredness, that stands between people and their Creator. As long as one thinks about the "I," it is nearly impossible to approach God. Our egoism, together with our perhaps reluctant tendency to want to control our lives (and those around us!) beyond our capability to do so is, to say the least, not conducive to serenity. Prayer opens our eyes to the higher reality that our will can only take us so far and that there is a Higher Will for us that, while often beyond our understanding, will surely take us further.

For Growth and Renewal: Establish a regular routine for your prayer. Begin with the common rubrics of *shacharit*, *mincha*, and *maariv*. Then grow beyond.

*Every drop that goes forth from Paradise
carries with it a drop of wisdom.*

—Zohar i, 125a

This historical fast day of the fifth of *Shevat*, no longer part of our regular calendar, recalls the death of righteous people who were among the generation of Joshua of Nun, the leader who, following the death of Moses, guided our people into the Promised Land. They brought Paradise with them—and suffused our surroundings with wisdom—their wisdom. We know what it is like to lose righteous people in our generation. I still remember the exact place I stood when I heard the news that John F. Kennedy was killed. That mental photograph is forever etched in my mind. There are others. Some I want to remember. Others I try to forget.

Look around the room. How many people should be there with you, but never made it, because their addiction made them? They were essentially good people who were lost in the world and never found their way home. They needed a leader like Joshua. We all do. That's why God created sponsors and spiritual guides.

For Growth and Renewal: Take a chance. Go to your rabbi and ask the rabbi for spiritual guidance. Ask your sponsor or Fifth Step advisor for help. Maybe you can take the trip together.

> *Let the dignity of one's friend be as dear and*
> *precious to you as your own.*
>
> —*Pirke Avot* 2:15

We ask ourselves, "What dignity is left to us who have done so many *un*dignified things in active addiction?" These things are all so painful to recall even though we realize that it is necessary and healing to do so. And so we tell our stories at meetings, repeating our story over and over again—as many times as is necessary—so that we and others may learn from hearing it, so we might regain our dignity through the process, having left it all behind us. In a sense, that's what Twelve Step recovery is all about: Regaining our dignity. In many cases, the story is the same—only the characters in *our* tale are different and they certainly are characters!

So we reach out to others as well, "carrying the message," hoping to help them restore their own dignity just as we have. And as we work each Step, we remember that we were made as human beings—not as angels (God has plenty of those)—in the image of the Divine.

For Growth and Renewal: Make a list of the aspects of dignity that you have lost as a result of the things that you did. Then restore them, one by one.

> *Those who study Torah*
> *give light wherever they are.*
>
> —Exodus Rabbah 36:1-3

It seems rather self-serving and certainly not very humble for those who study Torah to suggest that they have the ability to give light. But read this Exodus Rabbah text once again. It is really saying that it is Torah that is filled with light. We students of Torah are merely shining in *its* reflected glory.

I do feel an inner glow when I study sacred text. It is a reflection of my ongoing covenant relationship with God. No halogen lamps or fiber optics for me. Torah is all the illumination that I need. Rabbi Noah of Lechvitz once said, "If a person comes to God in prayer and says, 'God, let there be light—let me see Your light, for I do not want to sink into darkness,' immediately there is light for God illuminates the way for that person." That's Torah light. There's nothing like it. And what's more, it's not out of this world. It just seems that way.

For Growth and Renewal: Light a candle next to your study table. Consider the glow that it casts on you. Try to reflect its light in all that you do.

> *The end result of wisdom*
> *is repentance and good deeds.*
>
> —Babylonian Talmud,
> Berachot 17a

Some scholars suggest that the eighth day of *Shevat* is a sort of alternate historical fast day to 5 *Shevat*, both recalling the deaths of the righteous among the generation of Joshua. As Jews, we take every opportunity we can to remember the righteous men and women who have come before us. We pray that the example of their lives will stir us to follow in their footsteps.

What really is wisdom and righteousness anyway? According to this rabbinic text from Berachot, they are two paths which are inseparably linked, one to the other. If you are really wise, then you know the virtue of repentance. But if you aren't and are simply human like the rest of us, we take it on good authority. Repentance is the path to take. As Step Ten suggests, when we admit that we are wrong, we have taken another step in the path of repentance. It is the only path for us to take. Good deeds will follow.

For Growth and Renewal: Take the time to remember those who contributed to your recovery in one way or another, or who may no longer be among the living. Do Step Eight and make a list to help remember those others involved in your journey. Then do something to honor their memory.

*When a person stands facing the east, that person
needs but a turning about to face west. Likewise,
a sinner needs but a slight mental turning-about
to be far removed from one's transgression.*

—Rabbi Nathan David Sidlovtzer,
nineteenth century hasidic rabbi

Sometimes the gap between hope and despair, between active addiction and recovery, seems like an unsurmountable chasm, but it really isn't so. The slightest change of heart, a small degree of change in our perspective, a moment of sincere prayer, and we can turn it around. We really can.

The amount of work ahead of us may seem quite forbidding, but the important thing is that we are headed in the right direction. The beauty of recovery, the beauty of *teshuvah*, is that it allows us to leave the past behind and become spiritually reborn.

From the agony of her recent bottom, an addict raises her hand at a meeting to signify that she has been drug-free for 24 hours—and she is applauded. It takes a lot of courage to admit to a roomful of recovering addicts that you've had a slip. But most of all she is applauded because she has undertaken the turning-about necessary to choose life. To go from hopelessness to hope. What a difference a day can make!

For Growth and Renewal: Stop what you are doing and change directions. Sometimes a new perspective is all you need to face your addiction.

There shall be no strange god in you.

—Psalms 81:10

The rabbis writing in the Jerusalem Talmud say that one who obeys his or her evil inclination is like an idolater, and explains this text from Psalms to mean "Don't make the stranger in you your ruler." Good advice! As with our disease, that stranger, our *yetzer hara* (evil inclination), that feeling of wanting to do whatever we want to do whenever we want to do it, will always lurk within us. It is, perhaps, even an important part of us. After all, we can sometimes learn more about who we really are from our enemies than from our friends.

But the good news is that we don't have to be a slave to our *yetzer hara* or our addiction. We can't do it all by ourselves, but help is freely available for those who want it. We can live free of addictive or codependent behavior, one day at a time. We can begin to give our lives the hope and spiritual direction that it lacked before. In time, more will be revealed. But it begins when we lay down our weary idols.

For Growth and Renewal: According to the midrash, Abraham broke down the idols in his father's idol store. You can do the same thing in your own home. Nu? What are you waiting for? Start with your own home and remove the idols.

> *In one's approach to God there is no straight way*
> *of going up. It is always ascent and descent and*
> *ascent. Hence, authentic repentance—down and*
> *then up—is greater than constant piety.*
>
> —Hasidic teaching

Those who are just entering the program may mistakenly think that we can simply work the Twelve Steps and leave our addiction behind. For the lucky few, it may be possible. For most, the path of spiritual renewal is not a straight path. Deluding yourself into thinking that the only way to get sober or straight is to stay on a straight path may reflect the codependence that got you hooked in the first place. The Israelites could have made it from Egyptian slavery to the Promised Land in less than forty years, had they walked a straight path from Egypt to Canaan. But they didn't.

There were setbacks along the way for the Israelites. And there will be setbacks in your recovery and search for the holy. But our ancient Israelite ancestors kept moving forward, against the blinding desert sands, facing the heat of the desert and the wayward desires of their hearts. Eventually, they overcame their readiness to turn back at the slightest inconvenience. They made it. So will you.

For Growth and Renewal: Focus on your progress instead of your setbacks. Make signposts along the way. Celebrate each of them.

> *The center of the world*
> *is exactly where you stand.*
>
> —Babylonian Talmud,
> Bekorot 8b

One of the things that the Jewish calendar teaches us is that the center of the world is not always where we think it is. For we who believe, and we surely do, Jerusalem is the center of the world. Yet, the rabbis have taught us that there are really two Jerusalems, one heavenly and one earthly. In a spiritual sense, our recovery transports us to heavenly Jerusalem. Close your eyes and you are there. Golden Jerusalem. Peaceful Jerusalem. Then hold onto that feeling so that you can call on it whenever you need to—maybe even to help avert a relapse in your recovery.

The most important thing for you to remember at this moment and every moment *for the rest of your life* is that you *must* stay clean and sober. There are no other options if you want to stay alive. It's "tough Torah" for those who are willing to listen. But it will help you stay centered. Navigate your way through the cycle of this month of *Shevat.* Feel its moods; it will help you remember to stay clean.

For Growth and Renewal: Mark off the days of *Shevat* and count your clean time, one day at a time.

No one sins for someone else.

—Babylonian Talmud,
Bava Metzia 8a

We have wasted a lot of time blaming our addiction and our relapses on other people. "Had she not done that," the stinkin' thinkin' goes, "I would not have started drinking again." But the truth indeed is that "no one sins for someone else." The only one responsible for your addiction is you. Likewise, you are solely responsible for your own recovery.

But there is more to learn from this perceptive morsel of Torah. Things do not return to "normal" in recovery. We do not return to where we were—wherever that might have been. In recovery, our lives change drastically. We are not always fully aware of the changes—or ready for them—and certainly our loved ones, even those supportive of our recovery, are often caught by surprise, as well. So it is probably important for us to work the Steps together. Only the individual may be addicted, but all of us must recover. Thankfully, we are all reborn in the process.

For Growth and Renewal: Invite your family to share in the process of your recovery. Take them to an open meeting. Don't close the door in their face.

The prohibition against making idols includes the
prohibition against making idols out of mitzvot.
We should never imagine that the whole purpose
of the mitzvah is its outer form [the doing],
rather it is the inward meaning [the devotion
with which it was intended].

—Rabbi Menachem Mendl of Kotzk
early nineteenth century hasidic leader

Now that's real Torah, the kind of advice we have come to appreciate from the Kotzker rebbe. And we know exactly what he means. It is so easy to change one addiction for another compulsive behavior even if it looks benign—even healthy—on the outside. But be fore-warned. The evil inclination can get you even in the context of doing *mitzvot*.

Listen carefully to the words of Menachem Mendl. Imagine him standing there guiding you. And as you do your *mitzvot*, and you certainly should do them, focus on their inner meaning, the *kavannah* or intention with which you are doing them. One rabbi was once asked how he prepares himself for prayer. The rabbi responded, "I pray that I might pray properly." It certainly is a good way to begin your day.

For Growth and Renewal: Consider the motivation of the next *mitzvah* you do. Then consider it again. But don't forget to do the *mitzvah*.

You send forth springs which feed wadis
which flow between the mountains,
giving drink to all the wild beasts;
the wild asses slake their thirst....
You drench the mountains from your upper stories;
so that the entire earth is sated
from the product of Your work.

—Psalm 104:10-12,13

These lines from one of the psalms read on the festival of Tu Bishevat, the so-called New Year of the Trees, present us with powerful images for recovery. More reasons than you can count why it is important to allow our will to meet God's will. In the midst of winter—for those who live in the warmer climes of the country, you can follow this logic too—God is already setting the stage for the rebirth of spring. That's what is so special about Tu Bishevat. Through its celebration, we are filled with hope.

It's strange how Jewish tradition chose to celebrate nature when things seem so calm and serene, rather than simply when spring is exploding as would be expected. That's the beauty of the insight of Jewish tradition. Perhaps it is what draws us to it. We feel the same way about our recovery. Now that things are somewhat tranquil, we are able to feel life flow through our limbs again.

For Growth and Renewal: Get in step with Step Three: Turn your life and will over to the care of God. Read all of Psalm 104. Then read Psalms 120-134, as well.

> *Even tho' your dreams were dashed*
> *and knocked about,*
> *you are still that dream*
> *under everything you doubt.*

—Anselm Rothschild,
contemporary songwriter

These words were written by a contemporary Jewish musician just weeks before he died. They were words which eased him into death. While a disease progressively robbed him of his physical strength, he never lost the spiritual foundation which gave him strength and courage. The first time I heard these words sung, I really felt visited by angels. The words continue to resound in my ears. Perhaps it is because they speak so clearly to all of us who struggle to carve meaning in our lives even when the world seems to work against us. Spiritual renewal continues to allow me to hear this sweet message of truth. In active addiction, we will never hear it. The disease won't let us.

Throughout the month of *Shevat*, we think about rebirth. It seems crazy to talk about growth and renewal in the midst of winter, especially if you live in the cold climes of the north. But remember, our focus is on the seasons of Israel. Our time clocks are fixed east to Jerusalem.

For Growth and Renewal: What is the dream that you hold for yourself? It's never too late to pursue it. Take the first step toward meeting that goal. Then take it one day at a time.

Into Your hand, I entrust my spirit.

—Psalm 31:6

It takes a great deal of courage to place our lives in the care of the God of our understanding. Some will see it as an example of weakness. We know it as a sign of renewed strength. Whether it comes as part of your recovery or as a result of it, it really doesn't matter. What matters is that you do recover, that you do *teshuvah* (repentance), and that you return to God.

Admit it. You tried to go it alone, that is, with the help of drugs or alcohol. And when you felt alone as a result, you tried to draw close to others with your body. It's no news to you that the drugs and the alcohol and the sex didn't work. So now you are prepared to reconsider the covenant between you and God, the one which was established centuries ago atop that fiery mountain called Sinai. Don't take my word for it, take God's word for it. Follow the prophet's advice: "Take words of Torah and return [to Me]."

For Growth and Renewal: What activity makes you feel closet to God? Once you've discovered it, don't lose hold of it. And if you can't find one, read through the book of Psalms, one at a time. Within its lines, you will find yourself.

---

*One should not talk one way with the lips
and another way with the heart.*

—Babylonian Talmud,
Bava Metzia 49a

Now what does that mean? I understand how one talks with the lips—they're close to the mouth. But how does one talk with the heart? That's the point. Since you can't talk with your heart, make sure that what you say is indeed what you feel. No more beating around the bush. Honesty is indeed the best policy. And if you can't be honest (read Step Nine again), then don't say anything at all. Or as I like to say, say it to the wall.

God reads the heart, suggests our tradition. So you really are better off leaving the lies behind you, where they belong. They formed the foundation which "enabled" you to be an active addict. Without that foundation, guess what happens to your active addiction?

For Growth and Renewal: Spend the day being aware of how you may be closeting your feelings just to "put on a happy face." Be honest with yourself so that you can be honest with others.

> *The one who delves into Torah and discovers*
> *in it new meanings that are true*
> *contributes new Torah which is treasured*
> *by the congregation of Israel.*

—Hasidic teaching

It is this proclivity in our tradition which makes it possible for us to join recovery and Torah together. In the soul-searching dialogue with one another in Twelve Step fellowship, we're making Torah. Each time you share your story with others, you offer them hope and inspiration for their recovery while bolstering your own. And real words of Torah are spoken. We struggle with faith, with our belief in a Higher Power—just like all those who came before us. The Torah is a collection of stories which reflect the relationship of our ancestors with God through history. As we enter its pages, our struggles and theirs converge.

The journeys of Abraham and Sarah, Isaac and Rebeccah, Jacob, Leah and Rachel were not easy journeys. One of the reasons we continue to read them over and over, year after year is to gain new insight into those journeys. When our place is different, we often see them in a different light as well. A Divine light. But like the Steps, you have to work the Torah. Otherwise, the faith journeys of our ancestors will elude you and you will be left to struggle on your own. And you know where that leaves you.

For Growth and Renewal: What Torah have you learned today from your recovery? Share it with others.

*The laws of the Torah were given
that people should live by them
and not that they should die by them.*

—Hasidic teaching

*O*ne of the reasons why I chose to bring Torah wisdom to the Twelve Steps is in fulfillment of this teaching. As it is framed on this page, it is Hasidic, but it is a universal Jewish teaching. As a matter of *halacha* (Jewish law), there are only three things that the rabbis counsel that you must die before submitting to (and the truth is, they will kill you anyhow, if not in body, then certainly in soul): Idolatry, illicit sexuality, and murder. Otherwise, the overall command is to live. And all three are related to addictive behaviors. It may sound strong, but it is true.

Think about it for a moment. When your addiction becomes the most important thing in your life—and it surely was when you were active—it becomes an idol, a god. Often it leads to illicit sexuality or is included in it. For some, compulsive sex is the addiction. And murder, no one needs to tell you. In active addiction, you are killing yourself. So live by the Torah and let its teachings breathe life into you.

For Growth and Renewal: Take the time to identify the priorities in your life. Then make darn sure they stay that way.

If you spit in the air, it will fall on your face.

—Ecclesiastes Rabbah 7:21

No, all wisdom is not ensconced by lofty poetry. Some of it is basic, learned from the experience of life—whether yours or someone else's. Some of the most important things that I have learned have been taught to me in similar language—like the Twelve Steps. Just like this text from the midrash, it's pretty easy to understand. No one need explain it to you. And if you don't believe the words of the text or the experience of others, try spitting in the air. You'll soon feel this bit of wisdom—right on your face.

But don't wait to get a face full of spittle before taking to heart the other things that you can learn from your recovery. Every anniversary of your sobriety teaches you a basic lesson of living. You can recover. You can renew your life.

You are a good person who made some mistakes, who somehow took a wrong turn on the bumpy road of life. But that's all behind you now. Recognize the simple truths of your recovery and be reborn. Now that's real Torah wisdom.

For Growth and Renewal: Place this text from Ecclesiastes Rabbah someplace so that you can read it frequently. Let it serve as a reminder that the basic truths of life are indeed simple ones.

*Praised are You, Adonai our God, Guide of the
Universe, who creates innumerable living beings
and their needs, for all the things You have
created to sustain every living being.
Praised are You, the life of the Universe.*

This blessing for those foods not generally encompassed
by *Birkat Hamazon* (grace after meals) may be recited if
you do not have a *siddur* (and cannot recite by memory
the full prayer). It says all you need to say, a poetic
"Thank you God for everything." It is mentioned here in
connection with a historical day of feasting. (This twenty-
second day of *Shevat* commemorates the assassination of
the emperor Caligula and thereby the abolition of a
decree to erect a statue of his likeness in the ancient
Temple in Jerusalem.) It's one of those feasts that are generally no longer celebrated by the Jewish community and
are merely assigned to the history books. Perhaps the context of the celebration has been lost to Jewish history during the travels of our people. Or maybe we have grown as
a group of individuals to the point that we choose not to
celebrate the destruction of our enemies. As we know
from recovery, echoing the word of Beruriah to her
spouse Rabbi Meir, "It is not the end of sinners that we
seek. Rather, it is the end to their sinful ways." In the
spiritual growth of individuals and a people, there is
always more growing to do.

For Growth and Renewal: Get into the habit of saying
thank you to God after your meals. Slowly chant *Birkat
Hamazon*. And as you do, be mindful of the Source of all
life in the universe.

> *May the One who gives life to the living*
> *give you a long and stable life.*

—Babylonian Talmud,
Yoma 71a

What better blessing could you offer another? Long life and stability (or serenity if you prefer). It is probably a blessing many of our loved ones said in their hearts during our active addiction. Serenity is a key element in recovery. We might even say that it is one of the results of it. This blessing from the Talmud, which found its place among much of the legal material related to Yom Kippur (*Yoma* is an Aramaic word for *The* Day), is most appropriate for this twenty-third day of *Shevat*. On this day, the ancients fasted in recognition of a particular battle against Benjamin and the idol of Micah. It's complicated history (maybe that's why the historical fast day is no longer observed), but it is a simple blessing. Long life and stability to you.

When you are in recovery and attempt to live in the context of Jewish history, you can achieve serenity. While serenity means many things to many people, of one thing you can be sure: When you have serenity, you have your life.

For Growth and Renewal: Offer this prayer at the end of a meeting and share it with others you love.

> *To You, Adonai, I lift my soul.*
>
> —Psalm 25:1

How you lift your soul is really a matter of perspective—as long as your soul indeed gets lifted. When I am down, regardless of the cause, it is God who lifts my soul. I try, but I am not always able to do so. And you don't have to be an alcoholic or drug addict, a compulsive eater or gambler, to be down. We all feel down at various times in our lives. It happens to all of us. Don't let anyone tell you different.

My relationship with God elevates my soul and my life. It doesn't just happen. Like all good relationships, I work at it, constantly. I want you to develop the same relationship. It's well worth it. For those not yet accustomed to the presence of God in their lives, they may feel uncomfortable, even threatened by this constant reference to God or a Higher Power as Twelve Step programs like to refer to the Divine. Don't worry about all this Godtalk. It took Moses some getting used to it too. And he had prepared for it. Should you expect anything less?

For Growth and Renewal: Until you are ready to lift your soul, raise your body above your addiction. When you get up in the morning, say a prayer of thanks for your soul which has been returned pure to you and for your recovery which you have return pure to it.

> *The one who loves Torah*
> *is never satisfied with Torah.*
>
> —Deuteronomy Rabbah 2:23

Sounds funny, but Torah really does fill me up. Yet, I am never fully satiated by it. It sounds like something someone might say because they think you would like to hear it, the kind of thing that others might have said to you when you went for help. And you went away less than satisfied.

Some will say that this statement from the midrash does not sound much like serenity. You might even hear these words as just another compulsion, albeit directed in a more spiritual manner. But remember the goal of Torah is to bring the individual closer to the Source of all life. How can you ever get close enough? So it is a driving feeling of contentment. Maybe I grow as I learn so there's more to fill.

It might be better to say Torah is constantly satisfying me. That's what I love about it. I am never fully satisfied because Torah is a process, an expression of the on-going relationship between God and me. Just like the Twelve Steps, I have to keep working on Torah so that it can keeping working on me.

For Growth and Renewal: Don't put it off any longer. Start studying Torah and the Twelve Steps so that you might feel them working on you.

When a person goes to a place for prayer, that person must be clean in body and clothing.

—Abraham ibn Ezra,
early twelfth century Spanish poet,
grammarian, astronomer,
physician and philosopher

The book of Leviticus spends countless lines discussing the method for preparing oneself for the act of sacrifice. There is constant cleansing, consecration and the changing of clothing. We are inundated with countless details, many of which we have difficulty understanding. This is not something to be taken lightly. The entire sacrificial system was meant to help the individual get closer to God. In the ancient sacrificial cult or in the language of prayer, you can't get close to God unless you are clean. So start counting your clean time. When you approach the Guide of the Universe, be prepared. God is counting too.

What actually is a place of prayer? Is it merely a synagogue or designated place of worship? I think that we are being taught something more subtle. Abraham ibn Ezra is suggesting that we do not take prayer itself too lightly and simply utter them whenever and wherever we feel like it. Proper prayer takes proper preparation of body and spirit—and clothing!

For Growth and Renewal: Change your clothes before you go to a meeting, just as you would the synagogue on Shabbat. You're dressing up for the same purpose—to be clean before God.

A pagan once asked a rabbi, "Why did God choose to appear in a bush?" Came the reply, "To teach you that no place is without God's presence, not even a lowly bush."

—Exodus Rabbah 2:5

One of the things that spiritual renewal offers the individual is a renewed sense of passion about living. The bonus is that it comes through humility. You feel reborn. For some, passion is a funny word to express what we all feel. Perhaps that's why the burning bush is so fitting an image. A humble thorn bush, it burns with incredible intensity, but it never burns out. If you continue to work the steps, neither will you. No longer willing to accept life as something that is a simple measurement of years, oblivious to its majesty, the person who is renewed is overwhelmed by religious passion, actually overflowing. I guess that's why Step Twelve follows logically after the other steps. People don't really have to be told to work that step. In recovery, it almost works itself. It comes almost naturally.

It's ironic when you consider that this is the same person who, prior to recovery, was using drugs to fill an emptiness. But if truth be told, you are not the same person. In the past, there was a piece missing. In recovery, without chemicals to deceive you—and they do deceive you—you finally feel whole.

For Growth and Renewal: What is the passion that burns inside of you? Don't douse the fire. Instead, fan it with your recovery.

> *Every Jew must light a* ner tamid
> *[perpetually burning flame] in one's heart.*
>
> —Itturei Torah III, p. 229

This is one of those days when something from our past has left its trace on the religious calendar. On this twenty-eighth day of *Shevat*, we recall the anniversary of the death of Antiochus IV, the villain of the Hanukkah story. We have may have succeeded in erasing the recalling of the date from our daily lives but not from our collective memory as a people. In a sense, there are things in our recovery that work the same way. As a community, we remember each other's pain. Somehow in sharing the burden, it is lessened for each individual.

The image of the *ner tamid*, the eternal lamp as it is sometimes called in the synagogue, is an appropriate way to recall this day on our calendar. It was Antiochus, among others, who tried to prevent us from keeping it burning. When he was defeated, we immediately lit a lamp. Keep a *ner tamid* perpetually burning in your heart. Let its light shine on your recovery and be a beacon for those who might look to you for a shining example.

For Growth and Renewal: Imagine the *ner tamid* in your local synagogue as a symbol of your recovery. Just as we work to keep the *ner tamid* continually burning, you must work to keep your recovery constant.

Then shall every person give to Adonai a ransom for his soul. . . . The rich shall not give more and the poor should not give less—to make atonement for your sins.

—Exodus 30: 12,15, from the additional Torah reading on Shabbat Shekalim

More Twelve Step wisdom. Our souls have to be ransomed, but we have to be the ones to do the ransoming. Nobody can recover for us. When taking the first Step and every Step, we have to do it ourselves. And the measurement of one's ransom should not be compared with others'. We have finally grown beyond this need to assess the value of our actions by size—even of one's gift to God. That may be what helped fuel an addiction in the first place—by thinking that big houses, fancy cars, and "pretty people" put you in first place. Putting you first is the only thing that really counts. In recovery, let unhealthy comparison and competition die along with active addiction. Otherwise, it will kill you.

Give what is necessary, what is fitting. No more; no less. The Talmud cautions us, "sometimes adding on detracts" (Sanhedrin 29a). But remember, when you give of self to God, you'll get a lot more in return. But you have to return, to God, that is.

For Growth and Renewal: We thank God for what we have by sharing it with others. It's called *tzedakah*. It really helps us to ransom our own soul.

*I am Adonai your God who brought you out of
the land of Egypt, out of the house of bondage.
You shall have no other gods before me.*

—Exodus 20:2-3

There is a saying around A.A. fellowship meetings that if you make your #2s your #1s, you lose your #1s. It is the program's way of saying: Maintain your priorities. For us, the #1 priority is to avoid false gods. Notice that the edict does not command belief in God. Free-willed beings cannot be commanded to believe anything. Believe in God or believe nothing but no false gods. Anything we view as the highest good, be it money or sex or chemical substances, is as idolatrous as a ten-foot statue of Baal.

Living to use and using to live, we worshipped a substance with a devotion that led us to hell. In recovery, our #1 priority must be recovery. Anything that we place ahead of it puts our recovery at risk. By refusing to bow down to drugs, we are free to turn toward a Higher Power of our understanding.

The difference is as profound as that between slavery and freedom, as significant as that between evil and good, and as clear as that between life and death.

For Growth and Renewal: The text says, "No other gods but Me." Stop bowing down to anyone or anything else.

Adar

Joy

Late Winter

Whenever we talk about *Adar*, our voices are filled with joy. The fragrance of spring is in the air. Even in those leap years when there are two months of *Adar* and Purim is actually celebrated in the second, there is enough joy to fill up twice as many weeks. The Jewish people in ancient Shushan (Persia) were saved and we are forever grateful. That's why so many communities have their own Purims, to celebrate their own survival.

We can't always hide behind our Purim masks. There is much that we need to say and do. Thus, *Adar* is also very honest time. People come out of their winter recluse and wholeheartedly embrace the spring. And there are special Sabbaths which continue to pave a way to next month's spring celebration of Pesach and the liberation from Egyptian bondage. Shabbat Zachor, the sabbath of memory just before Purim, reminds us that our enemies continue to chase us. And we must protect ourselves. Victims no more, through recovery and renewal, we can make our lives holy. Shabbat Parah provides us with an opportunity to cleanse ourselves and, finally, Shabbat Hachodesh announces the beginning of the following month of *Nisan*. Wherever you are, no matter how far you have come or have yet to go, remember what our tradition teaches us, "Be Happy. It's *Adar*!"

159

With the advent of Adar, *we are to increase joy.*

—Babylonian Talmud,
Taanit 29a

It's really nice to have a full month (two in a leap year) whose message is one of sheer joy. That's the whole focus of *Adar*. No room during this month for self-pity. Our obligation is simply to increase joy in the world, and we do it by beginning with ourselves.

Notice that the text says nothing about happiness, thereby advising us not to confuse the two. Remember what the rabbis have taught us elsewhere: "Who is happy? The one who is satisfied with one's lot." Here we are speaking about joy, the kind that comes from a celebration of survival. And we do have great reason to celebrate. We are alive and ready to enjoy living once again.

Your joy is in your hands. Eating a lot or too little won't make you happy. You've learned that time and again. And gambling just brings you down even further. So provide yourself with real reasons to be joyful. Stay clean and sober. And stay in the program.

For Growth and Renewal: Share the joy of your sobriety with others.

> *To be is to stand for.*
>
> —Rabbi Abraham Joshua Heschel,
> contemporary theologian

*T*oo often in our consumption-oriented society, we fall prey to the spiritually dangerous notion that we are what we have. We spend our lives convincing ourselves of this myth until it is we who are spent. We believe it and so does everyone else. But some of us have learned the real truth the hard way: What we do after we have lost everything we had, as a result of active addiction, says more about what we are. Possessions come and go. There are many miserable rich people and many happy poor ones. Happiness is an inside job.

As Rabbi Heschel insightfully notes, our goals, values, and beliefs are what truly gives shape to our identity. Without purpose and direction, life itself becomes meaningless. The notion of placing "principles before personalities" is something heard at every meeting. That's what anonymity is all about. But it can also be said that healthy principles help make healthier personalities. Be your happy, healthy self.

For Growth and Renewal: Be an advocate for alcohol-free celebrations in your synagogue or in your community.

Accept your affliction with love and joy.

—Rabbi Eleazar ben Judah,
second century teacher
from Bartota

*T*wo students came to the Maggid of Mezritch, a Hasidic teller of tales, and asked how is it possible to fulfill the Talmudic obligation to praise God for misfortune with the same joy as one praises God for good fortune as instructed in the Talmud (Berachot 54a). The Maggid advised them to ask Rabbi Zusya, who lived in poverty and suffered from several painful ailments. The students asked Zusya, but he was puzzled: "I don't understand why the Maggid sent you to me. I have never experienced anything bad in my life. Only good things have happened to me."

While few of us will ever possess the spiritual fortitude of a Zusya, we can choose to look upon our affliction in a positive light. Bemoaning our "fate" in recovery can easily lead to resentment and to relapse. Instead, we can feel grateful that we have found the gift of recovery. It's hard to believe, but our disease could have been worse. And recovery is possible. We can keep the worst chapters of our lives behind us. We put enough stumbling blocks before ourselves when we were "out there." In Twelve Step programs, "easy" really can do it. So why not let it?

For Growth and Renewal: Others need your help too. Donate a few hours today to a local homeless shelter or soup kitchen.

Serve Adonai with joy,
for the joy of being human draws toward
the individual another joy from above.

—Zohar ii, 184b

Being fully human actually draws the individual closer to God. But how does one learn to be fully human? First stop trying to be someone else. Don't say, "if only I could do (*you fill in the word that fits*), then everything would be fine." I can never be like that other person. Nor should I try. That's powerful Torah.

There are three partners in creation. Mother, father, and God. I know that you may still have lots of family of origin work to do before you want to fully accept that notion. But it is something we can't avoid. We may have gotten into addiction on our own, but we didn't get into this world on our own. And it is God who has endowed us all as unique individuals.

What? You don't like what God created! To be dissatisfied with your essential self (not the self you created with drink and drugs) and to try to be like someone else, in certain ways, is blasphemy. Think about it. It's an affront to the Creator to reject what was created. So be the best you can be. That will help bring you closer to God or, at least, Twelve Steps closer.

For Growth and Renewal: Choose one bit of "unfinished business" in your recovery about your essential self and address it today.

Don't be so smart in your own eyes.

—Proverbs 3:7

If only the rest of the Bible and Jewish tradition were so easy to understand and spoke to us in such straightforward terms! You know what this bit of wisdom literature, as the Book of Proverbs is called in academic circles, is saying. The reason you know is because that's exactly what you thought when you were actively using and abusing, *before* you entered recovery. The words from Proverbs may be different, but the intention is the same nonetheless. How many times have people told me: "I really thought that I was so smart, in full control, that I could stop whenever I wanted. That was before I realized that I was out of control and that there was no stopping."

Whatever the case, I guess none of us are really as smart as we think we are. If that were indeed true, we wouldn't have started using in the first place. It makes sense: You can't get hooked on cocaine (or anything else) if you never use it. And for alcoholics and drug addicts in recovery, never is the new vocabulary word you have to learn. There is no other choice. No drinks, no more. No drugs, forever more.

For Growth and Renewal: What part of program don't you understand? Sit with your sponsor and work it out.

---

*A single instance of proper behavior is more
important than a hundred miracles and signs.*

—Rabbi Yehezkel of Kuzmir,
head of hasidic dynasty in Kuzmir,
nineteenth century

Too often we think that we need a miracle in order to recover. Perhaps such thoughts are just another item in a long list of excuses or denials. In a sense, recovery is a miracle. But there is nothing supernatural about it. It may be spiritual, but, in this regard it is quite rational. The essential requirement of recovery is only proper behavior. No other miracles are necessary or required. Consider it for a moment. You hold the key to your own recovery by what you do (or don't do).

Later in the month we will celebrate Purim. At that time, we will acknowledge and evaluate Mordecai and Esther's behavior. The account of what took place includes no real miracles. Only two people doing what they felt in their hearts—in their souls—was appropriate. They felt compelled to act. And as a result, we (their spiritual descendants) are here today. For some reason, you too felt compelled to act, and entered recovery. The results are clear: You are here today.

For Growth and Renewal: Start a new habit today, one that is good for your body and your soul. And remember to do it tomorrow. So you will be here too.

> *Righteousness begins when one sees*
> *the yoke which others bear.*

> —Yalkut Me'am Loez

According to Jewish tradition, this day marks Moses' birthday as well as the day of his death. And so in Oriental communities 7 *Adar* has become a day of fasting and commemoration for the pious because of the belief that a spark of the soul of Moses is found in every righteous person. Sefardic Jews still light candles for the ascension of the souls of the righteous. And in the United States, after *mincha* (afternoon prayers), eulogies are offered for Moses and famous rabbis and Jewish scholars who passed away during the past year. In Israel, it has also become the day to commemorate the unknown soldier.

In all these cases, we recall righteous people in our tradition. The great commentator Rashi reminds us, "When a righteous person leaves a place, that individual leaves a mark." We are always diminished by the death of others, especially righteous people who somehow find the way in their lives to feel the pain of others. For whenever we share the pain of another's burden, it is lessened for the one who has to bear it.

For Growth and Renewal: Take a look around you. Who has left a mark in your life? Choose one thing he or she taught you and try to emulate it.

I will commit my thoughts on the matter
to writing. Perhaps things will become clear
as they are written.

—Rabbi Moshe Feinstein,
contemporary Orthodox
legal authority

These comments, spoken by perhaps the greatest Jewish legal mind of this generation, were in response to one of the many questions posed of him. Often it is the actual act of writing down your thoughts that allows you to get a different perspective on things. We read Torah year in and year out, the same portions, and yet we can gain insights that evaded us only the last time we reviewed the same material. The Torah is the same, but perhaps we were in a different space when we read it.

We wouldn't know what happened on Purim—or any other festival—had someone not chosen (or been chosen) to write down the events and record them for us. Consider your own Step Four work. When we do a _cheshbon hanefesh_, an accounting of the soul, we actually write down these moral inventories. Writing things down allows us to be aware of the progress of our recovery. It keeps our recovery constantly in front of us. And if we don't keep it in front of us, we get behind.

For Growth and Renewal: Take out your Step Four inventory and your pencil. What things can you cross out? What things are you afraid to add?

> *Rabbi Hillel's students once asked him, "Rabbi, where are you going?" To which Hillel replied, "I am going to perform a meritorious deed." "And what is that deed?" they queried. "To take a bath in the bath house," Hillel responded. "And that is a meritorious deed," the students remarked somewhat incredulous. The patient Rabbi Hillel responded, "It is. If the statues erected to kings in the theaters are washed and scrubbed by those responsible to take care of them, how much more should we who have been created in God's image take care of our bodies."*
>
> —Leviticus Rabbah 24:3

Rabbi Hillel's message is clear. Take care of our bodies. They house our souls. According to some historic calendars, this ninth day of the month of *Adar* was set aside as a fast day in order to commemorate the controversies between Hillel and Shammai (Babylonian Talmud, Shabbat 17a).

Perhaps one of the most colorful aspects of rabbinic literature are these well-known discussions between members of the House of Hillel and the House of Shammai. Here were two rabbis who seldom agreed with each other. Doesn't sound so rare, does it? Ah, but the difference is that they both acknowledged that the discussions were for the sake of Heaven. I think such holy controversy has a unique way of helping us to keep clean.

For Growth and Renewal: Now that you are clean, do something nice for your body. Take a bubble bath.

Happy is the person who finds wisdom,
the person who achieves understanding.

—Proverbs 3:13

It's always the same quest. Happiness. We all strive to be happy. For many, it was this misguided search for happiness that got us in trouble with compulsive sex, chemical use and gambling in our active addiction.

Our tradition suggests that *Adar* is all about happiness. So why do we not always feel so happy—even on this tenth day of *Adar*? Don't get confused. Happiness is not a hollow feeling that is driven by some series of unplanned events. The same way spirituality doesn't just hit you and BAM! you feel close to God. Both happiness and spirituality have to worked at, struggled with. I believe they are connected, one to the other, but that's because I do indeed believe.

According to the advice from this verse from the Book of Proverbs, when we begin to understand the world in which we live, we can gain wisdom. Through such wisdom comes lasting happiness.

For Growth and Renewal: Write down something that you have just learned about your recovery. Then teach it to others so that you may learn.

169

Remember what Amalek did to you on the way as you came forth out of Egypt. Now he met you on the way, and smote the hindmost of you, all who were enfeebled in the rear when you were faint and weary. He feared not God.

—Deuteronomy 25:17-19,
from the reading for Shabbat Zachor

On the Sabbath before Purim, called Shabbat Zachor, we are instructed to recall Amalek, the enemy who attacked us on our way to Egypt. We were weak and he attacked us from behind—and we were unable to defend ourselves. Since that time, the name Amalek has been used to recall all of our enemies from history which are, unfortunately, too many to recall by individual name.

These enemies came from the outside, ready to attack on a moment's notice. Our calendar helps us to remember to them. But there are other enemies, as well, who live on the inside. Sometimes they are even hard to find in the deep, dark recesses of our inner selves. But they are there. Be sure of it. We got to know them in active addiction—until we finally threw them out.

And they are ready to come back, if we let them. Just don't let them. Remember Amalek.

For Growth and Renewal: What can you do to remember your own Amalek, your own enemy of addiction? Choose one thing that will remind you and instead of throwing it away, keep it in front of you at all times.

> *I will give you a new heart and put a new spirit*
> *into you. I will remove the heart of stone from*
> *your body and give you a heart of flesh.*
>
> —Ezekiel 36:26

Prophets always seem to say the most inspirational things. If only we were able to do the same. The prophets, according to Jewish tradition, speak on behalf of God. How can they help but be inspirational? So let's play close attention to the words of Ezekiel. He is indeed speaking directly to us.

Had we even considered the possibility that our heart was made of stone—so that it needed to be replaced? Probably not. Perhaps our feeling were so masked by alcohol that we couldn't discern them. One of the things that spiritual renewal encourages us to do is to take a good, hard look at ourselves. And when we do, we realize that we could always be gentler in our ways, in our reactions with others. Often, in fact, we are too harsh on ourselves.

Unburden yourself. Let God help rid you of that heart of stone.

Replace it with one of flesh. It's much more human.

For Growth and Renewal: There are many things that we have done with our hearts of stone. Choose one and repair the damage.

> *We cannot ask God in prayer to do something*
> *which is within our power, so as to spare us the*
> *chore of doing it.*

—Rabbi Harold Kushner,
author of *When Bad Things
Happen to Good People*

This thirteenth day of *Adar*, referred to as Taanit Esther (the fast of Esther)—and the day before Purim—was first observed as Nicanor Day, a feast commemorating the Hasmonean victory over the Syrian general Nicanor. But feast or fast, Rabbi Kushner's message speaks to both the victory of the Maccabees (of Hanukkah fame) and to the heroism of Esther (who saved the Jewish community of ancient Persia). While we may turn to God for inspiration and inner strength, we also know that there is much we have to do. Some call it a partnership, a covenant. Others simply quote Step Three and "turn it over." However you may choose to describe it matters not. What does matter is that you work the Steps and do what you need to do to stay in the program.

Esther has taught us a great lesson. Here a woman of humble birth sought the impossible in order to save our people. In recovery, we are doing the same. It takes humility and courage—and it takes doing what is nearly impossible to do.

For Growth and Renewal: Turn to God for inspiration and strength. Say a prayer and then go out and do what needs to be done.

> *The day in which the Jews had rest*
> *from their enemies and the month which*
> *was turned from sorrow to gladness,*
> *from mourning into a great day.*
>
> —Esther 9:22

People will continue to debate the historical details of the Purim celebration. "Are they accurate recollections?" they ponder. Yet, they are missing the point. Any time we have achieved victory over an enemy that seeks to destroy us is reason to celebrate. This day of *Adar* certainly is a great day.

Such victory gives us respite. It allows us to take a break from our zealous pursuit of self-protection. But such victory comes at a cost. The enemy was destroyed. Life was lost. How many do we know whose life was lost to the enemy of addiction! We must always be on our guard, cautious that recovery does not slip from our grasp.

Jewish tradition teaches us that Purim provides us with the mandate to just be happy. No strings attached. For today, set aside all of the worries you have (we all have plenty) and take this time in your life to just let it all go.

For Growth and Renewal: Today, be on your guard. Don't let some of the more frivolous traditions of Purim block your way to recovery.

> *The world is a narrow bridge.*
> *The main thing is not to be afraid.*
>
> —Rabbi Nachman of Bratzlav,
> late eighteenth century
> hasidic rebbe

I chose this well-known saying of Rabbi Nachman to mark the day called Shushan Purim because it acts a link to the Purim celebration. We normally think of Purim as a one-day celebration, but, in fact, it affects our people in various places over a three-day period. First there is Taanit Esther, the fast of Esther, then there is Purim. But because of the original celebration in Shushan (the capital in ancient Persia where the Purim story takes place), those who live in walled cities observe Purim on this fifteenth day of *Adar*. The world is indeed small, a narrow bridge, and we should not be afraid.

For me, this teaching of Rabbi Nachman has become a *kavannah*, a mantra-like phrase, which I repeat over and over as I prepare for prayer or even when I need to muster up inner strength to confront my day. For in his gentle wisdom is also encouragement and support. Like Esther, unafraid to confront the daily tasks of living, I know that I am not alone. And we are bound together through the history of our people and our relationship with God.

For Growth and Renewal: Make this advice of Rabbi Nachman your *kavannah* as well. Repeat it to yourself before you begin your day.

> *In the future, the Holy Blessed One will*
> *bring forth living waters from Jerusalem*
> *and with them heal everyone who is sick.*
> —Exodus Rabbah 15:21

While this day is not a day of special commemoration, the rabbis set it aside, saying that the sixteenth day of *Adar* should not be a day of mourning—regardless what happens in history—for on that day they commenced to build the walls of Jerusalem. Such is the great love for the city of Jerusalem. It's one of those feelings that is nearly impossible to articulate. It just is. For some, it is similar to the healing they feel as a result of spiritual renewal. You can't always explain it. All you can do is try to share it.

If you've been to Jerusalem, you know why the rabbis felt this way. And if you have not been able to visit this city of Peace, remember that the Hebrew word for serenity, *shelemut* (from which the word *shalom* is derived) is related to the word Jerusalem. Say it slowly and you can hear it. For those who have read my *Twelve Jewish Steps to Recovery*, remember "Heavenly Jerusalem was built out of a love for earthly Jerusalem" (*Tanchuma Pekudei* 1).

For Growth and Renewal: Imagine yourself in Jerusalem right now. Smell its fragrant air. Walk down its old streets. Rehearse the path of the prophets. Center your world and yourself in Jerusalem.

> *Let your house be a house of meeting*
> *for the Sages. Sit at their feet as their students*
> *and drink of their words with thirst.*
>
> —*Pirke Avot* 1:4

In Jewish history, the seventeenth of *Adar* was a feast day, commemorating the miraculous escape of the Sages of Israel from the Herodians (Roman enemies). Thus, it was a day of celebration of the Sages and their wisdom. I, for one, celebrate that wisdom everyday as I struggle to understand their message and the impact it has on my life. Each time I study a sacred text and am moved closer to God, I am mindful of my teachers who helped me find my way, who helped me find that place of centering in my life. As much as I might like to believe it, I didn't just get there on my own.

The Talmud teaches us that when you share something you learned from a teacher, you should imagine that that teacher is standing right there in front of you. Give him/her the honor they deserve by recalling them by name and teach in their name. Be humbled by their presence and the presence of God in your midst.

For Growth and Renewal: For your next fellowship meeting, begin with a bit of Torah and invite the memory of your teacher to share the joy of your recovery with you. Give credit to all those from whom you have learned.

It is a purification from sin.

—Numbers 19:9,
from the reading
for Shabbat Parah

This Shabbat, Shabbat Parah as it is called, is really a means through which one is purified before making the pilgrimage to the ancient Temple in Jerusalem during the upcoming (next month in *Nisan*) holiday of Pesach. And while we don't fully understand the sacrificial system of which this is part, only with a soul that has been cleansed do we have the right to stand before God and ask for ultimate redemption. Now don't misunderstand me. The life you led in active addiction does not taint you. Recovery is cleansing. It's no coincidence that you are called *clean* when you are sober. Shabbat Parah is spiritual detox. During Shabbat you scrub your soul in order to remove the dirt.

But be on guard. As the Kotzker Rebbe, Menachem Mendl, advises, "As the Sabbath departs, one must be extremely careful. Other forces—forces of evil—try to replace it." And you have to be ready to encounter the work week once again.

For Growth and Renewal: This Shabbat, add something to your observance that will help move you further from sin and closer to holiness, further from addiction and closer to joyful recovery.

> *According to the joy and a person's yearning for*
> *fulfilling the* mitzvot, *so one merits to hear, to*
> *attain, and to fulfill them.*
>
> —Rabbi Yehudah Aryeh Leib of Ger,
> the Sefat Emet, late nineteenth century
> founder of Ger hasidism

Is it joy that leads to the performance of *mitzvot*? Or is it the performance of *mitzvot* which leads us to joy? Perhaps it does nor really matter as long as the individual does the *mitzvot* and also experiences the joy. Why? Because doing the *mitzvot* brings a person closer to God. That's one of the main reasons we do them. What other joy *could* be better!

But the Sefat Emet is trying to tell us something else. One should not just "do *mitzvot*." Instead, one should long to do them. For in this longing comes the ability to fulfill them. Consider the Hebrew construction for a moment. The word *mitzvah* implies both the divine instruction (or command, if you prefer), and our response to it. And it is this combination which brings us real joy.

Hearing the *mitzvah* is a particular challenge in today's world, especially when you consider how noisy is our *yetzer hara*. It attempts to drown out the call to "be holy." But you know what you have to do. Stay in recovery and keep your ears open.

For Growth and Renewal: What *mitzvah* have you longed to do but not had the courage to do it? Now you can. We're all behind you.

> *As my ancestors planted for me,*
> *I shall plant for my children.*
>
> —Babylonian Talmud,
> Taanit 23a

*C*honi Ha-me'aggel (literally, the circle maker), a purported wonder worker who lived in the first century B.C.E., used to draw circles in which he would stand. Then he would speak these words: "Master of the Universe, Your children have turned to me because they believe me to be a member of Your household. I swear by Your great name that I will not move from this circle until You have mercy on us." So this day, the twentieth of *Adar*, became a feast day in Jewish history because in this unusual way Choni Ha-me'aggel effected deliverance from drought.

Once this Jewish Rip Van Winkle—as an old man—was observed planting a carob tree by the side of the road when a stranger happened upon him. The bystander mockingly said to Choni, "Old man, why are you bothering to plant this tree? You certainly will not be alive to watch it bear fruit." Came the now famous reply, "As my ancestors planted for me, I shall plant for my children."

For those in recovery, spiritual drought can be disastrous. And continuity in recovery is absolutely necessary. Plant for yourself and for your children.

For Growth and Renewal: Plant a tree and draw a circle around it. Even if others don't understand, you will.

Source of Mercy! With loving strength,
untie our tangles.

—from *"Ana B'koach,"*
translated by Reb Zalman Schachter-Shalomi,
contemporary leader in the Jewish Renewal movement

What a perfect way to describe our lives. It's exactly the way we feel sometimes, all tangled up in life. Maybe that's how our lives have become so unmanageable (re-read Step One), because we are so tangled up in them. And the tangles keep getting tighter. They seem harder to straighten out every day. *Ana b'koach*: Please, with loving strength God, help us to get those tangles untied and put our lives back in order. With the help of our Higher Power, as this prayer suggests, recovery helps us to untangle the knots. But we have to be the ones to make sure that we don't get unraveled in the process. That's where Torah comes in. It replaces the chaos in our lives with order and direction.

You don't have to be in recovery from an addiction to feel tangled up—nor to feel the loving strength of God and the healing balm of Torah. The rabbis have suggested that Torah is a blueprint for the world and our lives, as well. We can all seek guidance from God in an effort to find direction for our lives.

For Growth and Renewal: Take a piece of string. Tie it in a knot. Then place it on your desk or wherever you work. Let it be your symbol of sobriety.

> *The first time an event occurs in nature, it is called a miracle. Later it comes to seem natural and is taken for granted.*
>
> —Rabbi Israel ben Eliezer Baal Shem Tov, the Besht, eighteenth century founder of the hasidic movement

The Baal Shem Tov, the founder of Hasidism, goes on to say, "Let your worship and your service be your miracle everyday. Only such worship, performed from the heart with the enthusiasm of fresh wonder is acceptable." The miracle of recovery seems to work the same way. Think about the first time you entered a fellowship meeting, celebrated your first anniversary, or did your first Twelve Step work. The only way to recapture that feeling is by continuing to work the program. And there is no doubt about it, Torah supports your work in the program.

But how do you feel about your recovery now? Do you still marvel at it? When you start to take your recovery for granted, it can start dragging you back into the world of active addiction. Then by the time you realize what's going on, it may be too late. There will be temptations, even slips. But stay in program. And celebrate this miracle of your life.

For Growth and Renewal: Be on the lookout for miracles. They surround you. Each breath you take is a miracle. Never forget it.

> *Though my life is in danger,*
> *I do not neglect your teaching.*

—Psalm 119:109

That's why I do not neglect your teaching—because my life is in danger. Our lives are always in danger—whether we are in recovery or have never been addicted to anything. Life on this earth, however blessed we feel, is fragile for all of us. We are constantly reminded of this Torah wisdom. It is God's teaching that protects us from the many dangers of daily living—especially the danger of addiction to alcohol and drugs, eating disorders, compulsive gambling and sex.

In active addiction, we run through life. Always rushing at breakneck speed. Places to go; deadlines to meet. We go too fast to realize anything. Perhaps it is that fear of recognition that kept us running for so long. Too long! Recovery and spiritual renewal slow us down to a more regular pace. In recovery, we come to appreciate how delicate is that thread that keeps us alive. So we aim to protect it as best we can. And now, in the program, we can.

For Growth and Renewal: Stop running. Walk to your meeting tonight—if it's close enough. Or anyplace else. Give yourself a chance to clear your head and get ready to continue your recovery.

> *Do not say, "God has led me astray"*
> *for God does not desire sin. No one is*
> *bidden to be godless, and to no one*
> *did God give permission to sin.*

—Ben Sira 15:2

According to an old Jewish calendar, one which recalls dates that have been absorbed into history with little contemporary recognition, the twenty-fourth of *Adar* is remembered as the day on which King Uzziah contracted leprosy. The Bible understands leprosy as a punishment for sin. Thus, it prescribes various ways to rid oneself of this disease of body and soul. Today, we know better. One does not contract leprosy—or any other disease—as any kind of punishment. God doesn't work that way. Listen to the wise words of Ben Sira: "God does not want us to sin. Instead, God wants us to live good lives, far away from sin, and be joyful as a result."

But maybe the Bible is really talking about a spiritual leprosy, not a physical one. There are certain behaviors that leave spiritual disease in their path—and many of them are related to active addiction. The only way to protect yourself from contracting them is to stay away from your addiction and the behaviors associated with them.

For Growth and Renewal: There are still things left in your life that may yet be associated with your addiction. Today, remove another one from your home.

*This month shall be for you the beginning
of months; it shall be the first month
of the year for you.*

—Exodus 12:2

While Rosh Hashanah is considered to be *the* New Year because of the intensely introspective ten-day period it ushers in, the month of *Nisan* (immediately following *Adar*) is actually the first month in the Jewish calendar. While it makes little logical sense to have two new years (there are actually others too), it is one of those things we learn to live with and actually enjoy its peculiar and unique rhythm. To be sure, there are other things in this world that don't make perfect sense either. So stop trying to figure everything out with your head. Let your heart do the thinking sometimes.

In anticipation of the New Year which begins with the month of *Nisan*—and its implicit Exodus from Egyptian slavery—a special Sabbath is observed called Shabbat Hachodesh. (Sometimes it actually falls on the first of *Nisan.*) Now some will say, "Why not just forget it? Isn't one New Year enough?" I look at it this way: It gives me yet another chance to start the new year as a renewed person, a better person, and assign my past to the year which has already passed.

For Growth and Renewal: Here is another chance to look ahead. Consider where you have been and where you are going.

> *The heavens were opened*
> *and I saw visions of God.*
>
> —Ezekiel 1:1

*N*ow that's a religious experience. I guess it's the kind of experience that we all think we should be able to have, whenever we want to have it. For some, it begins as a lonely vigil on the top of a mountain. For others, the journey to the Divine begins at the shore of a majestic ocean or a peaceful country lake.

But not all of us are prophets or even mystics. If we wander through life thinking that this is the kind of experience that will confirm our faith, then we will be wandering a long time. The mystical encounter with a Higher Power, which I choose to call God, is a difficult one to achieve. For me, the other method, much more down to earth (somewhat of a contradiction in terms) seems less exciting. We find it in the study of sacred text. It is here where God and the individual meet in the pages of our literature. It is here where Martin Buber's "I and Thou" experience between the individual and God is so accessible. It is this path, the one for us non-mystics, that I invite you to share with me, because it is my path, the one that occupies my life that sets my soul on fire.

For Growth and Renewal: So open up a holy book and start reading. Begin with a *kavannah,* the repetition of a bit of sacred text. It helps us to get prepared. It's as simple as that.

*Praying at any place is like standing
at the very foot of God's throne of glory,
for the gate of heaven is there
and the door is open for prayer to be heard.*

—Pirke de Rabbi Eliezer 35

While we like to think that prayer belongs in the synagogue at prescribed times following a rather old traditional format, there is lots of room for prayer at other times
and at other places. And wherever you pray, you don't
have to send your prayers very far. God reaches out to
receive them. So don't forsake one on account of the
other.

Prayer has a way of sanctifying the space around you.
And it lifts us up, nurtures us—even as it links us directly
to God. People don't always like to talk about it. For
some, such a discussion is still quite awkward. But once
you are willing to open yourself up to the possibility of
prayer, then indeed you will feel like you are "standing at
the very foot of God's throne of glory" with the doors
wide open.

For Growth and Renewal: During your prayer today,
imagine that you are indeed seated at the foot of God's
glory. Let that image inspire your prayers and lift them
heavenward. And don't forget to include Step Eleven in
your prayers.

*It is true that an individual's temperament
may make it easier to act in a certain way,
but one is never forced as a result of it
to do something or not to do it.*

—Hilchot Teshuvah 5:4

Moses Maimonides, perhaps the greatest Jewish philosopher, prepared a set of principles for repentance based on traditional (Jewish law) which he called *hilchot teshuvah.* These precepts were designed for individuals searching for a means to find their way home. Some of these individual *halachot* (laws), like this day's affirmation, contain a bit of wisdom and direction for the individual. Maimonides is trying to teach us that because of our individual dispositions we may be more likely to do one thing than another. But he notes that a predisposition does not force us to do anything. We may be predisposed to addiction, but it is we who take the first drink—and the second and the third.

Likewise, it may be easier for some to enter recovery and work the Twelve Steps. (The truth is that recovery is not *easy* for anyone.) But no one really forces us to do it. Even if a court of law is involved, we are the ones who ultimately must stop doing drugs, gambling, and eating compulsively. It is we who are the only ones that can say no to our sexual addictions. God has given us a free will. But only in recovery can we use it freely.

For Growth and Renewal: Listen to the teaching and let it sing through your soul. No need to sing it to yourself.

The mitzvot *were given
in order to improve the human being.*

—Leviticus Rabbah 13:3

Many people question the relationship between Torah and recovery. You may be hesitant to change or add anything to your Twelve Step program, fearful that it will lead you out of recovery. These fears are understandable. Have you ever considered the reason why God gave Torah (and *mitzvot*) to Israel? Leviticus Rabbah offers us one reason and it's a good one for those who are puzzled about the relationship between Judaism and recovery. Neither can replace the other. However, for those in recovery, one enriches the other. And we can be better people as a result.

But like the Twelve Steps, the individual has to work at Torah. Pithy sayings like this one are nice to repeat—even to share, but are just nice mouthfuls of empty rhetoric when they don't help reshape your life. There may be other ways to do it. With Torah, one can improve oneself. Through Torah, you can really build your own stairway to Heaven.

For Growth and Renewal: Get one more synagogue in your community to open its doors and its eyes to the Twelve Steps.

Prepare to meet your God.

—Amos 4:12

According to the account of *matan Torah* (the giving and receiving of Torah) in Exodus, all of the Israelites who were present at Sinai answered in one voice. One commentary called *Torah Shelemah* interpreted this to mean that the great and the humble were all alike before God. That's why they were able to answer together. Such is the case in recovery. Addiction makes us all equal. And the truth is—addict or not—we are all humble before God. Or we should be.

But how does one actually prepare oneself to meet God? As a beginning, one should get clean and stay clean. Drugs, alcohol, compulsive eating, gambling and sex get in the way. Moses spent several days getting ready. But you don't just meet God on the mountaintops of Sinai. God is everywhere—as long as we don't crowd God out by being full of self. Jewish tradition teaches that whenever two people sit and talk about Torah, the Shechinah is present with them. Thus, even in our dialogue, through the pages of this book, when talking with others in the program, God is with us. Are you prepared to meet the holy in your life? Don't be afraid. Remember, be happy it's *Adar.*

For Growth and Renewal: Prepare to meet God in your life by seeing the godly in yourself and in others.

Nisan
Liberation
Early Spring

*O*riginally referred to as "The Month," and then later "The Month of Spring," *the* month of *Nisan* and the days anticipating Pesach, especially Shabbat Hagadol which immediately precedes the holiday, is the highlight of the Jewish year for many people. Spring is beginning. Once again, we enter Egyptian slavery—if only briefly—in order to remember our liberation and freedom. It helps us recall how our addictions and compulsive behaviors enslaved us so that we can appreciate the spiritual renewal that recovery has brought us. For those who are not in recovery—particularly friends and family—it gives us the opportunity to fulfill the dictum: "In every generation, the individual should look upon the self as personally delivered from Egypt." It's the closest others can get to your pain. Recovery is beginning.

Some say that the experience of liberation is not even possible without tasting the bitterness of slavery. That's perhaps why we were all in Egypt: To appreciate the sweet fruits of the Promised Land after journeying through the desert. But liberation is not enough. So we count the days one by one from the second day of Pesach until Shavuot, from liberation to revelation. Finally, through spiritual renewal, *one day at a time*, our suffering can stop.

> Nisan *is the month of the Exodus,*
> *the month of liberation.*

Although we celebrate the New Year in the fall, Jewish people have always began counting the months from the month of liberation in the spring. In this month, the religious life of Israel began with the erection and dedication of the Tabernacle in the desert of the first day of *Nisan* in the second year of the Exodus. Moses set up the house of worship on that day.

Moses devoted his entire being to this project, not just to the concrete task of building artifacts that would sit within its walls, but rather to the building of a community of men and women who believed in their spiritual potential and who were ready to have the presence of God in their midst. The *Shechina*, God's presence, belongs on earth, among us. No one is able to bring the *Shechina* in one fell swoop. All must do their part. Such work of spiritual rehabilitation is incremental. It proceeds in partial, patient acts of redemption, one at a time. The first month of spring is a time to take heart from the faith of Moses and all of the spiritual heroes, known and unknown, who have patiently and lovingly brought God's presence back into human lives.

For Growth and Renewal: Do your part to bring *Shechina* into the lives of others.

—Rabbi Gordon Tucker

For my sake, the world was created.

—Sanhedrin 4.5

Unlike other species, the first human beings were created as a single couple "to teach the greatness of the Holy Blessed One." For when a person mints several coins from a single die, they are all exactly like one another. But the Holy Blessed One minted each human being from the die of the first human. Yet not one of them is like another. Thus, every person is required to say, "the world was created for my sake."

Reflecting on the fact that every year on the first of *Nisan*, each Israelite was expected to contribute the sum of a half-shekel to support public worship in the Temple, this tradition from tractate Sanhedrin teaches us something extraordinary: We are God's coins. We all have the image and power of God in us, but we all activate it in our own way, at our own pace, in our own place and time. When each person gave that coin to the Temple, our ancestors enacted a powerful drama of faith: We are all equal—and unique—in the presence of God. We share the responsibility to be godly with every human being, but we reserve the inalienable right to bring the power of God into our lives in our own exclusive way.

For Growth and Renewal: Claim your birthright of equality, by deserving your divine gift of uniqueness.

—Rabbi Gordon Tucker

Always remember that you were slaves in Egypt.

—Deuteronomy 16:12

The theme of slavery and memory shapes the month of *Nisan*. Later in the month during the Passover *seder*, we will repeat: "*Avadim Hayenu.* We were slaves, but now we are free." We were in active addiction, but now we are in recovery, freed from the enslavement of addictions and compulsive behaviors. Yet we still have to remember. Always. We maintain our sobriety by keeping our memories green. Implicit in memory is the power to heal. What better evidence do we need than the history of our people!

During fellowship meetings we publicly tell our stories, detailing to one another the strained stories of our addiction—and our recovery. The first time you share your story publicly may be difficult. You may be fearful that others will repeat your story and your anonymity will be lost. There is a saying that "what you hear in here stays in here." We retell the tale of our journey in order to help others. Some listeners may be at their first meeting. Others who may be listening may be sober for years. Your story helps them both—and everyone else who is listening. Above all, repeating your story of struggle helps you.

For Growth and Renewal: After you "qualify" or share your story with others, hum these words to yourself: "We once were slaves; now we are free." And keep on humming.

A place has been left for me to labor in it.

—Babylonian Talmud,
Hullin 7a

When we speak about Egyptian slavery, our people's eventual exodus and their journey through the desert, we think of large numbers (600,000 people according to Jewish tradition). While we certainly resonate with the journey of the Israelites who left Egypt, such large numbers may be a bit off-putting. What about the journey of the individual? It takes individuals to make a fellowship, a community. We can't make the journey alone. But we, as individuals, have to work the program, to labor in it—ourselves. While the recovery of others is important (that's why many of us are sponsors), our main focus has to be *our* recovery.

We share the celebration of major milestones in our friend's recovery. Each anniversary is a celebration. One day sober. One week clean. A month without gambling. A year without compulsive sex. Ten years. Twenty years. We applaud. As we celebrate our friend's sobriety, we are also celebrating our own. If a relapse occurs, then the counting starts anew. It's one of the reasons why a place has been left for us to "labor in it," to continue to work at our recovery. As long as we work at it—even amid our occasional setbacks—we are moving forward in recovery.

For Growth and Renewal: Celebrate your sobriety by continuing to choose to do the work you do.

> *There is no room for God*
> *in a person too full of self.*

—Rabbi Israel ben Eliezer Baal Shem Tov, the Besht,
eighteenth century founder of the hasidic movement

This is the liberation time of year for us. This is the point of reading the Haggadah: It is my story. Each year I leave that narrow place (*Mitzrayim,* Egypt) which is too small for me now. It is a different place, because I am in a different place now. Growing in and out. One narrow place after another in a spiral movement. We never cover the same ground twice. With growing sobriety, the Twelve Steps take on a richer spiritual meaning.

It is time now to leave this year's narrow place. It is too small for me now, gotta go, don't have time to pack, will probably only take a few matzahs and a change of clothes with me. What sustains me on this journey is, as always, spiritual. I put out the *chametz* from my life for this journey. *Chametz* is anything that is inflated, puffed up: all the leavened food, all the inflatable aspects of self, too much me-ness, the narcissism of self. This is *chametz* and this is what I take out of my life during Passover. During the month of *Nisan,* I learn humility.

For Growth and Renewal: When I eat matzah, that substance of no *chametz,* I realize how *chametz* isolates the self from God. As you eat your matzah, remember: Less self, more Other.

—Rabbi James Stone Goodman

> *Go. Return to Egypt.*
>
> —Exodus 4:19

The story of the Exodus really begins with the concluding chapters of the book of Genesis. In those chapters, which recount the family history of Joseph and his brothers, the theme repeatedly is that of "going down." The book ends with Joseph in the most narrow and deep confinement that one can imagine—his remains are now confined in the tightest, deepest spot in the land of narrowness and straits [for that is what *Mitzrayim* (Egypt) means].

Who of us has not lived through repeated descents? Who of us has not felt confined, unable to break out of the tightest, narrowest of straits? Who has not had a personal *Mitzrayim*? The story of Passover is more than historical drama about the consummation of a love promised to an ancient clan from Mesopotamia. The account of the Exodus is not a story of a war, but rather a demonstration that seeds may be found in the narrowest of straits, an exhortation that birth to new life requires separation from Egypt, from bondage in every sense. The reality is that births are painful and difficult. The miracle is that they are possible.

For Growth and Renewal: Plant your own seed of redemption. Then nurture its growth.

—Rabbi Gordon Tucker

> *And God will turn the heart of the parents*
> *to the children and the heart of the children*
> *to the parents.*

—Malachi 3:27,
from the haftarah
for Shabbat Hagadol

The Sabbath just prior to Pesach is called Shabbat Hagadol, literally the Great Sabbath. There are lots of reasons why it is considered so important. For one, it anticipates the exodus from Egypt. But look at the words of the haftarah (the selection to be read from the prophets) for this Shabbat. Imagine how great this Sabbath has to be if it can help bring you and your parents (or children) back together. In order for families to leave Egypt, they had to do it together. In order to be delivered from their slavery, they had to detach themselves from all of the baggage of the past. But it took forty years in the desert to get themselves really free.

In recovery, you have to do the same. Getting clean means first to stay away from the chemical or behavior of your addiction that was keeping you enslaved. But addiction is a family disease. Recovery requires us to remove the chemical or compulsive behavior from the family system as well as from the body.

For Growth and Renewal: Do your "family of origin" work, making peace with the family of your childhood. As do the members of every generation, you have the ability to affirm the prophetic truth of Malachi's words.

*Have no fear. Stand by, and witness the
deliverance which God will work for you today.*

—Exodus 14:13

When we as a people left *Mitzrayim*, that narrow place which could no longer hold us, we charged into the Wilderness like 600,000 wild water buffalo. We smelled freedom. But we had the Wilderness still to cross, the next stage in getting free. That's the thing about liberation—it happens in stages, steps, one at a time—with our Higher Power at our side.

We count seven weeks in the Wilderness before the next step in our liberation: Torah at Sinai. Torah signified a wisdom that could not be anticipated, something entirely new. We are reminded that the most subtle aspect of control is thinking we can anticipate what we will learn. Freedom means accepting a teaching that is completely new. The way God led us through the Wilderness may be longer, but it is the way to our own wisdom. We may have the Wilderness yet to cross, but it need not be such a fearful place. There is no ownership in the Wilderness. We are lean and hungry and sustained by the miraculous and the spiritual. It is a time to savor because someday we will all be sitting on our mortgages, recalling the heavy boots and fleece jackets we wore in the Wilderness, signifying we had been to the peak.

For Growth and Renewal: Start packing. Bring only what you need to cross the Wilderness.

—Rabbi James Stone Goodman

> *God created the world in a state of beginning.*
> *The universe is always in an uncompleted state,*
> *in the form of its beginning . . . and requires*
> *continuous labor and renewal by creative forces.*
>
> —Rabbi Simcha Bunam of Pszysucha,
> early nineteenth century Polish maggid

Does freedom begin with being dragged out of *Mitzrayim*, out of the place where we got stuck? No. It begins earlier. Does it begin with the give and take between Moses and Pharaoh? No. Does it begin with a meeting with God at a bush full of fire, when Moses is introduced to a higher destiny? No. It begins earlier. Every act in the chain of action which leads to freedom is built on a previous act, contributing ultimately to freedom, in ways we may not be aware. Every act contributes to our freedom. No deed is done, no thought is thought, no dream is dreamed, for nothing.

When does freedom begin? It may begin today, with this thought, this action, that was preceded by the event yesterday, which may have been preceded by the dream the day before. Back beyond today. Every act has a liberating potential of which we may not be aware. When did we get free? When we stopped. When we decided. When we were willing to act. When we dreamed it. Back beyond, way beyond, before it came to be.

—Rabbi James Stone Goodman

For Growth and Renewal: Dream of your liberation today. Count your steps backwards and follow your path forward.

Even if a person has learned much Torah, that person should feel that he has yet accomplished nothing and consider herself a desert.

—Rabbi Menachem Mendl of Kotzk, early nineteenth century hasidic leader

What a powerful image for powerful Torah. It is especially appropriate for the month of *Nisan*, as we prepare for the Exodus from Egypt and our people's forty-year sojourn in the desert. In a sense, this humbling principle, taught by the provocative hasidic Rabbi Menachem Mendl of Kotzk, speaks as clearly to us as it does describe the folks who left Egypt. Each of our ancient ancestors had to leave Egypt the same way, on foot, with few possessions, in the middle of the night. A midnight move, as it were!

Addicted people know a lot about a lot of things, for they have experienced a great deal. They come from all walks of life, from a variety of occupations and professions—experts in various fields of human endeavor. But when they enter recovery, they have to set aside all of that other knowledge in order to learn new Torah. And that is both a humbling and liberating experience. As they move into recovery, addicted people are indeed deserts. As a matter of fact, we all are.

For Growth and Renewal: What did you take with you during *your* midnight move from slavery?

*The bush resembles a heart. It too can burn
without being consumed.*

—*Torah Shelemah*, Vol. 8, p. 123

Moses didn't just one day decide to lead the people from slavery to freedom. Each day, he prepared himself for the job—and God prepared him. During his life's journey, Moses envisaged a bush that was burning but not consumed. Realizing that he was on holy ground, Moses took off his shoes. And when he looked at the bush, he saw that it resembled a human heart. Not in its shape or size. Rather, in the way it burned with unparalleled intensity.

The heart *can* burn with passion, thankfully so. And that passion will fuel its burning, helping it to burn more intensely, with greater brilliance. But that same passion will protect the heart along the way.

For this passion is not driven by addiction. No alcohol, no drugs, no sex can produce such passion. Instead, this passion is the result of fulfilled spiritual hunger, nurtured by Torah and a relationship with God. It is a special kind of Twelve Step liberation from slavery.

For Growth and Renewal: Share your holy experience with a trusted friend, your sponsor or your rabbi. Let others feel the fire that burns in your heart.

---

*Others can gain control of you as long as
you possess a will distinct from God's.*

—Rabbi Nachman of Bratzlav
late eighteenth century
hasidic rebbe

It seems that Rabbi Nachman is speaking directly to those with a sexual addiction, as well as codependents for whom relationships with others have become addictive. Other people can gain control of you. We have learned this from our experience. Other things can gain control of you too. You have learned that in your active alcoholism and chemical dependency.

All the time we were worrying about what it meant to work Step Three, we didn't even consider what Rabbi Nachman comes to teach us. That's what happens when you get embroiled in a theological discussion. Mind games. They usually get in the way of belief. But no more. We are tired of making excuses, tired of avoiding the truth. Instead, as part of our recovery, we will work toward getting our will in sync with God's will. For that produces a sweet melody of its own. It's recovery music.

For Growth and Renewal: What have you done today to try to get your will in accord with the will of God for your life? If you haven't done anything yet, you still have a few hours to do it. So what are you waiting for?

The soul is the candle of God,
searching out all the innermost parts.

—Proverbs 20:27

Before Pesach begins, we are instructed to remove all of the *chametz* from our house. We rid ourselves of it through a cleaning ritual. First we take a candle and feather and search out all the innermost parts of the *chametz*. It is not upon me to search out your *chametz*. You must do that for yourself. What can I do? I can share my light. Second, we claim ownership of our *chametz*, and then we sell it. I cannot own yours, only my own. We accept ownership, then relinquish it, connecting the principles of ownership and being puffed up. I accept, and then I let go. Third, as if the word formula for accepting and relinquishing ownership were not enough, we burn our *chametz*. We find the deed that demonstrates we are serious about this inflated stuff we have searched out within. We want this *chametz* out and we want it out now. So we burn it.

Is it difficult to prepare ourselves this way for the Pesach of our liberation? What tools do we need to mine the *chametz*? We don't need a shovel, only a feather. You do not need a hoe and pick to mine your *chametz*, you need only a feather.

For Growth and Renewal: Here's your feather. You have been given the light. Now, go out. Do your work.

—Rabbi James Stone Goodman

> *Tell your child on that day saying that*
> *it is because of what Adonai did for me*
> *when I came forth out of Egypt.*
>
> —Exodus 13:8

According to the Torah, "God heard our moaning" (Exodus 1:24) and planned our liberation. On this day before Pesach, we prepare to leave Egypt once again. The firstborn among us fast (in gratitude for the lives of the Israelite firstborn spared during the last plague). And we symbolically burn (*biur chametz*) all of the *chametz* (leavened products) left in the house. All of these acts are part of the overall simulation of our slavery, a fulfillment of our obligation to retell the story of slavery and redemption.

For some people, this season is the most painful of the entire year. But it can also be the most healing. All of us feel enslaved by one thing or another. At no other time do sacred Jewish metaphors and rituals speak so cogently to our addiction. We have all been in Egypt! We all stood dumbfounded at the shore of the Red Sea when Nachshon ben Aminadav took that first step into the waters even as they threatened to drown him. And we all crossed over into freedom. These Passover rituals pave a path of redemption for all of us. As we hear in Twelve Step fellowships, "Let go and let God."

For Growth and Renewal: As you prepare your seder this year, remember to include stories of your own liberation from slavery.

> Ha lachma anya.
> *This is the bread of bitter affliction.*
>
> —from the *Haggadah*

*T*his is the first day of Pesach. The *matzah* is the symbol of our slavery—*and* our liberation. It is the day for which we have been waiting: A springtime seasonal signpost. Just as the fall holidays (of Rosh Hashanah, Yom Kippur, Sukkot) mark that time of year, Pesach stamps this season of recovery for us. We can breathe a little more freely. Redemption has indeed finally come.

Listen to the words of one who wants to share: "I was in a rehabilitation center during Passover. I had never missed a seder with my family before. There was just myself and another Jewish man there. He told the staff about our plight. A nurse took pity on us and brought us *matzah*. That was my first seder in recovery. I heard my friend never made it; I'm one of the lucky ones."

No you are not alone. We were in Egypt together. We will leave together, safely. We tasted the bread of bitter affliction. Bear in mind these words of Isaiah, Chapter 43, "When you pass through water, I will be with you. Through streams, they will not overcome you. When you walk through fire, you will not be scorched. Through flames, it will not burn you."

For Growth and Renewal: Place an extra *matzah* in the stack of three. Let it stand for the bread of affliction and addiction.

Praised are You, Adonai our God,
who has made us holy in Your mitzvot
and instructed us to count the omer.

—Blessing said on counting the omer,
in anticipation of the revelation of Torah on Shavuot

There are 49 days between this second night of Passover and the first night of Shavuot. Traditionally, Jews have kept a countdown, called an omer (literally "a measure"), during this period of time. Perhaps the counting provided a ritual framework for our agrarian ancestors when they worried about whether the crops would grow on schedule. Jewish rituals anchor us so that we don't drift out on open seas. Our sages saw the omer period as a bridge between Passover's liberation from Egypt and Shavuot's receiving of the Torah. This time of spiritual preparation helps us renew our Jewish commitment. We count what is important to us.

One addict told me, as he recently celebrated his tenth year clean, that he has his own tradition of tabulating his clean time. He counts weeks, days, hours, minutes, and seconds, and announces them yearly at his anniversary celebration. This is his personal "omer"—the measure of what is important to him. As we reach these anniversary milestones, they are truly achievements worth celebrating. It shows others that recovery is possible. In doing so, we prove it to ourselves. In a word, clean time *counts.*

For Growth and Renewal: Make an omer calendar to help you count your clean time. Then keep counting it.

---

*Ribbono shel Olam, Guide of the Universe, You
know that our desire is to do Your will. If we fail,
it is because of the* leaven *that works within us.*

—Babylonian Talmud, Berachot 17a

The ultimate prayer for Passover. The rabbis of the
Talmud knew what they were talking about. Leaven
reminded them of slavery and Egyptian bondage. The
only way to get free of it is to start from scratch using
fresh ingredients, nothing left over from past experience.
This is Step Three recast in a Jewish mold.

Why did leaven remind them of slavery? Because, just as
yeast "puffs up" bread, so do our egos inflate ourselves.
When we think that we are the be-all and end-all of the
universe, we inevitably become slaves to our own desires.
Instead of leaven working within us, we can have Heaven
working within us. But we have to get out of our own
way. We have to shift our focus from feeling good to
doing good. And, trickiest of all, we have to learn to love
ourselves without worshipping ourselves. The leaven,
yetzer hara (the evil inclination), our disease—whatever
you want to call it—will call to us from time to time. Let
us call to God for the strength and wisdom to not heed it.

For Growth and Renewal: Even as we are already in the
midst of the holiday, we may feel that there is still some
leaven around. Get rid of it.

Arise my beloved, my fair one and come away
For lo, the winter is past.
Flowers appear on the earth.
The time of singing is here.
The song of the dove
Is heard in the land.

—Song of Songs 2:10-12

The semi-sacred days of Pesach, referred to as the inter-mediate days or *Hol Hamoed*, have a special quality about them. They represent an infusion of the festival into daily life, of the holy into the routine. And Shabbat Hol Hamoed Pesach, the Sabbath that occurs during the festival celebration, has a particular flavor to it. This special ambience is expressed, to a great extent, by the readings of the Song of Songs, the book assigned to this festival.

The Song of Songs is a book of love, reflecting both an individual's love for another and one's spiritual yearning for God. That's probably one of the reasons the rabbis included Song of Songs when they edited the Bible. With active addiction behind us, the winter of our lives is past. Liberation comes now that spring is upon us—and we are in recovery. Flowers cover the earth of our lives.

For Growth and Renewal: Go out and sing a song of love. It's time.

*Generally, darkness is merely the absence of light
and can be expelled by lighting a fire. But this
darkness was so thick that it could be touched. It
was a darkness of a deeper nature.*

—Ovadiah ben Jacob Sforno,
sixteenth century
Italian biblical commentator

While all of the Passover plagues were heart-wrenching, darkness was perhaps one of the worst. People assume that it was simply night-like darkness. But, as Sforno the Biblical commentator suggests, "It was darkness of a deeper nature." There was no light whatsoever, the kind of darkness out of which addictions are fashioned. The Gerer Rav said that "the darkness was so dense that people could not see one another. That is the worst darkness: When people are unable to see their neighbors, that is, understand their distress and help them."

In recovery, that darkness has been banished by the light. The "night of watching," a name by which the evening prior to the Israelite departure from Egypt is known, is over. Sure, we still have to be on our guard. We are never fully free of the darkness. Each night, the sun leaves us— but it will return. And often, even before the stars appear in the sky, the moon is already apparent, lighting our way through the night.

For Growth and Renewal: Tonight, help someone find their way through the dark. You can help light the way.

> *But I will stiffen Pharaoh's heart.*
>
> —Exodus 4:21

We are told repeatedly in the story of the Exodus that God stiffened Pharaoh's heart. And that raises a very acute moral problem. How can God legitimately rain down destruction on Pharaoh after having caused him to ignore Moses' warning?

Many readers of the Bible have attempted to resolve this moral dilemma in a variety of ways. Among the most suggestive and far-reaching of these is the resolution offered by Joseph Albo, a Spanish Jewish philosopher of the fifteenth century. Albo noted that as God began to punish the Egyptians for the long years in which they oppressed the Israelites, they had the effect of softening Pharaoh's heart. It seemed, therefore, that he was not acknowledging God of his own free will and God needed to know whether his *teshuvah*, his repentance, was genuine. While this may seem like a neat solution to the moral problem posed by the text, there is great significance to Albo's observation. It is not only Pharaohs who lose their way and become destructive to others and to themselves. It is everywoman and everyman. A return under duress may be better than no return at all. But the ultimate test of inner strength is to be able to change one's ways.

For Growth and Renewal: Return to God of your own free will, but do return.

—Rabbi Gordon Tucker

*I am Adonai. I will free you from the burdens of
the Egyptians.*

—Exodus 6:6

It is rather ironic to me that at the time of year we feel closest to the possibility of redemption, the four promises of deliverance (this is only the first one) are connected to the drinking of four full glasses of wine, one for each of the promises. Here are the remaining three:

"I will deliver you from their bondage" (Exodus 6:6);

"I will redeem you with an outstretched arm" (Exodus 6:6);

"I will take you to be my people" (Exodus 6:7).

This is one of those parts in our ritual tradition with which we have to come to terms. Surely, Jewish tradition is not advocating the abuse of alcohol. And we want to experience the redemption of our ancestors for ourselves. So what do people who are addicted to alcohol or otherwise chemically dependent do during seder?

They do what our ancestors in Egypt did. In essence, they work Step Three, skip the wine, and make sure our will is in accord with God's will. Then get out of Egypt, fast! Tell yourself and those nearby, "Yesterday is past, tomorrow has not arrived . . . for today I do not drink."

For Growth and Renewal: Place the wine glasses on your table upside down. Acknowledge the redemption and your addiction.

> Leshanah haba'ah beyrushalayim.
> *May we celebrate together as a free people*
> *next year in Jerusalem.*
>
> —from the end of the *Haggadah*

We end each seder with these words. They represent our undying hope. It is the powerful hope that kept us alive as a people throughout even the darkest days of our history. Jerusalem. Even just saying the word brings with it a measure of inner peace, for Jerusalem is both place and a state of mind. Some say that the name Jerusalem means "city of *shalom*," of peace, of tranquility. That's why even Jerusalemites say it. They speak of heavenly Jerusalem, when they will be tranquil, as well.

On this last day of Pesach as it is generally celebrated outside of the land of Israel, we acknowledge our own liberation from bondage, hoping, praying, that our fellowship brothers and sisters will be together with us next year, that those who are still shackled by the chains of addiction will be liberated and join us, as well. We pray for the peace of Jerusalem. Next year, may we all be free. Through Jerusalem's golden vista, may we all be at peace with ourselves. For those of us in a Twelve Step fellowship, let us acknowledge the community of peace we have found. This new family will be with us wherever we go.

For Growth and Renewal: Using Jerusalem as a lens to your soul, recite a prayer for inner peace.

> *It is considered appropriate to clean the mud*
> *from one's feet before coming to pray.*
>
> —Shulchan Aruch,
> Orach Chaim 151:8

I have always found this particular *halacha* (law) rather amusing, perhaps a bit strange, and certainly, on first glance, somewhat irrelevant. But read it over again—as I have done so many times. When we finally are ready to come to God (Step Three), we realize how muddy our feet have become as a result of our journey to get here. Nevertheless, even as we are on the threshold of the synagogue—which is really the point of reference for this law—anxious to pray, to "turn it over" to God, we have to pause and "clean the mud" from our feet and our souls.

When you enter a mikvah (ritual bath), the goal is to remove everything that might separate you from the purifying waters, including jewelry, make-up, even fingernail polish. Somehow we feel that we are never quite clean enough. There is always some lingering mud left from our past. And so we work the Steps again, each time getting cleaner. We need to be kinder to ourselves, to allow a true cleansing of our selves to continue a day at a time. Isn't that what it means to be "selfish in a healthy way?" As they say in fellowship, "First things first."

For Growth and Renewal: Scrub it clean. When you go to your next meeting, "Know before Whom you stand."

The One who has created the day
has also created sustenance for it.

—Mechilta, Beshallach 2

As soon as the Israelites left Egypt, even after they passed through the Red Sea, a certain reality hit them. Getting out of Egypt is one thing, getting Egypt out of you is another thing entirely. There were setbacks along the way. You can read all about them in the Torah, week after week. Sure, God got angry, displeased, and chastised us. But God did not reject us. When the waters were bitter, God made them pure. When there was no food, God provided us with manna. Whatever our burdens, God provides us with the means necessary to face our challenges.

You are never really comfortable in the desert. You are always trying to do something to make it feel more like home. But it never does. It can't. During my first trip to Sinai (not the one with our ancestors) I remember praying with all my heart that the sun would rise to warm my body. But it was my soul that felt alone. I felt cold, but God sustained me during my journey there as God did with our ancestors. God will do it for you too.

For Growth and Renewal: Relive the Sinai experience in your mind. Feel its severe heat and its frigid cold. Then pray that the sheltering wings of *Shechina* might protect you. "Let go and let God" provide what you need in recovery.

> *You cannot find peace*
> *anywhere but in your own soul.*
>
> —Rabbi Simcha Bunam of Pszysucha,
> early nineteenth century Polish maggid

*B*ecause we desired to please others, at the expense of self, we pushed ourselves into active addiction. It was a slow process. We were generally unaware of it. Just one drink, a little toot, another dessert. If we couldn't please others, how could we ever hope to please ourselves! "Alcohol (or anything else) would make us more of what we wanted to be," went the logic of our stinkin' thinkin'. Or, "If I don't eat at all, then they will all find me attractive." Nothing foreign to the self and the nurture of our souls can make us more of what we essentially are. In recovery, we learn to bring our lives back into focus, on the self.

In active addiction, we sought solace in substances beyond the self, whether it was in alcohol, drugs, food, gambling, or sex. Nothing worked, nor could it. "You cannot find peace anywhere but in your own soul." Torah helps us to recognize that certainty. But such truths do not unfold instantly. Little that's worthwhile comes in a hurry. Instant gratification quickly fades. Time takes time. And a soul at peace with the self can last a lifetime.

For Growth and Renewal: Many begin to find peace during Shabbat. Begin there and bring those Sabbath moments into the rest of week. Find the Sabbath of your soul.

*You may find even madness
providentially beneficial.*

—Midrash Tehillim 34.1

During your time in recovery, you have probably attended a number of anniversaries—people celebrating their
first, second, fifth, or tenth year in the program. At nearly
every one of these very important occasions, there is a
common thread running through the grateful words of
each celebrant: My life is so much better now, more full
and fulfilling than I would have ever thought possible. It
is not necessarily about having more "things." Many of
us had many things before we put the Twelve Steps into
our lives—except that we derived little happiness from
them.

Recovery is about learning to live life better—with more
gratitude and a deepened sense of the holy—no matter
what life brings. And if it took us the insanity of active
addictive behavior to bring us to our bottom and move us
into recovery, well, how could there possibly be any more
fortuitous a form of madness? It took 400 years of Egypt
slavery before our people could be redeemed!

For Growth and Renewal: Liberate yourself. Get rid of
something you don't need. Give it to someone who really
does. Replace it with a feeling of fulfillment.

Ani Maamin. *I believe with tranquil faith*
in the coming of Messiah. Though Messiah may
tarry, even with all that, I still believe.

—From the Thirteen Principles of Faith
of Moses Maimonides, the RaMBaM,
twelfth century Jewish philosopher and theologian

With these words—and often their last breath—our people expressed their faith. This day which was all night, *Yom Hashoah*, the day of Holocaust memorial, altered Jewish history. After those years of horror, our people's self-conscience can never be the same. The Sefat Emet once wrote, "Israel orders its calendar by the moon for it is used to living in the night of history."

Some lost their faith as 6 million lost their lives; others affirmed their belief in God and the ultimate redemption that God would eventually bring. We share the legacy of both the faithless and the faithful, whatever is our lot in life. I do believe in the coming of Messiah. My faith may not always be as tranquil or as perfect (as others might translate this statement of belief) as it ought to be, but with my passionate belief I am serene. For those of you who had childhoods filled with fears, insecurity, and abuse, the Twelve Step fellowship family will be there for you, to provide safety and belonging as long as you need it. As they say in the program, "Keep coming back."

For Growth and Renewal: Repeat these words until you really believe them. And then once you do, keep repeating them.

> *Whoever is not ashamed to ask*
> *will in the end be exalted.*
>
> —Babylonian Talmud, Berachot 63b

You know the story. Someone once asked a Jewish person, "Why do Jewish people always answer a question with a question?" And the Jewish person replied, "Why not?" For all who seek to better understand themselves and the world, it is good to ask questions. Questions clarify. Questions challenge. Questions help us grow. Ours never was nor ever will be a religion of blind faith. Elie Wiesel, the noted author, recalls that when he came home from school, his parents never asked him, "Did you give a good answer?" but always instead, "Did you ask a good question?"

So let it be with your recovery. Especially in the beginning, there will be much that is strange, new, and puzzling. Do not ever be ashamed to ask someone—or the group—about anything recovery-related that you'd like to know. That is very much what meetings are for. It's hard—we know. Nobody wants to appear dumb—especially such self-sufficient lone wolves as us. But, as the recovery saying goes, "you can save face or save your ass"—but not both. We are here to learn, to do, to live. Stay open, stay willing, stay teachable. Ignorance is just another form of slavery. Learning from each other helps keep us free.

For Growth and Renewal: Learn something new about yourself today. Then share it with a friend.

> *You cannot be anything*
> *if you want to be everything.*

—Solomon Schechter,
early twentieth century scholar,
president of The Jewish Theological
Seminary of America

In active addiction, you are unhappy with who you are. Thus, with alcohol, chemicals and compulsive behaviors, you try to be someone else. It's a form of alchemy. Fool's gold. In this futile attempt, you often become the worst that you can be. That's generally when you bottom out. Just be who you are. In recovery, spiritual renewal can help you be the best that you can be. That alone is enough to keep you busy your entire life, one day at a time.

There are those who spend their lives trying to be someone they think they want to be. Unfortunately, they usually lose themselves along the way. God created us—each individual—in partnership with parents. We are miraculously unlike any other person who has been or who ever will be. You may share things in common with others. You may even try to look or dress just like them. Don't. Listen to the song in your own heart. Let it sing its sweet melody in your ears alone. Then transform it—through you—into a psalm of thanksgiving. Thank you God for creating me as me and you as you.

For Growth and Renewal: Do something today that is uniquely you, that others cannot own.

> *Praised are You, Adonai, Our God,*
> *Guide of the Universe, who has made the world*
> *so full that it lacks nothing and has created*
> *an exquisite creation with bountiful trees*
> *and human beings to enjoy them.*

—said in springtime
when the buds are beginning to bloom,
Shulchan Aruch, Orach Chaim 226:1

What a way to end the month! Grateful, humble, appreciating and enjoying the world in which we live, the lot that we have been cast. Such an awareness does not come to us overnight, nor even over the course of several months in the program. It takes a great deal to move to this point in our recovery. We get there one day at a time.

Blessings such as this one anchor us to the world, while offering us heavenly vision. This blessing is only to be said once a year when the buds spring forth into blossoms. The sheer beauty is exhilarating, but the creative genius that it represents is even more awe-inspiring. Night cycles into day. Winter moves into spring. And we feel liberated. While in active addiction we had previously felt out of control, this kind of order we have come to depend on.

For Growth and Renewal: Walk outside. Look at all the flowers. Smell their perfume. And say this blessing, so that we might all answer, "Amen."

Iyar
Independence
Mid-Spring

The name *Iyar* is related to the Hebrew word *or*, light. Prior to the Babylonian Exile (586-538 B.C.E.), *Iyar* was known as *Ziv* (a short way of saying "the brightness of flowers"), reflecting what was taking place in Israel, when the hillsides were blooming with spring flowers. Close your eyes. Breathe deeply. You can see the flowers and smell their fragrance. Both names reflect the time of year when finally we feel the warmth of spring light.

Kabbalists believe that, while reflecting a mood of mourning, the omer period (which entirely surrounds the month) allows us to go through the 49 gates of impurity imposed by Egyptian slavery. To make sure all of us have shed our slavery and are ready for the revelation of Torah, those unable to observe Passover because they were traveling are given a second opportunity through a Pesach Sheni, a second Pesach, on the 14th of *Iyar*.

In the modern period, the independence of the modern state of Israel was declared on 5 *Iyar* 1948, when our people was finally redeemed from its exile. But not without a cost. So a day of memory precedes it. Like the other months which have preceded it, *Iyar* reflects the travels of our people through history.

> *God spoke thus to Moses in the desert of Sinai, in*
> *the appointed tent, on the first day of the second*
> *month, in the second year after they had come*
> *out of the land of Egypt, "Take the sum of the*
> *entire community of Israelites."*

> —Numbers 1:1-2a

According to the Torah, Moses took the first census of the people in the wilderness on this day, the first of *Iyar.* The great medieval commentator Rashi suggests that the census was taken "because the Israelites were precious to God." So God asks Moses to count them every now and then. It's true. We count things that are important to us. Don't you count your clean time?

But there was much more to this counting of Moses. It was more than just arithmetic. For God asked Moses to take stock of the people, to get a sense of who they were now that they had come out of Egypt and had been traveling in the desert. Indeed, who were these people who had once been slaves? You probably ask yourself this same question, frequently and repetitively: Who am I now that my addiction is behind me? And how far have I progressed in my journey in the desert. Just remember, each step forward is a step further from slavery and addiction than the previous step. Forward counting for forward movement.

For Growth and Renewal: As you count your days, weeks, years in recovery, take an accounting of it as well. Ask, "Is my recovery better today than yesterday? Have I grown closer to myself?"

> *Solomon proposed to build a house*
> *for the name of Adonai.*
>
> —2 Chronicles 1:18

Seems rather presumptuous to build a house for God, especially when we realize that God is at home everywhere. Look carefully at the text: "Solomon proposed to build a house for the *name* of Adonai." Solomon wanted to enhance God's *reputation* in the world. In a way, I guess we all do. We want to share with others what God has done for us. Not everyone is comfortable with this notion, whether in the context of fellowship or synagogue or elsewhere. We don't go around building ancient Solomonic temples, but local synagogues and other institutions of caring and covenant, places where we might feel at home with God.

On this day which, according to Jewish tradition, marks the commencement of the building of the ancient Temple by King Solomon, we pledge ourselves to build God's home anew in our hearts. A great teacher once said, "God cannot dwell in a place where there is too much self." So we have to make sure that we make room for God in our hearts, in our souls, in our lives. We begin with humility, making sure that we are not too full of self. God will do the rest.

For Growth and Renewal: Make room within yourself for God. Then let God in.

Love your neighbor as yourself.

—Leviticus 19:18

Some of us, whether in a Twelve Step program or not, have trouble with the idea that an addiction is a disease. Somehow, they feel that an addiction—whether to alcohol, drugs, food, gambling or sex—is some sort of moral weakness, that addicted people are just no good. It's just not true. I want to scream it aloud at all of the people who shut their doors and close their eyes. I believe that it is this kind of misguided thinking that only serves to perpetuate the profound sense of shame that many addicted people have expressed to me.

So I turn to this text as evidence. Do we really believe that God would condone shabby treatment of our neighbors because we think too highly of ourselves? I don't think so. No, I think that the Torah reasonably assumes that most people care about themselves and look out for themselves. Thus, not loving yourself is not only not normal, it is not holy. It's not easy after all these years of self-hatred and abuse to love yourself. But that is what recovery is about, the renewal of genuine love of self.

For Growth and Renewal: Follow the teaching of Torah. Love yourself first. Only then will you be in a position to love your neighbor.

Have mercy on me, O Adonai;
See my distress at the hands of my foes.
You who lift me from the gates of death,
so that in the gates of tender Zion
I might tell all Your praise,
I might exult in Your deliverance.

—Psalm 9:14-15

This is a day of memory, literally *Yom Hazikaron*, for sacredly remembering those who have died in the struggle for Israel's survival and independence. For before we celebrate tomorrow, we must remember today. And so throughout Israel (and the Jewish world) Psalms 9 and 144 are read and reread, offering us some measure of comfort amid our pain. And at noon, the entire state of Israel stops for two minutes of silence. Traffic comes to a standstill. Buses pull to the side of the road and quiet their engines. Radios go off the air. All you can hear is the memory of the voices of people who have gone to their deaths. They have died so that we may live.

The best way to honor the memory of these brothers and sisters is indeed to live and enjoy life. And the only way to do that is to turn from active addiction and stay in recovery.

For Growth and Renewal: Be silent and reflect on the words of Psalms 9 and 144. In silence, there may be peace.

The ladder of heaven has only three steps:
Israel, Torah, and God.

—Zohar iv, 221b

Today is a day of celebration: *Yom Ha'atzmaut* (Israeli Independence Day). And if you go to Israel today, there is truly dancing in the streets. Parties. Parades. People. In the midst of such revelry, it is easy to lose sight of the long, hard journey that got us here. Israel was created out of the ashes of the Holocaust. Our recovery came at great expense, as well. Family. Friends. Painful separation. We cannot—must never—forget any of it. The rabbis of the midrash give us some perspective on our personal and collective journey: "When Israel reaches its lowest depths, she is lifted up" (Shemot Rabbah 1:9).

We have indeed all been lifted up. There is reason to celebrate. Those in recovery certainly understand the depth of this rejoicing. Thus, we all share this legacy of survival and are obligated to tell the story, to our friends, to our children, to all those born after us, to whomever will listen. It's a story worth hearing.

For Growth and Renewal: Do Twelve Step work and lift someone else up. Then you'll really have cause to celebrate.

*To follow the straight path, choose a good
colleague; to avoid the evil path,
avoid a wicked colleague.*

—*Pirke Avot* 2:9

It was easy and enticing for many to get sucked in by alcohol, gambling and drugs. Some of our friends were doing all three. We were a little bit bored, a little bit rebellious, and it was an age when the cardinal sin was to not follow the crowd. So down that path we went until, instead of doing drugs, the drugs were doing us.

My friend's mother was always very quick to quote a proverb at the proverbial drop of a hat. One of her favorites: "Show me who your friends are and I'll tell you who you are." Hey, once in a while even mothers are right! I've noticed that those who tend to stick with the program are the ones who start making friends. "Coming early and staying late" helps that happen. So does having a good sponsor. And so does reaching out to the newcomer. When it does happen, we are that much more connected to our program. It's not only a big part of how the program works, it's also a lot of fun. And, you'll quickly find that the people that you meet in fellowship meetings are about as crazy and as much fun to be with as the ones you've left behind!

For Growth and Renewal: Consider who you have been spending time with. Then start making friends in your fellowship.

*If a person should be humble in one's own house,
how much more should that person be humble
in the house of God.*

—Midrash Tehillim 101.3

Humility is a key to recovery and renewal. When humanity entered the modern era, we thought that we were in control of the world. No need for a Higher Power of any sort. We were our own "masters of the universe." Eventually we discovered how very wrong we were. Some came to this recognition on their own. For others, it was the voyage from active addiction to recovery that led them to discover God in their world and in their lives. And that is a humbling experience. We now realize that the bodies we tried to destroy with drink and drugs and food are also temples of God.

According to Jewish tradition, on this seventh day of *Iyar*, the Hasmoneans (of Judah the Maccabee fame) dedicated the walls of Jerusalem which they had repaired following their breach by the Assyrian-Greeks. (Remember the story of Hanukkah.) The Hasmoneans were committed to restoring a holy environment in which to live and extended their work beyond the ancient Temple to the entire walled city of old Jerusalem. Let us follow their example and "carry this message to alcoholics [and other addicted persons], and to practice these principles in all our affairs."

For Growth and Renewal: Bend your knees in prayer. Then go out and "walk the talk." On your way, remember to work Step Twelve.

*A person's temptation becomes more intense each
day, and were it not for God's help, it would be
impossible for an individual to resist.*

—Babylonian Talmud, Sukkah 52b

However you envisage your Higher Power, one thing is for sure: Only in covenant with that Higher Power are you able to resist the temptations that shackle you to your addiction. As you well recall, each day in active addiction seemed to move you further away from any real ability to enter recovery. Yet, there was something that finally made you realize that you "were powerless over alcohol [drugs, sex, food, and gambling]—that our lives had become unmanageable." Maybe it *was* your Higher Power even then.

Note well the words of Rabbi Harold Kushner, author of *When Bad Things Happen to Good People*: "Prayer, when it is offered in the right way, redeems people from isolation. It assures them that they need not feel alone and abandoned. It lets them know that they are part of a greater reality, with more depth, more hope, more courage, and more of a future than any individual could have by himself." Now that you recognize the covenantal aspect of your independence you are able to join together with your Higher Power and stay in recovery.

For Growth and Renewal: Ask for God's help to resist temptation in your prayers. You do your job and God will help you with it.

> *Meditation before God brings forth*
> *the holy spark that is found in every individual.*
> *It lights up the heart and thereby deprives*
> *the individual of all desire for evil.*

—Rabbi Nachman of Bratzlav,
late eighteenth century hasidic rebbe

Every individual has a holy spark. The rabbis tell us that it is there from birth—and even before. In the midst of active addiction, that holy spark hides beneath the surface. It seems to smolder, growing nearly cold, but it is there, nonetheless. In recovery, when we turn to our Higher Power, meditating before God, we are able to fan that spark into flames. In doing so, we are able to subdue the drive that fuels an addiction.

The recognition of the presence of God in our midst, of our relationship with God lights up the heart. We call this relationship covenantal, established between God and our people at Sinai and handed down to us through the generations. Martin Buber, a philosopher and theologian, calls this holy relationship with God "I-Thou." Buber encourages us to emulate this relationship in all our associations with others. Sounds a lot like Steps Eleven and Twelve to me.

For Growth and Renewal: Close your eyes and center yourself. Focus on that Divine spark deeply embedded in your soul. When you the urge to act compulsively threatens, ignite the spark. In such holy times, you can overcome your desire.

> *The enemy comes only on account of*
> *sin and transgression.*
>
> —Pesichta d'Rav Kahana 27

This tenth day of *Iyar* was once observed as a fast, because it marks the anniversary of the death of Eli and his sons (priests at the cultic center of Shiloh) and the capture of the ark by the Philistines. Jewish tradition has always recognized that "the enemy only comes on account of sin and transgression." So any defeat by an enemy demands self-analysis, introspection, *cheshbon hanefesh*, an accounting of the soul. In other words, while we try to figure out why the enemy has challenged us, we work Step Four again. And we know, the enemy of addiction is always tormenting us.

Logically, we may reject the rabbinic notion of reward and punishment and assign it to a distant past. But we still often feel that way in our hearts. And in terms of addiction, the transgression and the enemy are one and the same. So we seek to vanquish the enemy by removing sin from our midst. It's the only way to live.

For Growth and Renewal: While you try to figure out why the enemy of addiction has challenged us, work Step Four again.

All mitzvot *should be performed with the proper intention. There is one exception: Humility.*

—Rabbi Menachem Mendl of Kotzk,
early nineteenth century hasidic leader

Some people are confused about the meaning of *mitzvot.* They liken them all to good deeds. Nothing more, nothing less. While the Yiddish word "mitzveh" does well to capture the nuance of a good deed, the Hebrew word *mitzvot* means holy instructions (or commandments). The source for these instructions is no less than Divine.

When someone asks you to do something, you probably take into consideration who it was that made the request in the first place. You would do well to consider the giver of the *mitzvot* when you do them, as well. It this recognition that humbles the individual.

One does *mitzvot* for various reasons, but the end result is the same. Through *mitzvot*, we are able to get closer to God. We do *mitzvot* for this "One" purpose.

For Growth and Renewal: Before you do a *mitzvah*, pray that you might do it with the proper intention. That prayer will embrace you and your deed as it they both help to move you closer to God.

And the righteous will live by his faith.

—Habbakuk 2:4

It's difficult to be righteous and faithful at the same time. Temptations abound. It is easy to be seduced by money or power. And alcohol and drugs and other addictions present us with an even greater personal challenge. In today's world, I am not always sure what being righteous even means. But I do take the words of our prophets seriously, hoping to learn from them. I believe that we can all gain guidance and inspiration from their wisdom, for they viewed the world from such a vastly different perspective. And they were not afraid to speak the truth and be faithful to it. That is probably what draws me to them.

The prophetic book of Habbakuk numbers only three chapters in the Bible, a total of 56 verses. Yet, it includes the profound insight of a prophet who lived around the sixth or seventh century B.C.E. Like the other prophets, he wonders why it seems so often that the righteous suffer while sinners do not. He offers this text as a personal understanding of what others see as a paradox. If you believe, then act like you do. Live by your faith, the prophet tells us, do not die by it.

For Growth and Renewal: Being righteous can be as simple as being human. God has plenty of angels. Just be faithful to yourself. Be the best you that you can be—and God will provide the help.

If a person wants to know the Torah,
that person must work at it.

—Kevod Chacham

No matter how long we have been at it, we are all students of Torah. Like a cut diamond that shines and sparkles with the light, Torah radiantly illumines our lives. And each facet reflects new worlds of insight and understanding. There is no sufficient measure of Torah splendor.

People in recovery know what hard work is all about. They have been at it since the first day they stepped into a Twelve Step meeting. It's that kind of hard work that is necessary to learn Torah, as well. And it takes time. It's like a good physical work out. When you are finished, you feel exhausted but the exhaustion is renewing. And you know you have to keep at it. If you do not increase your learning, counsel our Sages, then you are decreasing it.

Recovery is worth the work. So is Torah: "It is a tree of life to all to cling to it, and all her paths are peace."

For Growth and Renewal: "Make your study of Torah routine" suggest the rabbis in *Pirke Avot*. It's the best way to learn. And you know what, they are right. Both Torah and recovery are as important to your soul as is proper food to your body. Find a partner and open up a book. Do it now!

> *When any of you . . . are on a long journey . . .*
> —Numbers 9:11

According to the tradition established by the book of Numbers, if an individual is unable to celebrate Passover on the established date (15 *Nisan*), then that person is given an opportunity to observe a Pesach Sheni, a "Second Pesach" one month later (at dusk, on 14 Iyar). While there are many reasons which may prevent someone from observing Passover, being far away seemed to be the basis for this flexibility in Jewish tradition. Since the Passover sacrifice had to take place at the Temple in Jerusalem, if you couldn't get there, you were not able to offer it.

While the Hebrew word in the text implies being "far away," the rabbis understand it more as "on a long journey." It was not always a matter of distance that prevented a person from going to the Temple in Jerusalem, where pilgrims went three times a year (Sukkot, Pesach, and Shavuot). Sometimes you could be physically very close and yet spiritually far away. Think about the time you may have spent in active addiction. You were far away, on a long journey going elsewhere. But when you come home, you are always welcome, even if you come home late.

For Growth and Renewal: If you didn't or couldn't celebrate Passover last month, here's your chance. Walking through the path of slavery with our ancestors may liberate you from your pain.

The gates of tears are never locked.

—Babylonian Talmud,
Bava Metzia 59a

Feminism has taught us a great deal about life and living, important things that many generations of women and men have avoided facing. It has even helped to bring about what has come to be called a men's movement. As part of this movement's ideology, certain emotions that seemed to have been inextricably tied to women have been reclaimed for both men and women. For example, it's now acceptable for men to cry, to express (rather than suppress) their emotions, to verbalize the yearnings of the soul.

Let's listen to what the Talmud is trying to teach us. It is acceptable to pour out one's heart, to unlock those inner feelings which may have been stored away for years, which we have previously been afraid to express. Together with your prayers, these tears can unlock the very gates of Heaven. Cries of the heart are always acceptable and accepted, from both women and men.

For Growth and Renewal: It seems like simple, even trite advice. But have a good cry—man or woman. In your tears, you can release the poison that is bottled up inside of you and flush out some of that pain.

> *It is greater to conquer one's anger than to fast*
> *for a thousand days.*
>
> —Rabbi Moshe Leib of Sasov,
> eighteenth century hasidic leader,
> known as the "father of
> widows and orphans"

Anger is poisonous. Just as an uncontrolled infection invades the body, likewise can anger consume the soul. It is nearly impossible to fully conquer one's anger. Perhaps it is one of the prices we pay for being human. But we can triumph over it. Once placed under control, we can move on in our recovery toward self-renewal and real independence. Like so many other things, we have to work hard at controlling our anger. We have to work at it hard. In active addiction those little annoyances which became major resentments seem to have been wrapped up in our codependence. Through recovery, we are able to gain new perspective on ourselves and on others.

Rabbi Nachman of Bratzlav taught that "An angry person cannot attain the goal to which one aspires." Anger, therefore, can actually prevent us from reaching our Twelve Step goals in recovery. No thousand day fasting is necessary. Our goal is recovery.

For Growth and Renewal: Let go of your anger now. Just let it go and be done with it.

> *If your heart becomes pure,*
> *the* Shechina *itself will sing within you.*
>
> —Rabbi Elimelech of Lizensk,
> eighteenth century hasidic leader

When your body is filled with chemicals, there's no way your heart can stay pure. And our goal is to get ourselves a clean heart. Even after drying out, after being clean for a while, we still have to go through a sort of spiritual detox. And "time takes time." Sounds pretty simple, but experience tells us otherwise. There are lots of forces working against us and, in active addiction, we helped those forces to overpower us. We lost control.

When you stop the drinking, the drugs, the compulsive gambling, eating, and sex—and all the things that got you there—then you have a chance to reclaim your heart. They clog up your arteries with spiritual impurities. Get rid of the anger and the resentment, all of the negative energy.

There is no sweeter sound than that of the *Shechina* singing through the soul of a person who has been restored. Music indeed speaks louder than words! I've heard it. Listen closely. You can hear it too.

For Growth and Renewal: Close your eyes. Listen for the melody. Then bring it to your lips and let it burst into song.

> *Rend your hearts and not your garments. Return
> to Adonai, for God is gracious and merciful.*
>
> —Joel 2:13

Remaining somewhat uncertain about the origins of the Omer, it is difficult to piece together the puzzle of its many traditions. Some contend that the Omer's somber mood is a reaction to the plague which killed many of Rabbi Akiba's students (in the second century B.C.E.). *Lag B'omer*, literally the thirty-third day of the Omer, somewhere in the middle, on 18 *Iyar*, may be the date on which the plague finally stopped ravaging these future Torah scholars. Thus, there is much to celebrate.

This eighteenth day of *Iyar* also marks the anniversary of the death of Shimon bar Yochai to whom tradition attributes the writing of the Zohar, the central text in Jewish mysticism.

Whatever the source, this twenty-four-hour period marks a separation from the anguish. To this day, Shimon bar Yochai's followers gather in Meron, light bonfires, and dance through the night in order to observe a *hillula* (wedding between heaven and earth). Other people observe Lag B'omer with their first spring picnic or outing for the season. The mourning is over—at least for a short time. We're on the road to Sinai, halfway there.

For Growth and Renewal: It's no longer time to "rend your garments." Rend your heart instead. God is waiting patiently,

The one who is obsessed with anger loses one's personal image of God.

—Rabbi Nachman of Bratzlav,
late eighteenth century hasidic rebbe

Rabbi Nachman of Bratzlav has a lot to say about anger. Perhaps it is because he knows the human condition so very well—or even his own condition. Or maybe it is because God is described as "slow to anger" and we are obligated to follow God's lead in order to live a holy life. Whatever the reason, Rabbi Nachman knows—as we all do—that anger is destructive, all-consuming. We are generally unaware of its strength. And when we allow anger to overtake us, we lose control. As a result, we strike out at whomever and whatever is in our path and thereby turn from it. Simply put, it gets in the way of our recovery.

As anger wells up inside of us, it saps our strength. In particular, it erodes our desire to work Step Two. When we entered recovery, "we came to believe that a Power greater than ourselves could restore us to sanity." But anger can drive you insane. Get back on the road to recovery and drive yourself elsewhere.

For Growth and Renewal: Keep an image of God present in your mind throughout your recovery. Let God be your constant companion. Wherever you go, you are not alone.

*If you see a person sinning or pursuing
an unworthy life, it is a mitzvah to try to
restore that person to the right path.*

—Moses Maimonides, the RaMBaM,
twelfth century Jewish
philosopher and theologian

Maimonides goes on to say, "Let your friend know that wrong actions are self-inflicted hurts, but speak softly and gently, making it clear that you speak only because of your concern for your friend's well-being." Sometimes, we get so involved in our own recovery that we lose sight of our responsibility to others. (Reread Step Twelve.) That's why we refer to Twelve Step programs as fellow-ships, and synagogues are called congregations. We are there to help one another.

Recovery is a path that ultimately has to be taken on our own, one step at a time. However, we *can* confront the challenges of daily living together and offer assistance to one another along the way. You might feel that after all you've been through, you have little to give. It's just not true. Because of all that you have been through, you have much to say. And plenty of us are ready to listen.

For Growth and Renewal: Take the advice of Rabbi Israel Salanter Lipkin, who said, "As long as the candle burns, you can still do some mending." You have a lot to give. Go out and give it.

The human soul is a tiny lamp
kindled from the Divine torch; it is
the vital spark of heavenly flame.

—Babylonian Talmud,
Berachot 10a

When I feel cold on the inside—and we all do at various times, whether as an addicted person or not—this thought warms me. It really does. I know that I am more than body, that I must care for it, as well. That means we have to totally stop polluting our bodies—beyond the alcohol and the drugs—beginning with smoke-free meetings and smoke-free recovery. Moses Maimonides, the great Jewish philosopher, taught that "the body is the instrument of the soul, to carry out all works." Our soul cannot be healed when our body is broken by active addiction.

It's a good thing that I don't have to exclusively count on myself to keep my soul on fire. Mine is but a tiny flame, kindled by a Divine spark. It is the spark of the Divine that warms my soul. When ignited, it sets my world afire. And I am healed.

For Growth and Renewal: This week, light your Havdalah candle outside. Watch how one wick ignites the other, how the flames dance in the air, until the candle is boldly lighting up the evening sky. The Divine spark lights up your life the same way, until your soul is ablaze.

> *When you climb the ladder,*
> *the lowest rungs are the first.*

> —Leon of Modena,
> Italian rabbi and scholar
> of the seventeenth century

Whenever I feel like I have just completed something but accomplished little, one friend reminds me, "That too is a *madrega* (a step forward)." It seems that we have to start on the bottom in order to get to the top. Without those first steps, you can't get anywhere. Even the angels in Jacob's dream (which we read about earlier in the year) started at the bottom of the ladder before they were able to reach heavenward.

Sometimes, our feet slip. The ladder is not always so steady. And urges to behave compulsively are going to occur. They come with the territory of being an addicted person (even in recovery) and they have absolutely nothing to do with whether we're working a good program or not. How we handle them, however, does. The more we hold onto the urge, the more it holds onto us.

So go climb your ladder.

For Growth and Renewal: As you consider Jacob's dream, imagine the angels going up and down the ladder. Then take a real ladder and place it securely against your house. Now start climbing. Pay attention to what is involved in each step. Then remember that feeling as you work *the* Twelve Steps.

> *Do not believe in your own wisdom
> until you can master your desires.*
>
> —*Mivchar Hapeninim,*
> fifteenth century ethical work
> attributed to Solomon ibn Gabirol

It is relatively easy to give advice to others. But that is no guarantee that others will accept what it is that you have to say. It sounds trite, but "You are what you do." Thus, you really have no business telling other people about controlling their desires until you can control your own. Of course, no one is in full control of their *yetzer hara.* Nor should they be. "Were it not for the *yetzer hara,* no person would build a house, marry, raise children, or engage in business" (Bereishit Rabbah 9:9).

According to Jewish tradition, the twenty-third of *Iyar* commemorates the expulsion of the Hellenists in 141 B.C.E. from Jerusalem's fortified area. For the Hasmoneans, it was a day of thanksgiving expressed in songs and feasts. Let *us* give thanks by being compassionate to ourselves, as we try to control our desires. "Give yourself a break" is a cornerstone of recovery and renewal. We cannot change our past, nor should we sugarcoat it. But we can come to terms with it by accepting what we were, by believing that we no longer have to be that way.

For Growth and Renewal: Try spending the day not offering advice to others. Instead, focus on overcoming your own desires.

*Know where you came from
and where you are going.*

—*Pirke Avot* 3:1

While traditions vary among communities, most have a custom about studying *Pirke Avot* on Shabbat, in the afternoon, especially this time of year. In a sense, such study aids us in understanding this teaching from the sacred text itself. As a result, it helps us to feel the rhythm of the Jewish week and the Jewish year.

People do drugs for various reasons. One person told me that she started using because she was "lost." And she really thought that drugs might be able to help her figure out where she was going. Well, she eventually found out where she was going and quickly changed directions! That's when she entered recovery.

There is only one way to go, but there are lots of ways to get there. Once you find your path, stay on it. It will lead you home.

For Growth and Renewal: Open up any edition of *Pirke Avot* and start studying. Begin at the beginning and read a little at a time. Then go back and read it again. Once you determine what the text has to teach you on living a holy life, everyday, begin to make some changes that will bring that life about.

*May the words of my mouth and the meditations
of my heart be acceptable to You, Adonai,
Rock and Redeemer.*

—Psalm 19:15

This well-known text from the book of Psalms helps to bring closure to the Amidah, the central prayer in Jewish liturgy, as we conclude our time for private reflection in the context of public worship. Here our prayers are joined with those who have come before us. In this context, perhaps the most focused recovery prayer we can offer is simply to ask God to help us become the best that we can be. We can ask for no more. And that's really enough. Making our best effort without fixating on the results frees us to accept life on life's terms. Once we are able to do that, we can go on living again.

What we say should reflect what we feel. While often missing elsewhere in the world, emotional honesty is something that we learn in the program. It is certainly something that others can learn from our recovery, as well. Teach it to others by living the truth of your recovery.

For Growth and Renewal: Use this text to bring a sense of closure to your prayers, elevating them and you at the same time.

Let days speak and many years teach wisdom.

—Job 32:7

Nobody in the Bible probably suffered more than Job. And he didn't deserve it. Ironically, that's likely the very reason why the book of Job was included in the Bible, to teach us that the righteous suffer along with the wicked. Sometimes life is the way it is, because life is the way it is. All we can to is try to learn from it—and try to change only what is in our power to change, starting with self. Nothing more, but certainly nothing less.

In active addiction, one suffers. It may have been suffering which led you to behave compulsively in the first place. But that time is long gone. We're finally ready for change. The season is right for it.

So let's listen to Job's advice. He advises us to allow our days and years speak to us, to offer the wisdom of their experience. Close your mouth. Open your ears and your heart and listen, listen, listen.

For *Growth and Renewal:* What is the one thing you learned about your life today? Write it down. Tomorrow, there will be more to learn.

---

*Sometimes one must look into the ashes
to find a solitary spark.*

—Dov Baer of Mezritch,
eighteenth century hasidic leader

It's true. We have all seen it. Even when someone is in the lowest depths of an addiction, an individual can pick oneself up and begin life again. Jewish tradition actually suggests that the possibility of renewal is presented to us every day. When we awake in the morning, we are reborn with pure souls, refashioned like a newborn babe. What we do with these souls during our waking hours is entirely up to us.

Consider your own journey. What moved you into recovery? Perhaps others joined you in your struggle. However, if you dig deeply into yourself, you will find that somehow you alone fanned the spark until it caught fire. Your addiction seemed to leave little left in your life but ashes. And yet one solitary spark was all it took. Perhaps that is one of the reasons why this twenty-seventh day of *Iyar* was once observed as the anniversary of another obscure Hasmonean victory. The Hasmoneans, a small group against the mighty armies of the world, never gave up hope. The message to you: Never give up hope.

For Growth and Renewal: Keep an unlit candle on your kitchen counter. Let it serve as a reminder that all it takes is one spark to ignite the flame.

> *Remember Adonai from afar*
> *and let Jerusalem come into your mind.*
>
> —Jeremiah 51:50

When Jerusalem comes into my mind, God is no longer far. It's part of the magic of Jerusalem, the city of peace. This twenty-eighth day of *Iyar* reflects the anniversary of the death of the prophet Samuel who moved the people from a loose confederation to an organized monarchy and named Saul as king. (Some say the date is 27 *Iyar*.) It was once observed as a fast. However, today we recognize 28 *Iyar* as Yom Yerushalayim: Jerusalem Unification Day, the day on which east and west Jerusalem were united in 1967.

For the individual Jewish person, Jerusalem *is* the center of the world. It is at the core, the very heart of the Jewish experience. As a people, we have built its walls, cried at its destruction, and wept at its rebirth. We have traveled its footpaths and wandered through its streets. The struggle of Jerusalem is our struggle. This sacred city is our anchor in a turbulent world. No matter how far we have traveled, in Jerusalem, we are forever home. When one envisages Jerusalem, one is helped to get centered in the world—with God close by.

For Growth and Renewal: For centuries, our people have dreamed of Jerusalem. It has brought them hope, comfort, and inner peace. When you feel alone, far from home, dream of Jerusalem. This vision will bring you home.

*Know that sexual intimacy is holy and pure
when it is carried out properly, in the proper time
and with proper intentions.*

—*Iggeret Hakodesh,*
attributed to Moses ben Nachman, RaMBaN,
medieval Spanish rabbi, scholar, and philosopher

Often we speak of addictions in terms of alcohol and drug abuse, maybe even food and gambling. There are still those who are unwilling to talk about (or admit to) their sexual addiction. No less real than alcohol or drug addiction, sexual addictions are just as destructive and deadly. The time has come to "admit that we are powerless over our sexual addiction" and can be healed.

The driving force behind sexual addiction is a desire to be loved. We think it may help fill the void that is created by the fact that we don't love ourselves. In active addiction, that perceived void is more like a black hole that, by definition, can never be filled. No matter how much we try, no matter how many people we sleep with, it is never enough. Never.

When we learn to love ourselves once again, we come to understand that there *is* a place for loving sex in our lives. Loving sex nurtures both partners. It enhances the self as it gives to the other person.

For Growth and Renewal: When you make love, imagine both you and your partner at the foot of Sinai, joining bodies and souls.

Sivan
Revelation
Late Spring

Inwardly impatient, we quietly conclude these last days of the Omer period. We have traveled many miles in the desert, through forty-nine gates away from the impurities of Egyptian slavery, say the mystics. Anxiously drawing to a close these final days of anticipating Torah, we yearn for God's revelation on Sinai, celebrating on Shavuot our covenantal relationship. But yearning is insufficient. Preparation is also necessary (*Shelosha Yeme Ha-gbalah*, "three full days of setting bounds" prior to Shavuot according to the Bible). We have waited a long time for this moment. We wish to make sacred the time and the space. Both the ground we walk on and the time we travel through is indeed holy.

As we anchor ourselves in the world, we continue to follow and count on its pattern of change. Nature prepares to cycle once again as spring is about to move into summer. Nothing stands still; there is always growth and renewal, even in the midst of what had appeared as utter destruction. The mourning period of Omer is over. Renewed, there is a sense of ease in the air. We seem to be able to breathe easily once again.

> *The giving of Torah happened at one specified*
> *time, but the receiving of Torah happens*
> *all the time, in every generation.*
>
> —Rabbi Isaac Meir Rothenberg Alter,
> the Gerer Rebbe,
> early nineteenth century hasidic leader

Anytime people study Torah, they are receiving it. Rashi taught, "Torah must be totally new to you every day." Like Torah study, recovery is a continually new event. It requires a "daily maintenance program," as some have said. Last week's meeting may not be sufficient to keep us clean today. The most inspiring stories quickly fade away because the disease helps us to forget, to despair, and to use. The one who is not busy recovering is busy dying. Recovery is a life-long process of fighting the disease of addiction, one day at a time. We get better, but we don't get cured. In the same sense, the study of Torah never ends; there are always new lessons to be learned.

The revelation of Torah may have begun at Sinai, but if it does not continue with us, it becomes merely a memory. For our recovery to continue, we must keep coming back to it. It must guide our lives. Recovery is being offered to us. Together like Torah—with Torah—it must be willingly received.

For Growth and Renewal: As you study ("Make your study a fixed habit"), imagine yourself at the foot of the mountain receiving Torah.

> *The counting from Passover to Shavuot is*
> *carried out "as is done by one who waits for*
> *the coming of the human being he loves best,*
> *and counts the days and hours."*

—Moses Maimonides, the RaMBaM,
medieval rabbinic authority and philosopher

The freedom of the Exodus is incomplete without the giving of the Torah. Freedom without Torah did not make sense. Until that time, the entry into the desert was without coordinates, focus-less. So we count as if the goal of our energies, of our days, is not yet here. And we wait impatiently, counting the days, until our objective is achieved, until our desire for Torah is consummated.

A nineteenth century Hasidic teacher, the Sefat Emet, sees the counting of the Omer as the days that preceded the making of the Golden Calf, which Jeremiah called "the devotion of your youth." Quoting the mystic Isaac Luria, the Sefat Emet suggests that a person ultimately draws on the innocent years of life for vitality, before sin and corruption. Though we may have slipped down the rungs of the ladder, we each have something onto which we can hold. Therefore, concludes the Sefat Emet, one should never give up or lose hope. That person still has the power to reawaken the strength that persists from the days of innocence. —Rabbi Gordon Tucker

For Growth and Renewal: Count your clean time (and the omer) the way you would count the time waiting for someone you love—you.

> *Warn the people to stay pure,*
> *today and tomorrow.*

> —Exodus 19:10

There are lots of ways to stay pure, but only one way to stay clean. That is to stay away from alcohol and drugs, compulsive eating, gambling and sex. But at the end of this text from Exodus, the Torah goes on to tell us to "wash our clothes." Actually the Torah is instructing to do much more than to put on clean clothes as part of readying ourselves for revelation. In a way, our clothes (that is, our outer selves) reflect who we are (our inner selves). And we have to clean them, as well. Or we won't be able to hear Torah even when it is revealed to us. While we usually think of revelation as Divine action, over which we have no control, *we* have to act, as well. If we aren't *ready* to receive Torah, we won't be able to do so. It is as simple as that. So whatever the addiction, stay away from it. Today and tomorrow.

This is the first of three days before Shavuot (called *Shelosha Yeme Ha-gbalah*, literally the three days of setting boundaries) in preparation for the revelation at Sinai. The main thing to do to get ready is to stop using and abusing—yourself and others.

For Growth and Renewal: Establish boundaries in your life. Stay away from one thing at a time. Then get ready for revelation.

> *Let them be ready for the third day;*
> *for on the third day Adonai will come down,*
> *in the sight of all the people, on Mt. Sinai.*

—Exodus 19:11

*O*ne day to get ready is not enough. In a way, we spend our whole lives getting ready. Once we enter recovery, we stay in it, because if we don't, we are no longer in recovery. Seems obvious, but it really isn't. Recovery and *teshuvah* are part of a long-term process. They are not tasks to be completed and then transcended. No, we are in it for *life!*

Like our first few days in recovery, this second day of boundary setting removes us entirely from the world we have come to know. It is only through such full and drastic separation that we are able to prepare ourselves for eventual re-entry into the world. The three days that the Bible sets forth might seem a bit arbitrary and altogether too short. And in a way, no time is sufficient to get ready to receive Torah. But the point is clear. It takes time to get ready to meet God at a place we consider to be our Sinai.

For Growth and Renewal: Consider what you do to get ready to go to a fellowship meeting. Carry that preparation into other activities.

> *You shall set bounds around the people round*
> *about saying, "Beware of going up the mountain*
> *or touching the border of it. Whoever*
> *touches the mountain will be put to death. . . ."*
> *When the ram's horn sounds a long blast,*
> *they may go up the mountain.*
>
> —Exodus 19:12-13

One more day before revelation, the last of three boundary days (*Shelosha Yeme Ha-gbalah*). We *finally* feel ready, having prepared ourselves in body and in spirit. The Torah warns us not to rush the process. So don't hurry. Just take it one day at a time.

There are always risks involved in such great moments. We take them every day in recovery. That's why proper preparation is necessary. No more quick fixes. No more instant highs. No more one-night stands. They are all behind us now. Let's keep them there.

Throughout the process of our recovery, we have learned what it means to wait until the proper time to do certain things. We do not put things off in order to avoid doing them. On the contrary, we delay until we are ready to do things right—or we end up like those who would approach the mountain too soon, dead wrong.

For Growth and Renewal: It was only when the shofar (ram's horn) had been sounded could the people then approach the mountain. Listen for its sound.

*Only in moments when we are able to share
in the spirit of awe that fills the world
are we able to understand what happened to
Israel at Sinai. Revelation means that the thick
silence which fills the endless distance between
God and the human mind was pierced. . . .*

—*Man is Not Alone*
by Abraham Joshua Heschel,
contemporary theologian,

There is a well-known story about a person who stares at a second person to the point of discomfort. Finally, the first person says to the second, "I know you from somewhere, but I just can't place it." With a smile, the second person replies, "From Sinai, we know each other from Sinai." I don't know exactly what happened at Sinai, but I do know that something spectacular happened. And in a mystical, metaphysical way, I was there. So were you.

Today's holiday of Shavuot celebrates that encounter between God and the people of Israel. Imagine the scene. Here you have a group of weary travelers, just like all of us, released and redeemed from slavery (sounds familiar, doesn't it?) who encounter the Divine in the midst of their journey. And their lives (and ours) are forever changed.

In the darkest hours of our slavery, we could not have anticipated such an encounter. Now we can imagine nothing else!

For Growth and Renewal: Imagine yourself at Sinai. Your life has been changed.

---

*Adonai is in the holy Temple. Let all the earth
keep silent before God.*

—Habakkuk 2:20,
from the Haftarah for
the second day of Shavuot

To be sure, God's presence cannot be restricted to one place or one time. In the desert *mishkan*, in the ancient Temple, in the synagogue, we find it comfortable to reach toward God. The Sinai experience epitomizes the relationship between God and the Jewish people. Thus, we should use it in some way to model our relationship with God. At Sinai, Torah was revealed to the entire Jewish people, but we are also told that each individual hears God's message according to our own ability to listen (both those standing at the foot of the mountain and those not yet born). While we are all part of God's covenantal relationship with the Jewish people as a whole, each individual's relationship with God is unique. Thus, we should live our lives reflective of that relationship and be sheltered by it.

Habakkuk is not suggesting that we should merely be quiet in front of God nor simply that we are dumbstruck by God's presence. Rather, this prophet is warning the individual to be silent. We must know before Whom we stand. God's power is awesome, but so is God's ability to heal.

For Growth and Renewal: Find your own individual place for prayer and meditation. Make sure it's comfortable. Then use it.

260

Then a great spirit lifted me up.

—Ezekiel 3:22

While this text is taken from the Haftarah for the first day of Shavuot, it also serves us well this first day after the holiday. During Shavuot, perhaps more than at any other time during the year, I feel closest to our ancestors and their experience at Sinai. I often try to imagine what it was like to have left Egypt, wandered in the desert and then waited in anxious anticipation for the revelation at Sinai. Various images dance in my mind as I am transported back thousands of years. During the holiday, all of those images that I have constructed are brought together. At the end of the holiday, I am not let down; rather, I feel lifted up.

I try to hold on to that feeling as Shavuot turns into ordinary time, as the rhythm of daily life regains routine, as the weeks of spring give way to summer. In the same way, you can hold on to the time you spend in fellowship meetings during the weeks ahead. When I want to recapture that time, I open up a book and engage the text once again. Likewise, you might call a sponsor and together recreate the message of the meeting.

For Growth and Renewal: Hold on to the feeling of Shavuot and be lifted by its radiance. How *do you* feel today?

The Torah makes wise the one who is naive.

—Psalm 19:7

Torah also makes wise even the person who is not naive. This text from Psalms is often translated as "Torah makes wise the one who is simple." My translation challenges this notion, for I understand Torah as a document in which is recorded the relationship between our ancestors and God, their struggles with faith. Thus, Torah makes wise the person who has not responded to a struggle with faith in his or her own life. That person is naive, because he has not decided to "make a decision to turn our will and our lives over to the care of God as we understood God." That person is naive because she sought wisdom and understanding through drink and drugs. Guess what? You didn't find it, did you?

We can become wise through Torah. It provides us with a perspective on life that no person or thing is able to offer.

In order to gain that wisdom, you have to open up its pages and enter into dialogue with the text of our ancestors. There is no alternative. It is a sacred study, the kind that can move us closer to heaven and Heaven closer to us.

For Growth and Renewal: What has Torah taught you today? Or what Torah have you learned today from life? Write it down and remember it.

> *The one who lives happily*
> *does the Creator's will.*
>
> —Rabbi Israel Eliezer Baal Shem Tov, the Besht,
> eighteenth century founder of hasidism

When we live a life reflective of the covenant that God established with us at Sinai, we are always doing our Creator's will. It is when we are out of touch with that sacred relationship that we return to compulsive behaviors and addictive substances that led us astray in the first place. *Mitzvot* lead to *mitzvot*; sin leads to sin. It's part of the spiritual logic of the universe. Put order back into your life. And restore balance to the universe. It's in your hands. It's really as simple as all that.

Our disease sets us up by convincing us to pursue a false version of happiness. It gets us to believe that our will for us will get us happier quicker. And then our disease influences us to look for shortcuts. . . . Or maybe it gets us to mistake excitement and titillation for *real* happiness. But we need to understand that what our disease wants most is for us to want—because then we are more easily led astray. If only we could pursue God's will as intensely as we pursue happiness! We'd wind up with both.

For Growth and Renewal: Consider your most important relationship. Work at it. What one thing can you do today to make that relationship better? It should mirror yours with God.

> *Direct me in the path of your mitzvot*
> *for I delight in it.*
>
> —Psalm 119:35

This is really the goal of the spiritual life, and such a life has serenity at its core. But can we really achieve it when there is still so much debris left in our lives to clean up? Will we be able to delight in a life that has given pain to others for a long time? Simply put, the answer to both questions is a resounding "Yes." And the key to such an affirmation is contained in this Psalm text.

Often people eat compulsively, because they do not feel inner joy. They are trying to fill with food the emptiness they feel. It doesn't work. It never did. When you allow God to direct you on the path to spiritual renewal, there is always the potential for inner joy and inner peace (*shelemut*). All you have to do is open yourself up to the possibility and work toward its realization. Healing will follow.

For Growth and Renewal: What path will you take today for your recovery? Map it out and then stay on it.

> *Tears may linger at nightfall,*
> *but joy comes in the morning.*
>
> —Psalm 30:6

It is at night that we probably feel most alone, most vulnerable, most in need of something to help us cope. The streets are empty and human activity returns to the privacy of the home. Strangers seem to hide behind shadows and familiar areas seem like uncharted territory in the blackness of night. Darkness seems to paint broad strokes of gloom across even the most hopeful parts of our world.

But we are not alone—even at night when it seems so. In fact, we are never alone. The God who was revealed to us in the desert is with us. The God who established a covenant with us thousands of years ago at a mountain called Sinai is with us wherever we go, whatever we do. Daylight illumines the world just as knowledge of the Almighty does so. The hours of the night may tick away slowly, but morning will always come. It may seem like it takes a long time to arrive, but it is that order in the universe, the knowledge that morning will indeed come, that offers us hope, gives us joy. All of this because it is God who brings it on and keeps us alive to enjoy it.

For Growth and Renewal: When you awake this morning, say a prayer of thanks. Your soul has been restored to you.

> *A people trained for generations in the house of bondage cannot cast off in an instant the effects of that training and become truly free, even when the chains have been struck off.*
>
> —Ahad Ha-am, Asher Hirsch Ginsberg, early twentieth century Hebrew essayist

Torah was given to a people who had endured Egyptian slavery. The state of Israel was born out of the ashes of the Holocaust. It seems that, as a people, we have reached many of our greatest spiritual heights only after we have experienced our darkest hours and deepest pain. It's part of the power of what some people call Jewish historical memory. The personal journey of the individual, our own journey to find meaning in our lives and be renewed, becomes fused with the collective journey of our people. Together, as a result, we share a past and a future.

Consider your own journey. For many, you could not have imagined in the midst of active addiction that you could even begin to enjoy such spiritual renewal. But just entering recovery, "even when the chains have been struck off," is insufficient. Recovery is not instantaneous. Hours in detox have proven that to you. Even more, you have to continue to work the program and live Torah every minute of your life. There are those who say that you have to actually "become Torah." And that takes a lifetime.

For Growth and Renewal: Do something today to "*be* Torah," to become that sacred gift: God's message to the Jewish people.

> Sachki sachki. *Laugh at all my dreams*
> *and I repeat anew.*
> *I still believe in [hu]man[kind]*
> *and I still believe in you.*
>
> —Saul Tchernikovsky,
> early twentieth century Hebrew poet

These lines have always intrigued me, drawing me to them. They are words which have fused pain with hope, memory with inspiration. I think they speak to every individual who has experienced disillusionment but has not despaired. While these are the classic words of a modern Hebrew poet, reflecting the hopes and aspirations of our people throughout our travels in history, the words also reflect one person's approach to life. Let's read them together. "You can ridicule my vision for a better life, a better world. That's O.K. I will still work toward it and help you do the same. We are all capable of reaching Heaven."

During your journey in recovery and spiritual renewal, there are going to be those who shut you out. They may be afraid of your history of addiction? They may be uncomfortable with all this spirituality and God-talk. So listen to the words of the poet. Believe in yourself and believe in others. Then continue on your way, striving with each step that you take.

For Growth and Renewal: What dream was forgotten in the midst of your active addiction? See what piece of it can be renewed. Then do something about renewing it.

*We have never been the same
since the voice of God overwhelmed us at Sinai.*

—Abraham Joshua Heschel,
contemporary theologian

I don't know if Rabbi Heschel was speaking about the people of Israel or the individual Israelite, both of whom were transformed at the foot of that mountain in Sinai. I suspect he was speaking of both. Moreover, I imagine that he was not merely talking about those 600,000 Jews who had left their slavery behind in Egypt and had readied themselves to receive Torah. Rabbi Heschel was speaking on behalf of each and every one of us whose life has been transformed through a recognition of the covenant that joins God and us together.

I, for one, have never been the same since I heard God's voice speak to me through Torah. No, I didn't hear it like Moses or the other Biblical prophets. Nor do God and I enjoy regular, routine conversation. Rather, it is the presence of God that I feel in my life, that I feel not only when I engage in the study of Torah, or when I am deep in prayer, or when a piece of music sends me heavenward, but also in my routine of daily living. Yes, I have heard God's voice in the world. And I continue to listen for it.

For Growth and Renewal: Where do you hear God's voice and how does it speak to you? Once you have discovered the answer, keep going back to that place and bring it forward to this time.

God's Torah is in the heart.

—Psalm 37:31

The giving of Torah on Mt. Sinai, celebrated earlier this month on Shavuot, shapes the mood for the entire month of Sivan. We think of that moment as among the most significant in the history of Jewish experience. It is there where Israel was transformed— and we with it. When we try to imagine what took place, we are nothing less than awestruck. Countless numbers of poets and artists, more articulate than we might be, have endeavored to try to recreate even some small aspect of that experience. But nothing comes close. Nor can it. It's all part of the mystery of Sinai.

The Torah is a folk history of the Jewish people in which is recorded its relationship with God. But its potential to transform the individual and sanctify life is meaningless unless you are willing to place "God's Torah in the heart." That's where it belongs, not on some mountain tucked away in the desert. But it doesn't get there on its own. You have to place it there. When we work the program, when we follow the path of Torah, when we stay in recovery, we continually stand at the foot of that mountain.

For Growth and Renewal: Put God's Torah in your heart. How? By working the program and then working it again.

> *When God spoke on Mt. Sinai,*
> *the whole world became silent.*

—Exodus Rabbah 29:9

When we recall the experience of Sinai, that loving dialogue between God and the people of Israel, we think of *words* of Torah. While the people were astonished at the time, even awestruck, we would still think that 600,000 people, men, women, and children, could make a lot of noise. But during the actual giving of Torah, we find silence. And in the silence of Torah, we can find God.

The mystics teach us that we can learn from every aspect of Torah. It is our touchstone for spiritual living. There is much to learn. However, not only do we learn from what is written in the Torah, but we can also learn from what is not written. Everything has meaning, even the spaces between the words, the silence. Such sacred silence helps us to remember that we are never alone. Wherever you go, God is with you.

For Growth and Renewal: Spend some silent time today. Get away from the distractions of profane noise. Listen for God's voice in the silent world that surrounds you.

The voice of God resounds to this very day.
But in order to hear it, one must prepare oneself,
just as the people did at that time.

—Rabbi Aryeh Leib of Ger, the Sefat Emet,
late eighteenth century Hasidic leader

According to the Bible, the people prepared themselves for three days before they were ready to receive Torah. We might say that their preparation started even earlier, perhaps as far back as during their days as slaves in Egypt. Thus, they yearned to hear God's voice and be delivered from Egypt. God didn't finish speaking as soon as Torah was revealed. Maybe people just stopped listening. Or perhaps the cacophony of secular noise was so loud that it drowned out our ability to hear God's voice (and us at the same time). The world just got too darned noisy.

Addictions and compulsive behaviors prevent us from hearing God's voice. As a result, in active addiction we could no longer hear God's voice. In recovery we refine our ability to listen, to hear God's voice. But it all takes preparation. We begin by getting clean and staying clean. And then we do *teshuvah*, turning back to the path of a good life that was established for us at Sinai. All it takes is a simple turn—in the other direction.

For Growth and Renewal: Prepare yourself to listen for God today. Get a good night's sleep. Do a little studying. Say a prayer. Stay clean.

> *Demons bother only those that bother them.*
>
> —Babylonian Talmud,
> Pesachim 110b

Someone once said, "No one can make you inferior without your consent." Ditto for one's drug of choice. We only give drugs their devastating power over us when we use them. And no one, no thing, no situation ever makes us use—not even ourselves. We use, ultimately, because we choose to do so. It is difficult to get that demon back in the bottle. That's why it's so important to keep away from it—which may mean new people, new places, new things. Tell yourself: No matter how bad my urge to use is, it's not as bad as using. Believe it! It's a liberating feeling.

Don't think yourself evil because the urge to do evil still lurks inside of you. It's all part of being human, what the rabbis call *"yetzer hara,"* a natural drive, an inclination, toward evil. Struggle with it. Overcome it. But don't try to control it. Don't beat yourself up over past mistakes. The God of our understanding does not want us to feel bad. We aren't bad people getting good; we are sick people getting better. And while you are at it, "If you have bundles of bad deeds, make bundles of good deeds to offset them" (Yalkut Shimoni, Proverbs 20). The more good we do, the better we will feel.

For Growth and Renewal: Go out and do one good deed. Not only will it help you feel better, it will help heal the world.

> *Let your tongue acquire the habit of saying "I do not know," so that you are not led to lie.*
>
> —Babylonian Talmud,
> Berachot 4a

"If only I didn't know then, what I don't know now," an addicted person in recovery once remarked to me. The realization that we can leave unlimited knowledge to God can be very liberating. No more pretending. We don't have to put up a false front. We no longer have to worry that our "ignorance" will be discovered. It means that we can accept that our knowledge gaps are not character defects. They are simply human. It means that we can ask for help from God, from others, from ourselves. Most of all, it makes it possible to learn that we don't know.

In active addiction, we thought we had everything under control. But look where all our street-smarts got us! Learning that we have a lot to learn—that we'll always have a lot to learn—is one of the greatest lessons of recovery and of life. It seems the more we know, the more we realize how much we don't know. And that's okay.

For Growth and Renewal: Stand in front of a mirror and practice saying, "I don't know" until the words flow easily from your lips. And then be ready to say it without feeling any need to have all the answers.

> *The human voice is calculated to be heard,*
> *but God's voice is to be really and truly seen.*
> *Why? Because all that God says are not words*
> *but actions which the eyes perceive*
> *before the ears do.*

> —Philo of Alexandria,
> first century philosopher

*E*ven after you entered recovery and began working the Twelve Steps, you might still have had a problem with the notion of a Higher Power. You are in good company. Consider those who came before us, whose struggles with faith are described in the Bible. Look at the great teachers of Israel who had trouble believing in God and in themselves. Like you, they too "came to believe." Belief in a Higher Power does not come instantaneously. I wish it were that simple, but it's simply not.

Maybe one of the reasons that we struggle to hear God's voice speak to us is that we are listening in the wrong places, expecting burning bushes and mountains of Sinai in the midst of suburbia. Or perhaps we are listening with our ears instead of listening with our hearts. Take a look at the world around you. God's voice speaks to us everywhere. If only we would listen in the right places!

For Growth and Renewal: Consider the words you speak today. Only use words that you imagine God might speak.

> *Each person only beholds in it*
> *what he [or she] is capable of seeing.*
>
> —Rabbi Menachem Mendl of Kotzk,
> early nineteenth century hasidic leader

I have often wondered why I can study the same text from Torah time and time again and each time see something new in it. And I had missed that meaning entirely during my previous encounter with it. It almost seems as if someone sneaked in and added additional meaning to the text in the intervening time between my study. Why didn't I see it the last time I looked at it? The rabbis suggest to us that we "Turn it. Turn it. For everything is contained in it." Perhaps it is I who have changed, not the text. And only when I am ready for the text to tell me something can I hear it speak to me that way.

Often, others point out aspects of the text that I missed. Why can't I see that either? Simple. Their experience in life is different than mine. It's one of the reasons that we tell our stories publicly in Twelve Step meetings. Our experiences in active addiction and recovery may be similar, but they are not the same. Our journeys are different. We have all taken different paths. Only when we are ready to listen to what another has to say can we hear that person. Each of us has become living Torah.

For Growth and Renewal: Rehearse today's events in your mind. What did you miss? Tomorrow, go back to it and make the repair.

> *The Torah is fire, was given in the midst of fire,*
> *and is comparable to fire. What is the nature of*
> *fire? If one comes too near to it, one gets burnt.*
> *If one keeps too far from it, one is cold.*
> *The only thing for people to do is to seek to*
> *warm themselves against the flame.*
>
> —Mechilta de Rabbi Ishmael to Exodus 19:18,
> collection of *midrashim* attributed to Rabbi Ishmael,
> early second century teacher

In some ways, Torah is like energy. Like fire, it can be beneficial or destructive. If it is to contain the potential to move us heavenward, then it has to reflect a measure of God's power. Some people don't like the image of Torah as fire. They would rather have Torah described as only gentle and nurturing. For me, that's not reality. Read the text. It speaks the stories of life, reflecting the real world and its ideal.

In Jewish history, this day in Sivan was a fast day marking Jeroboam's suspension of pilgrimages to Jerusalem. It was also a day of mourning in memory of the martyrdom of a number of early rabbinic teachers called the *tannaim.*

Our ancestors knew that Torah could warm them. They understood the force of its flame. And so they returned to it and kept coming back.

For Growth and Renewal: Wrap yourself in a *tallit* as you pray. Let it warm your body as it shelters your soul.

> *One cannot fully understand Torah*
> *unless you have stumbled in it.*
>
> —Babylonian Talmud, Gittin 43a

Look how really lucky you are. You stumbled, you fell. But now you are ready to share the Torah you have learned with others. And everyone has Torah to share. It may not be what was revealed to Moses on the mountaintop, but it will just as effectively help you find your way through the wilderness.

Mistakes are a vital part of all learning. Like the angels on the ladder in Jacob's dream, we are either going up or going down—it is *our* direction at any given time that is important.

Mistakes are a natural part of any learning experience and what is Torah, but God's game plan for how to live life. Sins are just "the errors of our ways" but only if, and it's a big if, we amend our ways. This notion of "descent for the sake of ascent," going down to slavery in Egypt so that we might go up to the Promised Land, is essential to *teshuvah* for it imbues even sin with redemptive value. As Rabbi Simcha Bunam so eloquently put it, "Failure to repent is much worse than sin. A person may have sinned for but a moment, but that person may fail to repent of it moments without number."

For Growth and Renewal: What have you learned as a result of what you stumbled on today? Once you have learned it, share it.

> *One must be open to the remote*
> *in order to perceive the near.*

> —Abraham Joshua Heschel,
> contemporary theologian

This text is one among many that reminds me to focus on my daily life and thereby helps me to elevate it. Too often, we are quick to dismiss as trivial the smallest of tasks so that we miss their meaning entirely. About many tasks we remark, "We are too good to do them. They are beneath us." Or so we thought. Addiction has taught us that nothing is beneath us. Many among us have been to places we never thought possible—and have returned, thank God.

I often think of the writings of Rabbi Heschel during the month of *Sivan,* because he has helped me to understand my relationship with God—which I usually imagine through the lens of Torah and Sinai. There is little in God's world that I do not try to understand, even if it means a struggle.

Like the twenty-third, this day marks a fast day commemorating Jeroboam's suspension of pilgrimages to Jerusalem and martyrdom of a number of *tannaim* (early rabbinic teachers), events lost in the pages of Jewish history. These too I try to understand.

For Growth and Renewal: Pay attention to the world which surrounds you. Note two things in particular: One near, one far. God has much to teach us.

To seek God is to strive for good.
To find God is to do good.

—Rabbi Leo Baeck,
twentieth century liberal Jewish theologian
who survived World War II in Germany

We now live in a time which philosophers and theologians call the post-modern world. Unlike the modern period which was marked by a belief that we could fully master our own destiny and our own world, we now recognize that the source for goodness must be found beyond the human experience. Actually, those of us who believe in God, who believe that God established a covenant with our people at Sinai, already knew that God is the source for goodness in the universe, that God is the only adequate measure of goodness in the universe. Others who did not previously realize that God is the source of goodness (and everything else) are now returning.

Rabbi Baeck reminds us that there is more to belief than a simple acknowledgment of our inadequacies and God's strength. No blind faith for us. Returning to God is a verb. It demands action. We can't just seek our Higher Power and hope that God will find us. It is a good start, but we have to do more. It is in our *doing* that we will find God.

For Growth and Renewal: Turn your prayers into an outline for living. Then follow the path you have set forth.

One is judged only by one's actions
at a given moment.

—Babylonian Talmud,
Rosh Hashanah 16a

Usually we think of our actions and God's judgments only during the Holy Day Season in *Tishrei.* But listen to what the text is telling us. At any given moment, at any time of year, we are being judged. And we are being judged for our actions at any given moment. Not for what we did yesterday or even for what we just did. Rather, we are constantly being asked, "What are you doing right now?" It's the same thing in recovery. Active addiction is in the past. Even our slips are behind us. God is only interested in our recovery *right now.*

But we must remember our past. Like other days in this month, the twenty-seventh of Sivan is marked as a fast day commemorating Jeroboam's suspension of pilgrimages to Jerusalem and the martyrdom of a number of *tannaim* (early rabbinic teachers). These dates may have been lost to the pages of Jewish history, but they are have become part of the historical memory of our people which gives us the strength and the sense of hope to concentrate on the present. Perhaps it is because we are here to enjoy it.

For Growth and Renewal: Always focus on the present. Complete today's recovery task (write it out) before you worry about what you need to do for your recovery tomorrow.

---

*Only as a soul comes to know itself can it come
to know its Creator.*

—Rabbi Abraham ibn Ezra,
early twelfth century Spanish poet, grammarian,
astronomer, physician and philosopher

People wonder how they can come to know God. Some travel the world, searching for secrets of the past. Few find the answers in distant places. The opportunity for self-knowledge is close to home. Just open up a sacred text and enter into dialogue with it. *See* yourself in it. Torah is a prism reflective of our souls. Many of us have avoided "looking in the mirror" for years, clinging, perhaps, to the childish notion that if we couldn't see ourselves, no one else could either. We may be fearful of all the old skeletons that lurk in the attics of our memories. The search may indeed unleash some profoundly unpleasant feelings—but the fact is that *not* looking at ourselves does even more harm.

Pray for the strength to look within yourself. Facing who you are is one of the bravest things a person can do. It is the turning point of spiritual change. It reveals the good and the bad. It lets the shame out and the innocence back in and restores our humanity. Tears and laughter can flow once again. It restores our spiritual self, for to know ourselves intimately is to sense the Divine spark within.

For Growth and Renewal: The Torah is the collective dream of the Jewish people. Which part of the dream is you?

Adonai is with me, I will not fear.

—From "Adon Olam,"
used to conclude the worship service

There are those who say that prayer is not meaningful for them. Perhaps they are expecting it to do something *for* them. It's the other way around. It is we who do something for prayer, when we bring our whole selves into the prayer experience and when we leave the outside world outside the synagogue where it belongs. Don't be critical of what's taking place. Just open yourself up to the possibility of prayer. It can take you heavenward. To you, I offer the rabbis' advice, "Pray before you pray that you might pray properly." The goal is simple. Prayer can bring you closer to God, and, in doing so, bring you closer to yourself.

This final line from the song "Adon Olam" usually concludes the morning worship service. It is the perfect note on which to end prayer. Just a simple, happy declaration of faith. Fear has aptly been defined as a lack of faith. And some of us may feel that we need to have faith in order to pray. Perhaps it's the other way around. Nothing is more effective than prayer for opening us up to the belief that we are in God's care. No, there's no need to fear.

For Growth and Renewal: Sing the "Adon Olam" slowly. Consider each word. Very slowly recite the last "I will not fear." And believe it.

The prayer is answered only of the one
who has lifted her heart in it.

—Babylonian Talmud,
Taanit 8a

Rarely does prayer come easy for me. Most of the time, I sit in the synagogue waiting for the words to come—and they sometimes just don't. It is not that I don't want to pray—I really do. It's just that the words feel awkward in my mouth. The poetry seems stilted. I open up a *siddur* (prayerbook) and thumb through the pages. I carefully consider the words that have worked so well for those who have come before me. But still I feel mute.

It took me a long time to realize that what matters is not my clever construction of prayerful language. Rather, it is the song that I sing in my soul that animates my prayers. With this song, my words of prayer are gently carried. And my soul, which longs for intimate dialogue with God, is sustained by it.

Recovery is prayer. Through it, we ask God to guide us so that we know what to do with our lives and turn away from the poisonous behaviors that dragged us down. And when our heart's not in it, it doesn't—it can't—happen. During those times, we continue to go to the house of prayer so that our actions protect our hearts.

For Growth and Renewal: Unlock your heart and offer your prayer. Just open your mouth. Your spirit will carry the words to Heaven.

Tammuz
Living
with Hope
Early Summer

In the radiant afterglow of *Matan Torah*, the giving of Torah, we are elated, poignantly aware of our special relationship with God. But all is not perfect, nor nearly so. Life continues to teach us that lesson. Beginning on the seventeenth of *Tammuz*, the day marked by the summer solstice, historically, the national decline begins with the breach of Jerusalem's walls by Nebuchadnezzar and later by Titus. Israel is in those narrow places once again, literally "between the straits," and begins a period of tribulation three weeks prior to Tisha B'av. To emphasize the pain, its Sabbaths are called the "Three Sabbaths of Affliction."

Thus, it would seem that *Tammuz* should be a month devoted to despair. Just as our hopes seem to be dashed, we are able to enjoy the perspective of history. We know that we will rise from the depths and be redeemed, that Israel will last beyond the nations which sought to destroy us. As individuals, we will survive. We have learned what history has taught our people: To live with hope. So we move forward, struggling toward a more perfect time and a more perfect world.

Rabbi Yochanan taught, "Whoever blesses the new moon at its proper time is considered as having witnessed the presence of the Shechinah.*"*

Rosh Chodesh, the beginning of a new month, each month, is a special day, a semi-holiday. It is also considered to be a celebration of women, perhaps because the lunar cycle is more in sync (than is the solar cycle) with a woman's menstrual cycle. While some women may feel burdened by menstruation, it presents us all with hope for the future. It is what I call one of God's rainbow promises, the potential for life inherent in us all. In recovery, there is a future and you are in it.

With the beginning of each new month, I feel a certain sense of rebirth and renewal. I honestly feel like I am welcoming the *shechinah* into my life once again, anticipating it when the cantor declares in synagogue on Shabbat that the new month will soon begin. In the midst of the sacred chant, I hear the *shaliach tzeebor* (the one leading community prayer) summoning me, "Prepare for it." And so I do. I have learned that whether I am truly able to witness the presence of the *shechinah* in my life solely depends on me. It is the kind of Torah wisdom that you also learn in recovery.

For Growth and Renewal: Go out and welcome the new month. It's a blessing.

Every person knows his [or her] own bitterness,
And in his [or her] joy, no one can share.

—Proverbs 14:10

No one can feel *your* pain. It's yours. Others, even those who are also in recovery, can approximate it, but like theirs, your pain is unique. But when we share one another's pain, when we tell our stories at meetings, cry aloud on one another's shoulders, weep compassionate tears for those who didn't make it and cry with elation for those who did, somehow our pain is lessened. In a community of fellowship, we are indeed renewed.

While such an approach to life may seem depressing to some, it affirms life for the rest of us and gives us hope. No one can witness another walking through the valley of death to return alive and not be lifted heavenward by the experience.

Your journey in recovery is also singularly unique. While others have followed similar paths, taken comparable trails, your particular journey is distinctive. And so you have the right to grab hold of the joy of recovery, as well. We want to share that joy with you just as we shared your burden. For your joy gives the rest of us hope.

For Growth and Renewal: Share your journey of addiction with your sponsor or a friend, but remember to share the joy also.

---

*And if I hear God, let me be the first to say
"Heneini."*

—*"Heneini,"*
Craig Taubman,
contemporary songwriter

Wisdom comes from all places. In this lyric from a contemporary Jewish song, Craig Taubman offers a note of hope and inspiration for us all. We really don't know how we would have reacted had we been one of our ancestors in direct dialogue with the Divine. Through our study and interaction with the text, we try to imagine our response. But what about the future? If God speaks to us, will we have the courage of our ancestors and say, *"Heneini"*? I am here, God. Choose me. Send me to do your work.

This *"Heneini"* posture is important to recovery—and not just for working Step Twelve. If we are truly willing to "turn it over," we also have to be ready to respond to God, to listen for God's voice in the world and respond to it. *Heneini muchan umezuman.* I am ready, willing, and able to do God's work in the world. Let me be a channel through which God's blessings flow into the earth.

For Growth and Renewal: Listen for God's voice in the world. And when you hear it, say *"Heneini."* Then do what needs to be done.

> *You cannot find redemption*
> *until you see the flaws in your own soul.*

> —Martin Buber,
> twentieth century theologian

This is probably one of the most succinct lessons of spirituality with special relevance to recovery that you will find. You can't get close to God (or others) until you take a good, honest look at yourself. Without such introspection, you will be unable to identify those factors that are causing the distance between you and self. Until you come close to yourself, you can't get close to God. Drugs, alcohol, overeating, bulemia, anorexia, compulsive gambling and sex: They all keep you far from yourself. None will fix the flaws in your soul. Only a relationship with God can do that.

Martin Buber, modern theologian and master of the "I-Thou" experience, wants to bring us close to God. That's why he taught us these things. Our obligation is to listen to what he had to say. But don't beat yourself up in the process. Through the process of *cheshbon hanefesh*, an accounting of your soul, learn to love yourself more, not less. It is knowing that all this is possible that gives us hope.

For Growth and Renewal: Make *cheshbon hanefesh* part of your Step Four recovery routine. However difficult it may be, love yourself through the process.

> *Rabbi Isaac Luria began his evening prayer*
> *by reciting "I hereby forgive whoever*
> *has sinned against me this day."*

If you are fixated on what others did to you during the day, you will not be able to pray in the evening with a full heart. Instead, your prayers will be flushed with bitterness and do you no good. As you walk into the synagogue, let go of all the baggage that you carry. By letting go of all of the minor (and even the major) grievances that you may have against others, you give others—and yourself—the freedom to pray. Don't forget to forgive yourself along the way. In the slavery of addiction, such forgiveness is not possible. But in freedom, the possibilities for renewal are endless. Recovery has well taught you that lesson.

Some may dismiss Rabbi Luria's tradition as noble but rather unrealistic. How can I simply let go of all the things that people have done to me during the day? Well, Isaac Luria was a mystic. Most of us cannot make the same claim. So we probably should get started earlier and not wait until the evening, when you get home or go to the synagogue. Don't wait until the evening. Let them all go now.

For Growth and Renewal: Try using Rabbi Luria's method for preparing to pray. Then pray that others may do the same—after you have worked Step Nine.

The reward is proportionate to the suffering.

—*Pirke Avot* 5:25

Most of us feel that if this statement were exactly true, then we would all be entitled to a rather hefty reward. Needless to say, we have all suffered a great deal. But what kind of reward are the rabbis of the Mishna speaking about? Surely, they were not interested primarily in monetary and material compensation. I suspect that they were talking about a reward that is truly immeasurable, one that is only experienced in what they perceived as a world-to-come.

Our notion of reward may be a little more down-to-earth, but it too is immeasurable by any monetary or material standards. The reward is recovery itself. Thus, this statement from *Pirke Avot* contains more subtle spiritual insight than even the rabbis had probably imagined. Recovery (with its spiritual renewal) is the reward for the suffering of an addicted person. As our tradition teaches, we had to go down to Egypt before we could go up to the land of promise.

For Growth and Renewal: Reward yourself by staying clean, then reach out to someone who needs a little extra help.

Praised are You, Adonai Elohenu,
who granted me a miracle in this place.

—Blessing said upon visiting a place
where one experienced a miraculous rescue

For the person new to recovery, this blessing represents the prayer said continually in one's heart. Feeling reborn, each day is a new day, each activity as if experienced for the first time. As one returns to daily living, each step taken in recovery—away from addiction and toward spiritual renewal—is like the step an toddler takes when first learning how to walk. And as we learn to navigate the world once again, we experience an even more mature sense of awe, for literally new worlds have been opened up to us.

For those not so new to recovery, too often, we may take recovery for granted. That's when you stumble. By saying this blessing you are reminded quickly and appropriately in a prayerful dialogue with God of the miracle of your recovery. And if you use the blessing as a guide for living, you won't forget.

Whether in recovery from an a disease of the body or the soul, many of us have experienced this sense of rescue. And we'd all be better off not to forget it.

For Growth and Renewal: Recovery includes the consecration of time and space. Include this blessing in the next anniversary you celebrate.

*Melodies I weave, songs I sweetly sing; longing
for Your presence, to you I yearn to cling.*

—From *Anim Zemirot*

This is what I try to do in prayer. I take the words that have been given to me by those who have come before and weave them with my own, hoping that the melody I write in my heart—this love song with the Divine—brings me closer to God. The *siddur* is filled with such melodies. I need only sing them and claim them as my own. In singing them, they become mine.

I really do long for God's presence in my life. Whether we are willing or comfortable enough to admit it, I really think that we all do. Such a recognition helps provide meaning and direction to my life. For some, this is one of the most difficult steps in recovery. We just aren't used to such Godtalk. That's okay. You'll get used to it. We may be afraid that if we accept God in this way we will lose self. The truth is that when we accept God, we regain self.

For Growth and Renewal: Repeat these words of prayer. If you can, take out a *siddur* (prayerbook) and slowly speak the words in Hebrew or English. You'll see, they will draw you into song.

---

*I am in deep distress. Let us fall into
the care of God for great is God's compassion.
Let me not fall into the hands of mortals.*

—King David to the prophet Gad,
II Samuel 24:24

King David was in bad shape. He knew that he had done wrong even without the prodding of the prophet Gad. He knew that he needed God's mercy, for David had already judged himself guilty. The rabbis teach us that if we pray then God must pray also (since we were created in God's image). But what is God's prayer? God prays, "May my *middat harachamim* (attribute of mercy) overcome my *middat hadin* (attribute of justice)."

We all deserve to be judged harshly by God: We have done a variety of things in active addiction. None of us lead even close to perfect lives. We try. We try hard. But we have to try harder. But our God is also a loving God. And so we pray that we are deserving of God's *rachamim*, God's mercy, and not subject to Divine judgment. At least, not yet.

For Growth and Renewal: As you work Step Five, be gentle on yourself. Although made in the image of God, you're only human. Keep it that way.

> *A generous spirit, a humble soul,*
> *a modest appetite, such is one who is*
> *a disciple of Abraham.*
>
> —*Pirke Avot* 5:21

The matriarchs and patriarchs of the Bible, these mothers and fathers of our people, serve us well as role models. While many of us were raised to believe that they were heroes, the truth is that they were all human, flawed, imperfect, struggling with their faith—even as God spoke to them. Thus, to be a disciple of Abraham (and we would add Sarah) is to be fully human.

So in recovery, we have a lot of learning to do. It's difficult to be generous in spirit, humble, and also maintain a modest appetite, as well. This kind of balancing act is what makes recovery so difficult. It is that middle ground that one codependent person told me was so hard for her to maintain. Give of yourself. But don't lose yourself. Instead, humbly, be of yourself.

The rabbis have taught us to strive to "Be Torah." As we have learned in fellowship meetings (and outside), "Model, don't meddle."

For Growth and Renewal: Be Torah today. Let others learn about their own recovery from you. Be generous in spirit. Humble your soul. Fulfill your needs in moderation. And stay clean.

> *Keeper of the light,*
> *I am your wayward child.*
> *Shine on so that I can see.*

—"Keeper of the Light,"
Doug Cotler,
contemporary songwriter

It is light that gives us hope. This plaintive lyric speaks directly to this month's theme (and every month's recovery message). In active addiction, we felt like we lived in darkness. And drugs and alcohol and compulsive eating, gambling and sex kept us there. Now in keeping with Step One, we willingly admit that we have been wayward. But we have returned, searching for holiness in the direction of that light. Where there is light, there is hope.

What is the source of that light? For some, this "Keeper of the light" is God. Others may consider it their Higher Power. One young person told me that her Higher Power was her sneakers, because that's what got her to meetings! Perhaps the light simply shines in different, and sometimes surprising, places. For me, the Source of that light— wherever it shines—is unmistakably God. And it is God's light that leads the way for us—whoever we are, whatever we have done, wherever we have gone.

For Growth and Renewal: Leave one light on in your home during the day. Let it remind you that even when the sun is shining, there is a need for light.

Adonai, do not rebuke me while You are angry
Nor discipline me while You are enraged.
Be gracious to me, Adonai, for I am
languishing away.
Heal me, Adonai, I am frightened in my bones.
I am also afraid in my soul.

—Psalm 6:2-4,
from the *Tachanun*

Baruch Spinoza, a great Jewish theologian, wrote in his book called *Ethics* that one should not love God and *expect* to be loved in return. We might even call that kind of expectation somewhat codependent. The Torah only spoke of Moses in those terms. Spinoza claims that God's love doesn't work that way. We love God for lots of reasons, but essentially because God *is* God. So we ask God to be God: to judge us, to have compassion on us, and to heal us.

Some verses from the *tachanun*, part of the morning weekday service, are said with the forehead resting on the forearm. It's one of the many postures for prayer. These various gestures for Jewish prayer help us to frame the words with our bodies. We feel depressed and disillusioned, can hardly keep our head up. But in a holy relationship with God, we are lifted up from our misery.

For Growth and Renewal: While you say these words of *tachanun*, rest your forehead on your arm. Then raise yourself up and go about your daily affairs.

Tammuz: Living With Hope   *Day 13:* Planting the Harvest

> *If you don't plant in summer,*
> *what will you eat in winter?*
>
> —Midrash to Proverbs

This may seem like a rhetorical question or down home farmer folk wisdom, but this bit of useful advice is indeed important to all of us, especially to those in recovery. We usually think of our recovery work along the lines of the major periods of the Jewish calendar with the primary period of introspection introducing the Holy Day Period. But if we wait until late summer (in *Elul*) to begin the process of *cheshbon hanefesh*, there may not be enough time. Start the process now, and keep it going.

For much of North America—and much of the world— summer is a playful time. School's out. Families go on vacation: Beaches, mountains, country lakes. For the Jewish community, however, for those in sync with the rhythm of the Jewish calendar, the history of summer and the events that occurred during this time are not so playful. We might consider the summer heat oppressive, even in its early period. Perhaps that is one of the reasons the Jewish calendar resonates so well for those in recovery. It isn't to say that there are no playful periods in recovery. There are many, but the lesson of living is this: One must always be conscious of his or her recovery.

For Growth and Renewal: Plant the seed of recovery and you will always grow.

Rab declared, "We give thanks to You, Adonai our God, because we are able to give thanks."

—Babylonian Talmud, Sotah 40a

While the fourteenth day of *Tammuz* reflects a celebration of a festive victory of the Pharisees over the Sadducees (remember who compiled the Mishnah and Talmud!), this little blessing is something that we might want to say every day in recovery. Active addiction obscured any willingness to give thanks. Could we thank God for the food we kept eating and eating while it was God's bounty which was destroying our bodies? The throbbing pain in our souls prevented us from uttering any words of thanksgiving, thinking that there was nothing for which to be thankful. Recovery has taught us the logic of Rab's prayer.

Every day is a day of thanksgiving—even when there is pain. We are never totally free of it. It is part of living in this world. Abraham Joshua Heschel wrote, "The focus of prayer is not the self. . . . In prayer we shift the center of living from self-consciousness to self-surrender. God is the center toward which all forces tend." The spiritual renewal that comes with recovery allows us to free ourselves from the pain and live beyond it.

For Growth and Renewal: It's easy to say thanks to God. Now try saying thanks to others, even those to whom it may be difficult: Parents, sponsor, children, friends.

> *Pray only in a room with windows.*
>
> —Babylonian Talmud,
> Berachot 34b

Any place in which you pray is supposed to have at least one window with a clear pane of glass, with some way to see outside. Stained glass, secured windows, and solid walls prevent us from looking to the outside, from breathing the air that circulates in the world. We become isolated. In our isolation, there is a tendency to be self-centered, pursuing only our self-interest. A total absorption in self may have led you to drink and drug in the first place. It was your way of protecting yourself, fallout from your low self-esteem.

Healing takes place in the midst of community, not isolated from it. Mordecai Kaplan once said, "Only by way of participating in human affairs and strivings are we to seek God." We become one with the world. You may have felt alone in your active addiction but in the community of fellowship, you learn that you are never alone. Your Higher Power is always with you.

For Growth and Renewal: Don't shut yourself off from the outside world. Always pray in a room with windows.

Hope for a miracle, but don't depend on it.

—Babylonian Talmud,
Megillah 7b

There is a story told about a man whose town was overcome by floods. A person went by in a rowboat and called out to him, "Come with me." "No, I will wait for God to rescue me," came the reply and the man climbed to the roof of his house. An emergency rescue team sent a helicopter to lift the man from his roof. Again he refused. A third time someone attempted to rescue him and he refused. Finally, his home was engulfed by the waters and he drowned. When he came to heaven and appeared before the Heavenly Court, he was bitter: "God, why didn't you rescue me?" came the man's anguished cry. "But I tried to help you three times and you refused to be rescued!" came the heavenly response.

I believe in miracles. Not the kind depicted when the Red Sea was separated or when the sun stood still. Those are part of the religious folk history of our people, assigned to sacred literature. I accept them as part of Torah tradition. There are plenty of other miracles too, like the miracles of love and life, of recovery and spiritual renewal. How else could you describe your journey from active addiction into recovery if not as a miracle?

For Growth and Renewal: Pay attention to the miracles around you. Accept God's help in whatever form it comes.

301

> *Judah is gone into exile because of affliction . . .*
> *and finds no rest. All her persecutors*
> *overtook her* between the straits.

—Lamentations 1:3

It's no coincidence that the Bible uses a word to describe this period of time that sounds like the Hebrew word for Egypt (*Mitzrayim*). Whether we are slaves in Egypt or forced to live in Babylonia, we are in exile—from our home and from ourselves. In active addiction, we are never home. Whenever we are vulnerable, our enemy tries to seize the opportunity to seize us. Our addiction works the same way. Let's not give it the opportunity.

This day in Jewish history is filled with pain. We continue to observe it to remind us of where we have been so that we might appreciate and be thankful for where we are now. Thus, we are taught that "whoever mourns for Jerusalem will be privileged to see her in joyous time" (Babylonian Talmud, Taanit 30b). The seventeenth day of *Tammuz* begins the period of time twenty-one days prior to Tisha B'av known as the time "between the straits." You know the feeling. We've all had our difficult and distressing times "between the straits." Perhaps it is because we have been there and returned that we have learned to live with hope.

For Growth and Renewal: When you see a friend "between the straits," reach out and help. Remember Rabbi Nachman's words, "The world is a narrow bridge."

Unless you believe that God renews creation every day, your prayers will grow habitual and tedious.

—Rabbi Israel ben Eliezer Baal Shem Tov, the Besht, eighteenth century founder of the hasidic movement

The Baal Shem Tov spoke from his own experience—as we do from ours. He was reacting to what he perceived as an intellectualization of Judaism. If you get up each day and simply run through the routine of morning prayers without recognizing that you have been created anew this very day, then indeed your prayers will become habitual and tedious. They will do little to help you start your day nor move you forward in your recovery. And there is nothing better than a good prayer to start the day (even better than a good cup of coffee!). Rabbi Yisrael, the *maggid* of Kuznitz, was often heard to say, "Nothing gives me greater pleasure than a good prayer."

Our tradition teaches us that when we awaken each morning, we awaken as a new child enters the world, innocent, clean, full of potential—regardless of what took place the night before. We have a chance each day to begin our lives again. In this regard we are totally free to take what God has given us and do what we will. Our prayers have a way of directing us, of making sure what we will is also God's will.

For Growth and Renewal: Acknowledge your birthday today and include in your prayers a prayer for a birthday tomorrow.

I have put words in your mouth.

—Jeremiah 1:9

This text is taken from the Haftarah portion from one of the Sabbaths of Affliction, those three weeks when we are "between the straits." God speaks to Jeremiah in order to tell him what to say to the people. While we may not have prophets in our time, God still speaks to us. The challenge is learning how to listen.

When God spoke to the people at Sinai, there was total silence. No outside noise. Torah communication has to be crystal clear. Therefore, we have to make sure that we rid ourselves of the noise, anything that will prevent us from hearing what God has to tell. Addiction makes a lot of noise. How do we know? When we are active, we can't hear God's voice in the world. It is only when we enter recovery that it is possible to hear the words of healing and be heard.

For Growth and Renewal: According to *halacha* (Jewish law), one does not speak (or enter into idle conversation) between saying the words of blessing and then completing the act for which the blessing was intended. After you pray, keep silent. If you keep talking, how will you hear God's voice?

Return to Me . . . and I will return to you.
—Zechariah 1:3

This is a beautiful statement of the spiritual equivalent of Newton's Second Law. It is expressed in what a friend shared with me: A summer camp counselor was talking about God with an young girl. The camper said that she wasn't too sure about God, but she did know a little about physics. It fascinated her that, as Newton stated, there was an equal and opposite reaction for every force exerted in the universe. The counselor said she was glad that their camp was different than the rest of the universe because she got back a good deal more than she put into it. The kid wondered about that for a moment or two, and then mused. "Well, maybe that's God."

Concerning all acts of initiative, creation, and spiritual renewal, there is one elementary truth—that the moment one definitely commits oneself and moves toward God, then God moves toward us, even one step further.

For Growth and Renewal: As you take a step on your journey, know that you are moving two steps closer to God. So keep taking (and working) those Steps.

Tammuz: Living With Hope *Day 21:* Getting the Message

They will fight against you but will not prevail.
I am with you.

—Jeremiah 1:19a

These words, spoken by God to the prophet Jeremiah, were taken from a haftarah of one of the Sabbaths of Affliction. Even a prophet is sometimes afraid to speak the truth, fearful of the reaction of those who are not likely to respond favorably to what the prophet has to say. And the prophet *has* to say it. During your recovery, you will want to say lots of things to lots of people. Apologies. Rebuke. Words of love. Not everyone will be ready or willing to hear what you have to say.

Others will tire of hearing what the program has taught you or what you have learned from the Twelve Steps. They will tire of hearing Twelve Step sayings and the language of recovery. Remember what God told Jeremiah, "They will fight against you but will not prevail. I am with you." Few people are ever *ready* to hear prophetic truth spoken. So we ready ourselves instead. They'll get the message.

For Growth and Renewal: When you work Step Twelve and "carry the message" to other addicted persons, some will not hear you. Nonetheless, you must speak the truth . . . and be ready to help.

Wisdom begets humility.

> —Rabbi Abraham ibn Ezra,
> early twelfth century Spanish poet,
> grammarian, astronomer, physician and philosopher

So the question is, "How does one get wisdom?" I think that it is the question that everyone asks, regardless of whether they are in recovery from an addiction or not. How many times have you said to yourself, "If I had only known then what I know now"? Often the recollection of the event itself is a humbling experience. Some people seem to be born with wisdom. Even at a young age, they are insightful and wise. Others among us are not so lucky. We have to depend on what life teaches us in order to get wisdom. For many of us, even what we learn from life is insufficient to make us wise.

Perhaps that's one of the many reasons why our Jewish tradition is so important. Through it, we are able to look through the eyes of those who came before us, to relive their struggles and learn from them. Each time we read a text, in a sense, we become that text. Our lives become sacred texts. It doesn't sound very humble, but let's look closer. The responsibility of being Torah is a humbling experience. It's a wise thing to learn!

For Growth and Renewal: Before you run to tell somebody what they are doing is wrong, consider how you learned about it in the first place. Maybe they can join you on your journey.

---

*Even an angel can't do two things
at the same time.*

—Genesis Rabbah 50:2

Some people in the recovery community do not like to consider addictions of any sort except those that involve chemicals—substances that are habit-forming drugs. Yet, there are other addictions, as well. We know them all to well: Compulsive gambling and sex, compulsive eating, anorexia and bulimia. But there are other compulsive behaviors that are addictive, as well. If there are those who suffer from them, then we have a responsibility to talk about them and draw from our tradition and our experience healing for them too.

Workaholism is one of those compulsive behaviors that is addictive. When our work consumes us, when we lose ourselves in it, when it overwhelms the rest of our live and we can't do anything else but work, we may be addicted to it. Hence the wisdom from the midrash, "Even an angel cannot do two things at once." We all have our limitations. No matter how much we work, no matter how hard we work, no matter how long we work, there will always be more work to do *tomorrow.* So let's leave some of that work for tomorrow and work on our recovery today.

For Growth and Renewal: When you are confronted with a decision today concerning work or family, work or self, follow the advice of the Torah "choose life so that you may live."

308

> *As a long as a person breathes,*
> *that person should not lose hope.*
>
> —Jerusalem Talmud, 9:1

This is the essential message of Jewish recovery and spiritual renewal: Where there is life, there is always hope. In active addiction—where the *malach hamavet*, the angel of death, stalks its prey—we seem to lose all hope, blaming it on the presence of death. And the risk of death in active addiction is real. But one must never despair, no matter how dark one's world seems.

When I listen to people tell their stories at meetings, I am filled with hope and inspiration after the retelling of their harrowing tales. People who inhabited hell have returned alive to tell us about their journey.

Just because you are in recovery does not mean that there will be an end to disappointment. But in recovery, you will not succumb to disillusionment and despair. Instead you will be renewed in spirit.

Stay alive. Stay hopeful. It's the only way to live.

For Growth and Renewal: Focus on your breathing. With each breath you take, breathe in life. Exhale death.

> *The road to Heaven bears signposts based on the Torah. Those who study it will therefore be able to find their way to Heaven.*
>
> —Zohar i, 175b

People forget. The Torah is not just the spiritual history of our people. It is more than just a recollection of our ancestors' individual struggles with faith. For us, the Torah is a guide for redemption. It will take us as close to Heaven as we are willing to go. Codependence and addiction take us the wrong way. We have to get back on track. And the only way to do it is by staying clean and staying sober.

I'd like to believe that it is a straight path. Maybe it is for some people. For most of us, it isn't. The Israelites probably thought the same thing. Why couldn't we just go straight from Egypt to Canaan and avoid all the problems along the way. Had they taken the most direct path, maybe they wouldn't have stopped for Torah along the way. Then where would we be?

If you want to get to Heaven, stick with us. That's where we are all trying to go. Occasionally, we may get sidetracked, lost in the midst of our own direction. Eventually, and that's the most important part, we get back on the proper path.

For Growth and Renewal: The Torah can only help you if you claim it as your own. Carry it. Caress it. Study it. Stay on its path.

The one who preserves Torah is the one who makes oneself like the desert, set off like the rest of the world.

—Rabbi Samson Raphael Hirsch, foremost exponent of Orthodox Judaism, nineteenth century Germany

Some of you might read Rabbi Hirsch's advice and be puzzled, thinking that recovery has to take place in the midst of community. While we must recover on our own, we do not recover alone. Rabbi Hirsch is not contradicting that principle. He is suggesting that it is hard to be holy. No matter how hard we try, there is much and many in the world competing for the opportunity to compromise our holiness. So we have to stay away from it and from them. Some will taunt us, try to get us back to where we came from. And we must stand our ground.

Recovery is not easy. You know that. But neither is spiritual renewal. It takes just as much work. Some say even more. Therefore, we have to go to meetings and to the synagogue. We have to work with a sponsor and a rabbi. We have to read *the* Book (Torah) and the Big Book of Alcoholics Anonymous. There really is no other way.

For Growth and Renewal: Set yourself a recovery goal for today that will allow no compromise. Then be prepared to muster all your spiritual resources in order to reach it. If you don't quite make it, that's okay. There will be more tomorrow to work on.

> *On enduring pain: "It is always a question of a moment, for the pain which has passed is no longer, and who would be so foolish as to concern oneself with future pain?"*
>
> —Rabbi Yitzchak Eisik,
> av bet din of Cracow

To answer the rabbi's question (all together now!): We would. So much of our time and life is wasted fretting over horrors that never occur—or, if they do occur, don't seem quite as terrible as we thought they would be. And what about all the bad stuff that just hits us like a bolt out of the blue? Should we set aside sufficient time to worry about that too? Worrying has got to be one of the most useless emotions around. It does nothing constructive—although in our hearts, we somehow feel that worrying about things might prevent them from happening. In reality, worrying about life prevents joy from happening.

In the Jewish folk tradition, there is the notion of the *ayin hara*, the evil eye. (When my *bubbe* used to mention it, it was always accompanied by a "pooh, pooh!") We don't talk about our good fortune or situation so as not to jinx it by calling this to the attention of the ever-lurking evil spirit. Maybe it's time to give the evil eye an evil eye of its own.

For Growth and Renewal: Let go of the pain. It does not help our recovery. It hinders it. Just let it go.

> *The happy person is the one*
> *who constantly searches one's actions*
> *and regrets every unworthy act.*

—Abraham ben Isaac Weinberg, the Slonimer rebbe
nineteenth century hasidic rebbe in Bylorussia

This is a Twelve Step strategy for living, a Step Four and Ten combination. We rebuild our lives around the Steps, working them again and again. And as soon as we nearly finish, we start again. The first time I climbed Mt. Sinai, my companion stopped near the peak of the mountain and started to turn back. Panting, sweaty from our climb, I asked him where he was going. He replied, "I always like to save a little for the next time. When we return, perhaps we'll finish our climb."

We work the Steps over and over, because we never really finish them. Life continues and so much of our scrutiny of it. There are those who claim that one can only work Step One all the way through. Other Steps, particularly Four and Ten, require our constant attention. The Slonimer Rebbe would probably agree. It's funny how finding faults can make us happy. Those who do not understand Twelve Step or *teshuvah* logic would probably label this a paradox. But lots of people don't understand us anyway! Why spoil a good thing?

For Growth and Renewal: Regretting an unworthy act is not enough. Make amends, fix what is broken, gather the splintered shards of holiness that are scattered around the earth.

---

*Keep sin at a distance
and it will turn aside from you.*

—Ben Sira 7:2

*O*ften, after being sober and clean for years, we think that we are finally in control, that no temptation is strong enough to entice us. We figure that it's finally okay to be near people drinking and drugging since it doesn't affect us. Or visiting Atlantic City for the shows is all right as long as I don't go near the casinos.

But it is wise not to tempt temptation, for just as we say that God turns toward us as we turn toward God, so it is with sin. Sin turns toward us as soon as we show it any interest. Like the snake in Eden, it knows just what to do and what to say to entice us to it. All we have to do is listen to its seductive whisper. Ben Sira may be right, but in our case it is impossible to keep our self-destructive inclination at a distance. It is, after all, within us. We are never too far from the door.

The pursuit of Torah and an attempt to reach God is a lifelong endeavor. So is recovery. We are never really free of our addictions. Acknowledging this truth helps us to live with hope.

For Growth and Renewal: Take Ben Sira's advice. Stay away and stay alive. Let Torah nourish your soul. Sin will find another companion.

Av
Beginning
Again
Mid-Summer

Known to the rabbis as *Menachem Av*, the *Av* of consolation, this month focuses on the destruction of the Temple on the ninth of *Av* (*Tisha B'av*)—epitomizing all of Jewish tragedy—and the weeks of consolation that follow. Preceded by Shabbat Chazon (the Sabbath of Vision) and followed by Shabbat Nachamu (the Sabbath of Comfort), Tisha B'av casts its dismal shadow on the entire month. In Taanit 4:6, we read: "When *Av* comes, gladness is diminished." But all is not lost. Beginning with the Shabbat which follows its observance, there are seven weeks of prophetic consolation which take the ritual form of special *haftarot* for the Sabbath. It takes time to bear our pain. Humbled by what has taken place, it forces us to take another good, hard look at ourselves. And that's exactly what we do. And then we begin again.

Rabbi Shneur Zalman of Lyady once said that during *Elul*, the thirteen attributes of God's mercy are shining. On Yom Kippur (during the month of *Tishrei*) these attributes also shine, but in the season of repentance it is we who must approach God. During the month of *Av*, God approaches us and joins us on our journey back home.

Av: Beginning Again   *Day 1:* Lightening Burdens

This is the day that Adonai has made.
Let us rejoice and be joyful in it.

—Psalms 118:24

It is Rosh Chodesh, the first day of the month of *Av.* What better prism can we have than through this well-known Psalm text to view the world? When one recognizes that the entire world has been touched by God, that everything we do is filled with the Holy Presence, then all of life is transformed. It's difficult to feel holy when we are still wallowing in our own filth, when the pain we caused challenges us to return. But once on the way home to recovery, we regain our ability to see the God-given beauty in the world even in the smallest, most inconsequential things. For God is not only the Creator of the world but also the Source of all life in the universe— including our own.

According to Jewish tradition, this is also the day when we commemorate the death of Aaron. God shares our burdens, making them easier for us carry. God created the world, set the laws of nature in motion, and created the human species to enjoy the lush fruits of paradise. Every day is the day that God has made and we are alive to enjoy it.

For Growth and Renewal: Begin your day by welcoming the new month.

Get washed, get yourselves clean.
Stop doing evil things that I see
Stop doing evil
Instead, learn to do well.

—Isaiah 1:16-17a,
from the Haftarah for Shabbat Chazon

This text from the prophetic writings of Isaiah, taken from the Haftarah for Shabbat Chazon, literally the Sabbath of vision, the Sabbath prior to Tisha B'av, also called Shabbat Eicha among Yemenite Jewry, helps prepare the community for healing even before the ultimate destruction of the Temple in Jerusalem takes place. It is as if the prophet is saying, "I know what is going to happen and maybe it is too late to prevent it, but I can help you prepare for the healing that will follow so that it does not happen again."

It's nearly the same thing in recovery. We know what active addiction is like. We can't prevent ourselves from being addicted people. We already are and will always be. But we can help in healing our souls, in order to prevent ourselves from returning to active addiction. All you have to do is follow the advice Isaiah gave to our ancestors a long time ago. Get washed. Stay clean. Stop using and abusing.

For Growth and Renewal: Treat your body to a spa treatment in fulfillment of Isaiah's directive.

Av: Beginning Again   *Day 3:* Learning to Walk
Again

> *Walk in the ways of your heart*
> *and the sight of your eyes and know.*
>
> —Ecclesiastes 11:9

Ecclesiastes, known in Hebrew as *Kohelet,* offers us basic wisdom for everyday living. He spoke from the perspective of a long, full life, filled with a myriad of experiences. His message is simple: Trust your own instincts and don't be deceived by others who would try to dissuade you. Menachem Mendl of Kotzk added his own gloss (comment) to the text. He said, "You are to walk in the ways of your heart but based on knowledge, after investigating your course in life."

What an apt message for Twelve Steppers. The program helps you to "investigate" your course in life. Now you know that you can trust your heart—in covenant with a Higher Power—to lead you in the right direction for your life. Listen to the message of the Psalmist: "Happy is the one who has not taken the advice of the wicked, nor went the way of sinners, nor kept company with those who scorn [the Torah]. Rather, your delight is Adonai's Torah and on it should you meditate day and night" (1:1-2).

For Growth and Renewal: Ecclesiastes has a lot of wisdom to offer. Take out his words and give them the attention they deserve.

Keep your sin before you always.

—*Shaarei Teshuvah,*
Rabbenu Yonah of Gerona,
thirteenth century Spanish rabbi, author, and moralist

Some will suggest that once you have made amends for all you have done (see Step Nine) that you may forget about it and just go about the struggle of daily living. But experience tells us that it is not so easy to simply forget the wrongs we have done. We may not even remember some of them since they were clouded by the fog of active addiction. So Rabbenu Yonah teaches us (in his own little book on repentance of *Shaarei Teshuvah*) that to begin again means that you have to "keep your sin before you always." Remember what you did wrong and to whom. Keep that list in your mind. Refer to it as needed. It may help prevent you from doing in recovery what you did in active addiction. Recovery is not a solution for all problems. There will undoubtedly be lingering issues that will require your attention. (See Step Ten.)

Some may feel that this approach is an additional burden. As they say in Yiddish, *Genug es genug.* (Enough is enough.) But the truth is that once you admit to your sins and call them your own, you can be liberated from them. Then you can really begin again.

For Growth and Renewal: Place a reminder of your sin on your desk at home or at work. Each time you see it, be reminded of the work you yet have to do to sustain your recovery.

---

*A person's pride will bring her low,
but the one who is humble will be raised up.*

—Proverbs 29:23

People are in constant motion. When you're arrogant, God humbles you. And when you are distraught and disillusioned, God raises your spirits. It is a perpetual up and down movement. This view of the book of Proverbs always reminded me of a child's toy in which the people on the bus go up and down, up and down. It's a kind of spiritual physics: "For my sake the world was created, but I am only dust and ashes." One motion demands another.

If you can learn in your recovery that your self-esteem is not dependent upon your arrogance (usually a good indicator of low self-esteem), there will be no need for God to bring you down. Some may call this finding the middle ground (which many codependent people have told me is very difficult for them to find). Others will suggest that it is simply finding the appropriate action for every reaction. (Recovery logic is not always what you would expect!) That's when you know you can begin life again, when you feel good about yourself and don't have to tell everyone about it.

For Growth and Renewal: Consider how you reacted today to your latest recovery challenge. Were you boastful, full of self? Or meek and submissive? Find the middle ground and find yourself.

> *Holy One of Blessing,*
> *Your Presence fills creation . . .*
>
> —from the traditional form for blessing,
> translated by Rabbi Lawrence S. Kushner

While this is the basic formula for all blessings in Jewish ritual (*Baruch ata Adonai, Elohenu Melech Ha-olam*), as translated by Rabbi Kushner, for me it is a *kavannah*, a sort of meditative Jewish mantra. It helps me to frame my prayers and my life. God's presence does indeed fill all of the world. I believe it. See for yourself.

"If that's the case," you might ask, "then how is there room for everyone and everything else?" That's part of God's mystery, part of spiritual physics. Only in God's case can two things occupy the same space at the same time. In that space a special union is possible—what the program calls a relationship with a Higher Power, what we call covenant, what the theologian Martin Buber calls the "I-Thou" experience. Whatever you call it, when you experience it, you know what it is.

For Growth and Renewal: God has blessed us with many things in our lives, whether or not we always realize it. As you recite these words of blessing (*Baruch ata Adonai . . .*), consider how God's presence indeed pervades the world in which we live.

Help us to lie down O God in shalom
and raise us up to life.

—from the "Hashkivenu" prayer,
said in the evening service

At the end of a tough day—and sometimes they all seem to be difficult—we want a little rest, a little *shalom* to help carry us through the night. *Shalom*, from the word *shelemut* (tranquility, wholeness, serenity), is what we all ultimately desire. It's not something that money can buy. Nor can we get it from anyone or anything else. The key to inner peace lies buried deeply inside the self. We have to work hard to release the potential for *shalom* that is locked away inside our soul.

And so we ask God to guide us, to help us. And in the morning, feeling renewed, we are ready to begin again. Every day we are given the chance to start over, to begin life again. That seems to be the essence of *shalom*, a release from all our worldly burdens in order to be at peace with ourselves. The key to such *shalom* is acceptance. It's amazing what happens in only a few short hours—and while we are asleep. It's all in a day's Twelve Step work!

For Growth and Renewal: As you prepare yourself for sleep, release the potential for *shalom* that lies locked away inside your soul. Begin with your own prayer for inner peace.

*I will put my Torah on their innermost parts
and I will write it on their hearts.
I will be their God and they will be My people.*

—Jeremiah 31:32

One of the ways we prepare for Tisha B'av is by eating boiled eggs with ashes on them. We know what happened on Tisha B'av and we try to prepare to live through that awful memory once again. Critics might say, "Why bother remembering the past and all of the pain that it contained? Better to look toward the future and what it has in store for us." But that's not the Jewish way. Nor is it the Twelve Step way. Memory is an important part of our identity as Jews. And the memory of active addiction is an important part of our recovery. When we hear friends tell their stories, it helps to remind us of our own personal struggles.

We know that recovery is not a straight path. There are ups and downs, successes and setbacks. Tisha B'av is one of the setbacks in the life of the Jewish people. We went into exile. The Temple was destroyed and we were forced to wander the earth without a place to call home. We have listened to the prophet Jeremiah. Through the experiences of our journey, we have allowed God to write the Torah on our hearts. The wandering is finally over.

For Growth and Renewal: Take the initiative and write God's Torah on your heart. Claim the faith journeys of our ancestors as your own.

> *Let not the wise person glory in wisdom.*
> *Let not the strong person glory in strength.*
> *Let not the rich person glory in riches.*
> *Only in this should one glory:*
> *In one's earnest devotion to Me.*
> *For I Adonai act with kindness,*
> *Justice and equity in the world.*

> —Jeremiah 9:22-23,
> from the Haftarah for Tisha B'av morning

This ninth day of the month of *Av*, Tisha B'av, is a difficult day in the life of the Jewish people. While it is the day which marks the destruction of both of the ancient Temples in Jerusalem, Jewish tradition has also assigned the memory of other calamities in Jewish history to this date. Even God's decision that the people should die in the desert was issued on Tisha B'av, according to rabbinic tradition. Yet, somehow we survived and began again. Perhaps it is because we listened to the wisdom of our tradition, as the prophet Jeremiah teaches us in the Haftarah portion designated for Tisha B'av morning.

There is a rabbinic tradition called *nechemta* (consolation) which requires that we not end any instruction on a note of rebuke. The rabbis suggest that the prophets learned this from Moses as he led the people through the desert. In the midst of the tragedy of Tisha B'av, there is hope. We are consoled and can begin again.

For Growth and Renewal: Practice *nechemta* in your own affairs. Be gentle with your neighbors, your friends, your coworkers.

> *Help us to return to you, Adonai.*
> *Then we shall truly return.*
>
> —Lamentations 5:21

We always think that we can do it on our own. We got into this mess by ourselves and now we are going to get out of it the same way, somehow. Yet, even if we find the means to begin our recovery without anyone's help, it is an empty process without God. There is no other way to say it. You will be back where you started from—perhaps even worse. God's presence fills the void we used to feel and takes us beyond it. Faith in God establishes a firm foundation for recovery where only our flimsy self used to stand.

The destruction of the Temples took place over a period of two days, but the rabbis thought that one day was enough. We had to pick ourselves up and begin again. This verse from Lamentations, the Biblical book identified with Tisha B'av and this season in the Jewish calendar, is found near the end of the entire book. It epitomizes the message of the month and of our recovery. It is essential spiritual renewal.

For Growth and Renewal: As you recite these words (as the Torah is returned to the ark during the morning service when it is read), say these words aloud. Let them guide you throughout your day.

Seek Adonai while God can be found
Call to God while God is near.

—Isaiah 55:6,
from the Haftarah for
the afternoon of Tisha B'av

If you believe that God is indeed responsible for the destruction of the Temples and the dispersion (and original exiles) of the Jewish people, then even in the midst of all that pain, you know that God is near. That's the message of consolation that the prophet Isaiah seeks to offer us in this passage which is designated to be read on the afternoon of the somber observance of Tisha B'av. Although we are undergoing exile, we can be comforted by the fact that God is near to us.

In the rejection of God, there is usually acceptance of God. It sounds contradictory, but it really isn't. If you are angry with God (and in recovery you will want to work through much of that anger), you are accepting of God's place in your life. Otherwise, there would be no need for anger. Belief and faith are struggles. Just because we are in recovery does not mean that the struggle of faith is ended. For many, it is just a beginning.

For Growth and Renewal: Take your complaints and concerns to God. Together you can work them out, but you have to work them.

Let us search and try our ways,
And return to Adonai.
Let us lift our heart with our hands
To God in the heavens.
We have transgressed and rebelled.

—Lamentations 3:40-42

The book of Lamentations and its doleful chant permeate the entire month of *Av*. Some may see as depressing the constant rehearsing of the woes of our people. Even the special *trope*, the notes for cantillation, that are assigned for its reading are dirge-like. But history has taught us to look at the month of *Av* in a different way. We simulate the experience of our ancestors in order to understand it. Their pain is indeed our pain. It is one of the many things that binds us together through time and space, across the generations. But just reliving the experience is insufficient. In the midst of our exile, we are taught to "search and try our ways." It is the Jewish way to learn from our experience and grow as a result of it.

Recovery works the same way. As we move from active addiction into recovery, we too can learn to "search and try our ways." And in this searching, we admit to our shortcomings. We have indeed transgressed and rebelled. But no more.

For Growth and Renewal: The book of Lamentations is rather cathartic. Read the words which express the pain of our people so that your pain may join our ancestral pain. And feel release.

*One cannot escape the eye of God, but in trying
to hide from God, one hides from oneself.*

—Martin Buber,
twentieth century theologian

Now that's something to think about. While it may remind us of Noah in the garden, it really speaks more directly to how we lead our lives. We know that God can see what we do and yet we sometimes act as if God can't. We do things secretly, thinking that we get away with misdeeds. And sometimes it appears as if we do. But then we have to live with ourselves. We are only as sick as our secrets. Progress, not perfection.

In recovery, we learn to live with ourselves once again and not try to escape through drugs, alcohol, food, gambling, or sex. Rabbi Abraham Isaac Kook wrote in his *The Lights of Teshuvah* (Chapter 15): "When one forgets the essential nature of the soul, when one averts one's thought from the quality of introspection, everything becomes confused and in doubt. The principal of *teshuvah*, which illumines the dark places, is the return of humans to the self, to the source of one's soul and immediately the individual will return to God, the soul of all souls, and will progress higher."

For Growth and Renewal: When you do something wrong, don't hide from God. Admit what you have done and come clean!

Comfort ye! Comfort ye, my people.

—Isaiah 40:1,
from the Haftarah
for Shabbat Nachamu

On Shabbat Nachamu, the Sabbath which follows Tisha B'av, we offer comfort to one another. It is part of praying in a community. Taking our lead from the prophet Isaiah, we recognize that we are able to gain strength from one another. Sometimes it is the only way to do it. When we share our burdens, however formidable they may be, they are lessened as a result of the sharing. And we feel a bit better. It is one of the reasons why traditionally Judaism requires a *minyan* (a prayer quorum of ten people) for certain prayers, especially mourner's Kaddish. It is the community's way of imposing on itself an obligation.

The Twelve Steps work only in community also. We gain strength from one another, sharing our stories and our burdens. There may be some who enter recovery on their own and stay there. But they are rare. And even so they miss out on the fellowship of fellowship.

For Growth and Renewal: Join a *minyan* today. Help support someone in your community. That's what friends are for.

> *Serve Adonai with fear*
> *and rejoice with trembling.*
>
> —Psalm 2:11

While this text is often associated with the month of *Elul*, it seems to me to fit perfectly with Tu B'av, the fifteenth of *Av*. This joyous day in the Jewish calendar takes the form of celebration only six days after we have commemorated Tisha B'av. In the days of the Temple, it was a day of wood offering, celebrating the harvest of trees (and is also often associated with the fifth, seventh, tenth, and twentieth day of the month).

So why the fear and trembling? For me, because it *is* still so close to Tisha B'av. These feelings of contrition linger with me in the days and sometimes weeks which follow. It often takes me a full week to get back to a normal routine. I am chastened by Tisha B'av (and the entire month of *Av*), as I am reminded of all that God can do (and has done) in the universe and in my life.

This fear does not diminish my love for God. Sometimes, I think that it might even increase it. There is a well-known Jewish folk saying which suggests: "Fear without love is incomplete. Love without fear is nothing."

For Growth and Renewal: Add one thing to your recovery routine. Then express your love for God by keeping clean and working to stay that way.

> *Fools attempt to learn the entire Torah*
> *all at once, at the same time. When they fail,*
> *they give up completely. Wise people*
> *study the Torah a little every day.*

—Deuteronomy Rabbah 8:3

People in active addiction think they can quit whenever they want. Denying that they have a problem, they say to themselves and to others something like: "Just one more drink and then I'll stop." You probably said something similar to yourself. And then something finally made you seek recovery. But in the early days of recovery, you wanted to recover all at once. Chances are you came to a meeting or two while you were still actively using. You figured one meeting would do it and when it didn't, it was back to the bottle or the needle or the craps table or the refrigerator or the bed of another stranger. You just couldn't figure out the way the program works. Time takes time.

Like recovery, Torah takes time too. Just like you will always be a recovering alcoholic or addict and your recovery will take the rest of your life (or it will take your life), Torah is a lifelong pursuit, as well. And it will give you life, real living. Perhaps it is the study of Torah every day that makes people wise. That's what makes them want to study a little more.

For Growth and Renewal: If you haven't fixed a time for regular study, do so today. If you have, then invite someone to join you.

Only those of a broken heart can find God.
For the broken heart—repentance, complete
emptying before God—is the breaking of the
stubborn isolation and self-sufficiency that is
the root source of our troubles. It releases
the stopped-up fountain of faith.

—Will Herberg,
twentieth century theologian
and social critic

It doesn't take much to find someone with a broken heart. Addicted or not, we are all broken in some way. So I guess we all have the potential for finding God. I think that that's Will Herberg's point. When you recognize that you have a broken heart, then you are able to find God. It is that recognition that allows you to empty yourself before God, removing the delusion of self-sufficiency and filling up the space with faith.

One addicted person told me, "I felt empty inside so I tried to fill that emptiness with food. It didn't work." Like this friend in recovery, you may have tried other things, as well: Alcohol, drugs, sex. Nothing worked nor will it. That emptiness you feel cannot be filled with something from outside of self. But it can be filled in covenant with God. This is the essence of humility.

You do the work (all Twelve Steps). God will do the rest.

For Growth and Renewal: Take your broken heart and present it to God. You'll be amazed how, with God's help, it can be mended and you can be healed.

*The best remedy for those who are afraid, lonely,
or unhappy is to go outside, somewhere where
they can be quite alone with the heavens, nature,
and God. Because only then does one feel that all
is as it should be and that God wishes to see people happy, amidst the simply beauty of nature. As
long as this exists, and it certainly will, I know
that then there will always be comfort for every
sorrow, whatever the circumstances may be.*

—from the diary of Anne Frank,
young woman who perished in the Holocaust

Of the many historical fast days that dot the ancient Jewish calendar, the eighteenth day of *Av* is designated as such because the eternal light was quenched on this date during the reign of King Ahaz. It is just another reason for the gloom that cast its spell on the month of *Av*. But listen to the words of the young Anne Frank. If she could be positive in the midst of a world that was literally falling apart around her, certainly we can be positive even in the midst of the month of *Av*.

Yes, we can be positive because as difficult as recovery may be—and, at times, it will be difficult—we are moving in the right direction. Let's begin our recovery today again—and *we should* consider every day in recovery as if we are starting anew—and take Anne Frank's advice.

For Growth and Renewal: Follow Anne's advice. Be alone with nature, with God. Then you'll realize that you are never alone.

God forgives all of your sins,
heals all your diseases.

—Psalm 103:3

This short text from the Psalms has given tens of thousands of people hope and faith. You can return to God even after the mess you have made of your lives through alcoholism, chemical addiction, compulsive eating, gambling and sex and just plain sinful behaviors. Through *teshuvah* (repentance), you can be healed. Throughout the book of Psalms is the gentle, healing guidance to transform the individual. It is especially important to consider this text as we prepare to finally enter the Promised Land. The Bible tells us that all of the slaves went forth. We are not told that God only took some of the Israelites out of Egypt. God took all of them—slave and sinner alike. Rabbi Joseph B. Soloveitchik suggests that sin is an illness and that healing is implicit in repentance.

Addiction is a disease, but everything that is associated with it is not. In recovery, we stop all of the dishonesty that seemed to be inseparable from our addiction. With the healing power of recovery, the sinful behaviors seem to fall by the wayside. We have no interest in them any longer.

For Growth and Renewal: Put a book of Psalms by your bedside and read it each night. Select one line and focus on it before you sleep. Let it guide your dreams and your recovery.

In the body, the soul is not enclosed, but held,
as by the end of a shoe string, like a bird
capable of traversing the heavens, that is
held back by a thin silken thread.

—Rabbi Abraham Isaac Kook,
early twentieth century rabbinic
authority and thinker,
first chief rabbi of Israel

For some, the idea of a soul, separate from the body—and distinct from the mind—is hard to understand. Some have the notion that the body is actually a prison, holding the soul captive against its will. Others contend that since the body is part of the earthly, material world, it is, by definition, tainted, corrupt. None of these views are essentially Jewish. While we are alive, body and soul are joined together by mutual desire. Each one, body and soul, holds within itself the potential to nurture the other.

Yet, in active addiction, the soul seems to be totally controlled by the body. Weighed down by out-of-control needs for alcohol, drugs, food and sex, it upsets the natural balance that was established for you even before your birth. In recovery, through spiritual renewal, you can free the tethers on your soul and allow it to work with your body, not against it.

For Growth and Renewal: Release your soul. Let it do its work as you work the Twelve Steps into your daily routine.

It is not the place that honors the person,
but the person who honors the place.

—Babylonian Talmud,
Taanit 21b

Many of you may be concerned about the location of your Twelve Step meeting. Although more and more synagogues and Jewish Community Centers are opening their doors to A.A. and other Twelve Step program meetings, it is likely that your regular meeting takes place in a church basement. It is too easy to let the location of a meeting become just another brick in that wall of denial that has been built around the Jewish community and isolated us from the truth. Jews do drink. And there are Jewish alcoholics and addicts. And you are probably one of them.

Together we are working to make changes so that you can feel more comfortable in your recovery, at home in the synagogue with Jewish sources and resources. In the meantime, don't let the location of a meeting stop you from going. Remember, "it is not the place that honors the person, but the person who honors the place." And the best way to honor it is to stay in recovery.

For Growth and Renewal: Make an effort to make the space in which you hold your Twelve Step meetings holy space through what you do there.

Send, send Your words to me
that I might write the song.
Send to me Your melody,
that I might sing Your song.
Your message flowing through me,
so that I might speak the words—
That wanting to be ever close,
is all we need to be near to You . . .

—Sharon L. Wechter, contemporary songwriter

As we near the end of the month of *Av*—with its pain and its consolation—we may feel somewhat confused. We yearn to know God, to come close to God. That's what is so instructive and warming about these words of search of a Jewish woman. Would that we could all be the channel through which God's message and melody could be sung! Perhaps it might help us to understand God and, in the process, we might come to know ourselves.

Rabbi Jediah Bedersi said that "The sum total of what we know of You is that we do not know You." This rabbi brings us to a profound spiritual understanding that provides us with a foundation for recovery and our entire life. While some might take this as meaning that God is beyond all comprehension, what it really means is that as close as we get there is so much to know. Thus, we are always motivated to seek more of God, to long more for God, and to do more for ourselves.

For Growth and Renewal: Ask God to send God's words to you, so that you might be God's voice in the world.

*It is Adonai your God who marches with you
to do battle for you against your enemy
to bring you victory.*

—Deuteronomy 20:4

Often I translate *Adonai Tzevaot* (Lord of Hosts) as "God is my army." Such a translation assumes some poetic license, but I think that it captures the spirit of the original Hebrew. When we are forced to do battle, when we go about the tasks of daily living, we want God to lead us. We are reminded of Zechariah's message, "Not by might, nor by power, but by my spirit, says Adonai." Unfortunately, sometimes it takes war to gain peace.

For the addicted person, the greatest enemy is what the rabbis call the *yetzer hara*, our impulse to do evil. And so you must do battle with your evil impulse. While the book of Deuteronomy includes a whole litany of rules for us to follow should one be forced to go to war, these same rules apply when we clash with our evil impulse. And we all have one. So we are warned, "Do not rejoice when your enemy falls" (Proverbs 24:17). Even when we finally conquer the evil impulse and have left active addiction, we must recognize that we have left a bit of ourselves behind. It is part of the cost of doing war.

For Growth and Renewal: Now the battle is over. You can begin again. Rejoice not when your enemy falls, but when joining her or him in celebrating *shalom* (tranquility, wholeness, and peace).

> *As a person thinks in his or her heart,*
> *so is that person.*
>
> —Proverbs 28:7

Thinking doesn't always make it so in reality, but it usually makes it so between our ears. Ironically, few of us ever stop to think about how enormously our thoughts affect the quality of our life. Perhaps that's why the program encourages so much honest self-expression and self-scrutiny: Unless and until we come to terms with our "inner reality," we don't even know who we are.

The way we think about a situation can literally either make it easier to handle or make it almost impossible to deal with. Said the great contemporary sage Rabbi Moshe Feinstein, "When you think that you will not be able to do something, these thoughts prevent you from accomplishing what you really could if you believed more in your abilities."

Are we plodding through life or living with a purpose? Letting go or festering in resentment? Running scared—or Higher Powered? Only the voice of our heart can really clue us in on how it feels to be us. We need to listen to it. And to realize that a more positive mental attitude makes more positive living possible.

For Growth and Renewal: Write down what it is that you want to do today to foster your recovery. Make sure it is in your heart. Then do what you have written down.

Let a good person do good deeds with the same zeal that an evil person does bad ones.

—Shalom Rokeach, the Belzer Rebbe,
nineteenth century rebbe in Galicia

My friend Aaron Z. (who co-wrote *Renewed Each Day* with me) told me, "It always seems to me that bad habits are so much easier to fall into than good habits. Maybe that's just me—or maybe it's human nature. Or maybe I just have more enthusiasm for the things in life that are illegal, immoral and/or fattening. Lord knows, I am not alone!

"They say that we make recovery as easy or as hard on ourselves as we wish. I happen to like going to meetings. It took me a while, but I made friends, got connected, and there are very few meetings that I walk out of without having heard something that I needed to hear. Would I have been as likely to remain in recovery if I hated the meetings? I doubt it."

Going to shul, to the synagogue, is the same way. If you go with a chip on your shoulder, ready to criticize everything that takes place, you won't get anything out of it.

For Growth and Renewal: Take counsel from Aaron Z. Go to shul and go to a meeting and leave your baggage at the door.

The wise will remain serene in the face of trouble.

—Solomon Ibn Gabirol,
eleventh century
Spanish poet philosopher

Fear and panic distort our ability to think clearly. Decisions made in haste are often ones that we come to regret. Trouble is trouble enough. We don't have to make things worse by letting it overwhelm us. Situations that seem so terribly urgent may just be God's way of telling us that we are too hung up at the moment.

Addicted people tend to be hard on themselves. We were born in a hurry and have an itchy trigger finger when it comes to pushing the panic button. We need to learn that "one step a time" isn't just the way to go through the program, it's a good way to go through life. We live in a hurried society, but we don't have to buy into that craziness any more than necessary. We are the keepers of our own internal time clock. And if that clock is running too fast, it isn't working right. If we do the best we can, and have a little faith that things will work out for the best, we might find that they do. Taking a calm, measured approach to life may not come easy to us, but it is *possible*—and it does work. See for yourself.

For Growth and Renewal: When you are troubled, take a deep breath, give yourself some time to think. Talk things over with a friend. And pray for guidance.

> *If I ascend to heaven, You are there;*
> *If I descend to Sheol, You are there too.*
> *If I soar with the dawn and come to rest on the*
> *western horizon,*
> *even there Your hand will be guiding me,*
> *Your right hand will be holding me fast.*

> — Psalm 139:7-10

Perhaps the reason why you can find God wherever you go is because God is with you wherever you go. Like it or not, you can't escape God. Some of the prophets tried to do so, but they soon learned that their journeys—sometimes as far as halfway across the world—came to naught. God was there too.

Some say *teshuvah* is a journey to God. Others say that it is a voyage back to the self. However you describe your recovery, just remember that the joy is in the journey.

In active addiction you certainly found your way to Sheol, and now, in recovery, you are looking for heaven. It's a long way to travel in one lifetime, sometimes back and forth in a short span of time. But consider how you got there and where you yet have to go. How are you going to get there?

For Growth and Renewal: Find God today in a place where previously you had not realized God existed. And remember to do a better job of looking next time!

> *I surrender my soul into your care . . .*
> *You are with me. I will not fear.*
>
> —from the hymn "Adon Olam"

Sounds a lot like Step Three to me: "Made a decision to turn our will and our lives over to the care of God *as we understood God*." Yet, there are still those who will try to debate the Jewishness of this step (and all of the Twelve Steps). They are probably still in denial. It's really a shame: They could be renewed. Look at the hymn from which this text is taken. It is probably sung more often with more melodies than any other Jewish hymn. Its message is pretty clear. Maybe if we sing loud and long enough, we can help open their hearts and their heads.

I've probably heard a hundred different reasons for people who are not ready for recovery and therefore still actively using and abusing. But it is mostly people outside of the program who argue that the Twelve Steps are not Jewish. And it's that argument that keeps them outside of the program—and outside of recovery. As for me, an addicted person or not, I sing these words of "Adon Olam" nearly every day: "I surrender my soul into your care . . . . You are with me. I will not fear."

For Growth and Renewal: Don't rush through the words of Adon Olam today. As you sing out each word, work Step Three. Let go and let God.

Shiru lAdonai shir chadash.
Shiru lAdonai kol ha-aretz.
Sing to God a new song.
Sing to God a new song, all the earth.

—Psalm 96:1

For lots of people it takes a long time to get into the program. And a lot longer to really *get into* the program. Usually the first time you enter a fellowship meeting is not really the first time. You may have come once or twice before, but you were still in denial, perhaps still actively using. You had yet to admit to your addiction and only wanted to *see* what A.A. (or N.A. or G.A. or O.A. or whatever Twelve Step program you are in) was all about.

When you finally make it into recovery, even with the pain and the remaining work you have to do, you may feel like singing. And you may want the whole world to sing with you. But maybe not. Not everyone feels like singing, especially the kind of singing which you may be thinking of. That's okay. Some still feel like crying. And that's okay too. Because we all sing different kinds of songs to God. And in recovery, they are all *new* songs. Just sing out whatever is in your heart.

For Growth and Renewal: Sing out whatever is in your heart. I think that singing presents us with another opportunity to do Step Nine work.

> *Wisdom is before a person with understanding*
> *but the eyes of a fool are in the ends of the earth.*
>
> —Proverbs 17:24

Whether addicted or not, we all struggle for meaning in this world. But in active addiction, you can't even see where you are going. So you don't even know that you are going in the wrong direction. You know *teshuvah* (repentance and renewal) literally means a turning or returning. Maybe you couldn't find what you were looking for because you were looking in the wrong place. All you had to take was one step (the first out of twelve) in order to change directions and return to the path you strayed from sometime earlier in your life.

The wisdom of your recovery is not far out of your reach. Listen to these words of Torah. Let them guide you.

Surely this instruction which I enter into covenant with you today is not too much to comprehend, nor is it beyond your grasp. It is not on heaven to prevent you from saying "Who from among us can go to heaven and get it for us and teach it to us that we may comply with it?" Neither is it across the seas to prevent you from saying, "Who from among us can get to the other side of the sea and get it for us and teach it to us so that we may behave in accordance with it?" No. This teaching is very close to your mouth, in your heart, so that you may observe it. (Deuteronomy 30:11-14)

For Growth and Renewal: Wherever you stand, there is still more turning to do. So start turning.

Elul
Introspection
Late Summer

This final month of the religious calendar is devoted to one thing: Introspection. As we prepare to begin the religious year once again (whose counting takes precedence over the calendar year), our thoughts turn inward. We turn our attention to questions like: "What kind of a life have I been living? What changes must I make before I dare stand before God?" The penitential prayers (*selichot*) that color this month—and are said daily—help us to prepare. They provide us with a posture for our *teshuvah*, our repentance. By uttering the words of prayer, we ask God to help us to change, to grow.

Some say that the name of the month is an acronym for the words from the Song of Songs *Ani l'dodi v'dodi li* "I am to my beloved and my beloved is to me" (2:10), emphasizing the renewal of the relationship between estranged lovers (God and the people of Israel), following the near end of their relationship with the destruction of the Temple. Simply put, sin separates us from God.

Daily, the shofar is blown as part of our preparation and we recite Psalm 27. Toward the end of the month, we are awakened to our task by the shofar which is sounded even before the sun rises.

Adonai is my light and my help.
Whom shall I fear.
Adonai is the foundation of my life.
Whom shall I dread?

—Psalm 27:1

On this *Rosh Chodesh*, the first of a new month, this introductory verse introduces Psalm 27, said every day during the month of *Elul* as a warm-up for your own *cheshbon hanefesh*: Soul-searching and introspection. It actually frames the entire month. I would probably add this to the Psalm verse: "What I shall fear? What shall I dread?" And it's true that with God at your side, you need fear no one and nothing. A connection to God and godliness strengthens a person's resolve to withstand evil.

But such faith in God and your covenantal partnership with God does not mean that you don't have to work at holiness. You can't simply dump it all in God's lap, so to speak, and be on your merry way. You have to work and work hard, doing Step Four, recovery's version of *cheshbon hanefesh*, along the way. Then work some more especially during the month of Elul. It may be the summer and nearly the end of the religious year, but it is only the beginning as far as the Twelve Steps are concerned.

For Growth and Renewal: As you prepare to do your *cheshbon hanefesh* in *Elul*, Step Four work, be mindful of Psalm 27. Let it lead the way to soul-searching healing.

> *One thing I ask of Adonai*
> *only that do I seek*
> *to live in the house of Adonai*
> *all the days of my life,*
> *to gaze upon Adonai's beauty*
> *to frequent Your temple.*

—Psalm 27:4

In Psalm 27, we find a mix of the two images that dominate the Psalms and are translated into the liturgy. God is either described as king-like (we would say sovereign) or a judge holding court. In the context of the ancient world, both images may, in fact, be the same. However, those of us who see God as merciful and gracious (*El rachum vechanun*), may want to adjust the image a bit. We see the house of Adonai in kinder, gentler, more spiritually nurturing terms. God's house is thus neither palace nor courtroom. Rather it is the world in which we live, where God's sheltering presence can be experienced anywhere.

But life is more than survival. We only *live* in God's world when we abandon all of the things that drag us out of it, all of the dishonesty and deception that accompanied an active addiction. If you seek such a world for your life, you will find it.

For Growth and Renewal: Clean house. Do your inventory and rid yourself of what you no longer need. Let's work not to be attached to it.

> *Hear Adonai when I cry aloud.*
> *Have mercy on me, answer me.*
>
> —Psalm 27:7

Often we think that if we pray, then God will answer our prayers, as if God has an obligation to answer them. The truth is that God can do whatever God wants. That's why God is God. And that's why through this Psalm (every day during the month of *Elul*), we ask God to hear our prayers and answer us, to have mercy on us. As we peer deeply inside our souls, we come to realize that we don't always deserve what it is we ask for—but we ask for it anyway. It is part of what makes us human. Yet, if we really want God to hear us, to respond to us, then we have to show God that we are serious about the changes we are prepared to make in our lives.

This is the essence of real *teshuvah*.

Asking God for things is part of our unrelenting desire to control. Face it: We are not in control. Be more reflective instead. So we begin the process of *teshuvah* with Step One. But it doesn't end there. And it doesn't end in *Elul* either. Each step (and each month) runs through the other.

For Growth and Renewal: Repeat the words of Psalm 27 and reflect on them as a *kavannah*, a mantra of sorts, to prepare you for your prayers. It helps you to make the transition from the regular routine of life to the holy.

> *Do not forsake me, do not abandon me.*
> *O God, the One who delivers me.*
>
> —Psalm 27:9

In the midst of active addiction, we may feel abandoned by God. Some may even feel that they started using or abusing because of a perceived sense of abandonment. Regardless of the cause or the case, when things don't go our way in life, we may feel deserted, neglected, abandoned. Sometimes, we do the abandoning. We walk out on our jobs or our spouses or anything else as soon as the going gets rough. It seems easier than confronting rejection and pain. Or we may try to ease our way through the pain with the "help" of drink or drugs. But the pain gets worse, not better.

And so we turn to God, our Higher Power, knowing in our hearts, as the Psalmist goes on to say, "Though my father and my mother abandon me, Adonai will take me in" (Psalm 27:10). Many people read this and think that this is an indicator of some unresolved "family of origin" work. And maybe it is. But it has more to do with accepting the responsibility for the adult self than it does anything else. Getting clean also means growing up.

For Growth and Renewal: With this psalm in mind, do the remaining "family of origin" work that remains unresolved. You'll grow from it.

Show me Your way, Adonai,
and lead me on a level path
because of my ever-watchful foes.

—Psalm 27:11

There are those who wait anxiously for you to stumble and fall, just looking for the chance to keep you down. Some even plan for it. And so, instead of reaching out a hand to help, they extend you credit at the bar or on the street, pushing you into active addiction even further. They are the ones who say, "What's the matter? You don't like the food? Eat a little more." Or, "If you really loved me, you'd sleep with me." And so, as part of our recovery work for the month of *Elul*, we turn to God and ask "Show me *Your* way" and then follow it.

Walking on a holy path is not easy. But all it really takes is placing one foot in front of the other. And then moving forward. Take your time and God will lead you on a level path in life, but you have to be the one who does the walking: One foot in front of the other. That's what it takes—and more.

For Growth and Renewal: And when the opportunity to use or abuse confronts you again, walk the other way!

> *Look to Adonai [for hope]*
> *be strong and of good courage.*
> *Look to Adonai [for faith].*

—Psalm 27:14

This last verse of *Elul*'s daily psalm ends on a note of inspiration, as your work in Steps Four and Ten should do, as well. The goal of the program and *cheshbon hanefesh* (introspection) is to heal, not hurt. As the Psalmist tells us in this psalm, it takes a special kind strength and courage to do such spiritual recovery work. But consider who your partner is!

Don't think that God is going to do the job for you. Whenever you err, you have to be the one to make amends—when possible. That is one of the responsibilities of adulthood. Sometimes the damage can't be repaired. Destroyed relationships may be irreparable. Through working the active Step Nine, real healing takes place. So if you can't fix what is broken, then go fix something else!

For Growth and Renewal: Go fix something that is broken in your life that needs repair. And remember to look to God for the strength to help heal.

> *First judge yourself, and using the same yardstick,*
> *judge others. Do not be lenient with your faults*
> *while judging harshly the same faults in others;*
> *do not overlook sin in yourself*
> *while demanding perfection of others.*

> —*Toledot Yaakov Yosef,* Rabbi Jacob Joseph,
> eighteenth century rabbi from Polonnoye

It is so easy to be critical of others and so hard to be critical of oneself. Often, we avoid an honest look at ourselves by busying ourselves with others, especially by doing someone else's inventory for them—and they didn't even ask. Such criticism has unfortunately become so commonplace that we often don't even realize that we are guilty of it. It's no coincidence that one of the ways the rabbis understand leprosy in the Bible is as slander and idle gossip, through a bit of Hebrew wordplay. And the avoidance of self-scrutiny provides yet another way for us to discover what we may have been running from in active addiction in the first place.

On first glance, this statement look likes a contradiction to Twelve Step program philosophy, but read Yaakov Yosef more closely. If you learn to evaluate yourself properly (and *Elul* is *the* main month to do it), then you probably won't judge your neighbor at all! Let God be the judge. You stick to being human.

For Growth and Renewal: Take the time today to transform something of which you have been critical in others into a measuring stick for yourself.

---

*For two and a half years, the House of Shammai
and the House of Hillel argued whether or not
human beings should have been created.
Both houses concluded that it would have been
better had they not been created but since they
had, let them examine their past deeds.
And then they added: Let them consider their
future actions, as well.*

—based on Babylonian Talmud, Eruvin 13b

For people who have not heard of this infamous discussion, they are astonished by it. Most people think that Judaism is overwhelmingly supportive of the potential for good that lies deep inside of each individual—even if dormant—that such a compromised statement seems to be totally out of character with the great rabbis. Perhaps the rabbis were simply troubled by the world that surrounds them, as we often are. But they didn't despair. They came to their conclusion and then suggested that we all move forward. Any discussion concerning whether God should have created human beings is not only a bit presumptuous, but it is also moot. We have been created and so our obligation is to live up to being worthy of our creation.

Maybe the rabbis wanted to use this statement as a goad. Look at their last statement. It was as if they were inviting all of us to prove them wrong. Let's see what we can do about it!

For Growth and Renewal: Consider your past actions. Let what you have learned guide your future.

> *I am a sojourner in the earth.*
> *Do not hide from my mitzvot.*

—Psalm 119:19

Reflecting on this verse from the book of Psalms, the Medziboner Rebbe commented: "A traveler came to a town where everyone was a stranger to him and he had no one with whom to converse. Later another stranger arrived and both became friends, impelled by their mutual loneliness. They agreed to have no secrets from one another. Here the Psalmist says,'I am a stranger in the earth of evildoers and You, O God are likewise unwelcome. Let us become friends and have no secrets from one another.'"

When we enter a fellowship meeting for the first time, we sometimes feel the same way. Strangers to ourselves, we feel like the people around us—even as they reach out a hand to help—are also strangers. As we reach out to one another, and allow others to reach out to us, we learn that we are not strangers at all. Rather, we are friends who have as of yet not met each other.

In your recovery, hide no secrets from yourself or your sponsor. In *Elul*, hide no secrets from your God.

For Growth and Renewal: Reach out to someone in recovery and make them feel welcome by giving them the hug of life.

> *One needs to make* teshuvah *as an act of*
> *preparation for the study of Torah.*
> —Rabbi Yaakov Yitzchak, the Seer of Lublin
> early nineteenth century rebbe,
> founder of Hasidism in Poland and Galicia

And we thought that it was the other way around, that the study of Torah was necessary to ready oneself for *teshuvah*. For me, they are really one and the same. One engages the text *as* one makes *teshuvah* and is thereby spiritually renewed. Some people think that you have to be well-trained before you can study Torah. The study of Torah is a unique experience, but it is available to all.

It's kind of like looking for your first job. "You need more experience," says your potential employer. But you can't get the experience you need without your first job. Torah is different in that it gives you the insight of experience as you study it. While more learning helps to prepare for its study, we are never fully prepared for it. And so we keep on studying it. *Teshuvah* is the same way. We never quite finish the journey.

For Growth and Renewal: Prepare yourself for today's study of Torah by working the Steps, one at a time. Then do both: Torah and the Twelve Steps.

Rabbi Baer of Radoshitz once said to his teacher,
the Seer of Lublin, "Show me the best way to
serve God." The tzaddik *replied, "It is impossible*
to tell people the way they should take.
Everyone should carefully observe which way
one's heart is drawn, and then choose this way
with all one's strength."

Often we are led to believe that we all reach the path of spiritual renewal in much the same way. We think that *teshuvah* journeys should be the same for all people— whether they are in recovery from an addiction or not. As a result, when we see the liberating feeling that it can offer one person—but not us—we are quickly disappointed and disillusioned. There are those among us who even return to active addiction as a consequence. Like most things in life, there is no simple formula for success. Spiritual renewal does not provide us with *the* way. It helps us to find *our* way.

But you can't find your way in the dark. And active addiction dims the light in your world. Nor can you find your way if you are not looking for it. And in active addiction, you are only looking for one thing—your next drink, your next fix, whatever it is that keeps you from getting anywhere except down. That's where the Higher Power comes in. God illumines your path so that you can get where you are going.

For Growth and Renewal: Leave your front light on during the day, as well as during the night. Let it remind you of your recovery.

As they were walking in the valley of Arbel,
as the light of dawn was breaking through
the darkness, Rabbi Chiyya remarked to
Rabbi Simeon ben Halafta, "My friend, behold
how the dawn grows stronger and stronger.
So shall our Redemption be: At first, a little,
then more and more."

—Jerusalem Talmud, Berachot 1

How do you transform the actions of your past? *You* do not, God does. The godliness of the transformation reaches outside of time to transform the past in a way that I cannot, but that only God can. Only God moves out of time this way. When one makes *teshuvah* transformation, one transforms at the level of *neshama*, the divine soul which sits inside all of us, that non-local quality of soul that comes directly from God. Indeed, it is godliness itself.

In the Talmud, it states that a person who makes *teshuvah* is closer to God than one who has been thoroughly righteous. How is this so? Think of all human beings as being connected to God by invisible fibers of relationship. Think of it as a rope. When we sin, we cut the rope. We sever the invisible fibers of relationship that connect us to God. When we make *teshuvah*, we repair the rope where it had been cut, shortening the distance, bringing us closer.

—Rabbi James Stone Goodman

For Growth and Renewal: Take a past action that had previously given you pain and renew it so that it brings you *shalom.*

359

> *One must repeatedly confide in another person,*
> *whether spiritual counselor or trusted friend, all*
> *improper thoughts and impulses which come to*
> *one's heart and one's mind, whether these occur*
> *during meditation, while lying idle awaiting the*
> *onset of sleep, or at any time during the day, and*
> *one should not withhold anything because of*
> *shame or embarrassment.*
>
> —Rabbi Elimelech of Lizensk,
> eighteenth century hasidic rabbi

For many people, this is one of the hardest things to do in the program. This kind of disclosure requires us to be honest with ourselves and trusting of other people. What makes it difficult is that we had given up on both during active addiction. Coming back to them takes time.

Elimelech's advice, almost coming right out of the Twelve Steps, is a spiritual exercise. It helps us to vanquish our *yetzer hara*, our libidinal inner drives. When asked "Who is strong?" the rabbis answer, "The one who conquers his [and we would add her] *yetzer hara*." But to take control of one's *yetzer hara* (instead of letting it control us) takes practice. And so we share all of our "secrets," with sponsor and friend, taking all that we have learned about ourselves in the process to a spiritual advisor so that our recovery might be guided forward in our renewal.

For Growth and Renewal: Keep a journal of all of your "improper thoughts and impulses" and take them to your spiritual counselor. Use them to help you prepare yourself spiritually for the next day.

---

*A reconciliation that does not explain that error
lay on both sides is not a true reconciliation.*

—Genesis Rabbah 54:3

There are always three sides to every story: Mine, yours, and the truth. The sooner we accept this truism as truth, the sooner we can get on the road to recovery. My colleague Rabbi Lawrence Kushner likes to share how Yom Kippur is observed in the foyer of his synagogue, Congregation Beth El in Sudbury, Massachusetts. You may find it a bit strange, but it is in the foyer where the rapproachment between people takes place—before the individual enters the sanctuary in order to pray to God for forgiveness. It is there where honest reconciliation takes place.

In terms of spiritual time, the month of *Elul* functions just like the synagogue foyer operates in terms of physical space. *Elul* provides us with the time we need to reconcile and make peace with others—and with ourselves—before we stand before God and ask for forgiveness. It takes time for us to recognize that we, too, are at fault even when it is we who have been wronged. Therefore, we share in the sin of another. And so we pray in the plural: "*We* have sinned. *We* have transgressed. *We* have acted perversely."

For Growth and Renewal: When you have done something wrong, admit it. Then seek *shalom* in all your relationships.

Your command, seek my face, my heart repeats.
Your face, oh God, do I seek.

—Psalm 27:8

We are taught that the mechanism of transformation, *teshuvah*, was built into creation, at the end of the sixth day, "between the suns," that time of mystery and uncertainty when something had ended, something new not yet begun. It is a place many of us find ourselves in when we enter recovery. It is an exceedingly holy time, full of possibility. When God finished the six days of creating, there followed a holy period of possibility when the miraculous was sewn into the fabric of Creation, to unfold when it was appropriate, when it was needed. Dusk, when the sixth day had ended, the night not yet begun . . . the Talmud tells us that is when *teshuvah* was created.

In *Elul*, we turn to the centrality of *teshuvah*. *Teshuvah* is transformation, the ability of a human being to change in a deep, inner sense. This implies that we have to be careful what we identify as "defects in character." They may be transformable, through *teshuvah* transformation, into our greatest strengths.   —Rabbi James Stone Goodman

For Growth and Renewal: In the midst of your *teshuvah*, seek out God and share God's shining presence with others. Let it help strengthen them, as well, and help you see your own "defects."

> *You don't stumble because you are weak,*
> *but because you think yourself strong.*

> —Yiddish saying

Such all-or-nothing people we are. If we aren't feeling woefully inadequate and worthless, then we tend to get a bit too full of ourselves and we start to think that we're bullet-proof. But we're not. How often and how painfully have we learned that it is our own thinking that is our biggest stumbling block. With some time in the program, it is very easy to get complacent—or over-confident. The increased self-esteem and mastery of living life on life's terms that recovery fosters can indeed be very heady. But running with that headiness is just the sort of insidious self set-up that has caused more than a few of us to fall.

The rabbis teach that haughtiness and humility are both part of the same dimension of human existence. When humans are too haughty, God brings them down low. When they are too humble, God raises them heavenward. Be humble in the presence of God. Yet keep your head upright. Know you are both "dust and ashes" and "a little lower than the angels." Live a life reflective of both.

For Growth and Renewal: Be conscious of bowing the head and bending the knee during your prayers. Then stand straight. Be aware of both movements as you seek to live a holy daily life.

> *Rabbi Hillel said, "If I am not for myself, who will be my advocate? But if I am only for myself, what am I really? If not now, when?"*
>
> —*Pirke Avot* 1:14

How many times did we promise ourselves to quit? And how many times did we fail? We even became comfortable with our problems since it allowed us the opportunity to not deal with them. That's why the rabbis teach us to repent the day before our death, since we never know when that day will come. We live a life constantly seeking to return to the path that God has set before us. It's easy to quit until we are seized by our next urge. We can fool others, even ourselves but never God. Addicts know about urgency. Always in a hurry, no wonder quick fixes look so appealing.

Hillel's classic challenge offers us a different kind of urgency. He teaches us that life is so preciously short, that spiritual priorities are necessary, that getting sidetracked is dangerous and will prevent us from achieving our goals. If recovery is not our first priority, we risk losing it. Don't focus on the "easy" in "easy does it." Pay attention to the second part: Do it! When it comes to recovery, "later" is too late. Together we can make our best effort to keep our recovery active, growing, and strong. Today! Now is the only time we ever really have.

For Growth and Renewal: In whatever you do, use Hillel's statement as a measuring stick as you preserve your self.

> *Once a person repents,*
> *stop reminding her of what she did.*
>
> —Babylonian Talmud, Bava Metzia 58

What you did is not who you are. What you now do—
and do with the rest of your life—is what's most important. Now that you are ready to forgive others, be ready
to forgive yourself. While in recovery, you are still an
addicted person—something you will always be—*active*
addiction is part of your past. Just keep it there. Then no
one will feel inclined to remind you of where you've been.
You're a long way from the spiritual destitution that
brought you down. It's been a rough journey home. But
know that you got here—and you're here to stay.

My friend Aaron Z. (with whom I wrote *Renewed Each
Day*) told me that many people are surprised that he does
his work anonymously. "You should be proud that you've
turned your life around," they told him. But, to para-
phrase Tevye in *Fiddler on the Roof*, Aaron quips, "It may
be no great shame being an addict—but it's no great honor
either!" He tells me, "I am not proud of what I did while I
was an active addict. I would rather that it not be a factor
in any of my relationships outside my fellowship and chosen circle of friends. Going to meetings and listening to
people share stories is a sufficient reminder of what *I* did."

For Growth and Renewal: Remember what you did during your active addiction? Now work to keep it in your
past.

> *When can penitence atone for a person's sin?*
> *Only when one's conscience still troubles him*
> *regarding it. If a person's conscience ceases to*
> *trouble him, atonement will be of no avail.*

—Zohar i, 27a

Recovery does not release us of the responsibility of conscience. Just because we repent does not mean that we do not have to worry about staying on the right track. What's life anyhow without worrying? God may guide us, *mitzvot* will help shape our behaviors, but the decision to lead a good life is still our own. And once we decide, then we have to act. No coasting allowed!

Guilt is not a great feeling, but not all guilt is bad. We need to learn to distinguish appropriate and inappropriate guilt. For example, some people feel guilty about things going well in their life—as if they somehow don't deserve to be happy. That's the kind of guilt we really don't need. On the other hand, you show me someone entirely guilt-free, and I'll show you a liar. Guilt is our God-given moral compass. If we do something wrong, it's *supposed* to feel uncomfortable.

For Growth and Renewal: As you take a look at your life, remember that the nature of our world is such that we will be tempted. Sex. Food. Alcohol. Gambling. Drugs. It is not easy to lead a good life. It is only better and healthier.

Wicked people teach their bad habits to others.

—Hasidic teaching

One of the many things that the Twelve Steps teach us—and there are many things indeed—is that we should focus our critical faculties on ourselves. We have enough work to do on our own. Let others do what they need to do to better themselves. And so, this Hasidic teaching has always troubled me. We have learned that we cannot blame others for our mistakes. Regardless of how we got there or why we stayed in active addiction, it is we who were the active addicts. Others may have "enabled" us, even joined us in our active period. Others may have taught us bad habits, but we willingly and often quickly learned them.

Maybe recovery and renewal don't give us all the answers. Rather, it makes it possible to see clearly enough to find the answers. Perhaps it is enough sometimes to just ask the right questions. It is something with which we have to learn to live. Just like we really don't know why we are addicted people and others are not. And so, we turn this hasidic teaching on its head and ask ourselves, "Can wicked people *really* teach their bad habits to others?" I don't know, but I am going to stay away from them anyway. So should you.

For Growth and Renewal: So wicked people can't teach bad habits to others. So teach the truth to others.

May the One who answered Abraham
on Mt. Moriah answer me.

—from the Selichot liturgy

Rabbi Simcha Bunam said that if he were the one writing this penitential prayer, he'd reword it as follows: "May the One who has answered me until now answer me at present as well." Because there exists no person whom God has not answered many times. You don't even have to actually pray to be answered by God. Prayers come in different forms, not all of them words. Discovering a recovery fellowship may be a perfect example of how often God gives us what we need, whether we ask for it or not. That doesn't exempt us from asking. Especially when it comes to forgiveness, we need to ask God, the ones we have wronged and ourselves.

The mystics of Safed taught that if one prays at the graveside of the pious, then one's prayers will be speedily answered. People have "found" various ways to make their prayers more efficacious. Some people think that they are undeserving of prayer. Perhaps it is because we think that we are unable to find the right words in our entreaty to God. Will that place God's response in jeopardy? More important than the words we choose is the intention with which we pray.

For Growth and Renewal: It is said that artists and writers do best when they work from their own experiences. Take yourself to God. And shape your prayers out of your life.

Rabbi Simeon ben Lakish said, "Repentance that springs from love of God causes willful sins to be treated as righteous deeds."

—Babylonian Talmud, Yoma 86b

Among other things, *teshuvah* means the ability of a human being to reorient to time: To the past, present and future. The mechanism of *teshuvah* transformation is similar to the mechanism of Steps Four and Five. Maimonides explains that *teshuvah* transformation begins with a spoken confession, a verbal expression describing from what you are turning (making *teshuvah*). Like the difference between the Fourth and Fifth Steps, speaking it is different from thinking it. The confession expresses one's regret at the past error. One then resolves not to make the same mistake again. These are basically the two parts of *teshuvah* transformation, one referring to the past, one to the future.

"Willful wrongs are transformed as if they were merits." The negativity of the past is changed into merit. What a concept! What you once experienced negatively empowers you positively. It is the transformation of darkness into light. Your light is brighter, because you have harnessed both the energy of light and of darkness.

—Rabbi James Stone Goodman

For Growth and Renewal: Try a *teshuvah* transformation exercise: Think the change. Say it. Then do it.

> *Do not separate yourself from the community.*
>
> —*Pirke Avot* 2:4

The term "twice-a-year-Jews" has been used to describe those who limit their synagogue attendance to Rosh Hashanah and Yom Kippur. More often than not, they fail to get the "religious fix" they were hoping for. They may even wonder why they keep coming back, year after year, despite getting so little out of it. Maybe they have a sense of obligation. Or even a sense of tradition. Maybe these Jews are reluctant to sever this last tie to the community. We welcome them at any time.

But just think about it! How would your recovery be if you only attended meetings twice a year? This is not to say that it is impossible to maintain a prayer relationship with God in private—or even to recover. It is possible. But Judaism and Twelve Step fellowships have always recognized the value and power of group prayer. To limit one's experience of that power to two holy days—and expect to have this wonderful sense of reawakened religious fervor or communal connection—is an almost certain set-up for failure. "Giving time time" applies to all commitments. "Quick fixes" don't work in the synagogue either.

For Growth and Renewal: Forge a path back to the synagogue. Begin by joining (or starting) a Torah recovery group. Give time to your recovery commitment by also attending meetings regularly.

While sinning, repent!

—Ben Sirach 18:21

Don't wait until next Rosh Hashanah and Yom Kippur, thinking that you have to find the right time to get on the road to recovery. You might never find that "right time." It will always be "I'll start tomorrow" or "just one more" or "I know what I'm doing. I can stop anytime." By that time, it may be too late. So begin your recovery and your return even in the midst of what you are doing—right now. If you can start now in the shadow of an active addiction, then you'll remember the pain for a long time. And that's what you need to do. Forgive yourself, but don't forget what you've done. Then keep on forgiving.

Some have said that the program "takes all the fun out of getting high." And it may. Once you know enough to know better, you can't use ignorance as an excuse anymore. So, even through the haze, we realize, maybe more sharply than ever, how some controlled substance, or even an uncontrolled one, is controlling us and our bottom gets a little lower. Being aware that what you're doing is wrong—even *while* you're doing it—can be the first step toward repentance and recovery, if you want it to be.

For Growth and Renewal: Begin your recovery *now* by stopping one sin. Ask for others to help you. It's the right place to start.

By mercy and truth iniquity is atoned for.

—Proverbs 16:6

Forgiveness of ourselves and others is one of the most powerful forms of spiritual healing. And truth—which can mean the honesty and willingness to look at ourselves—can continue to keep us clean.

We can learn a great deal from sharing with one another. Through Torah, our ancestors have shared their struggles of faith with us. In program, our friends share their struggles with recovery. We do both for the same purpose: To learn, to grow, to live holy lives.

One person commented to me on his shortcomings as an active alcoholic quite candidly: "I am not, by nature, a crook or a liar, but put some alcohol in me, and I am all those things and worse." A statement of fact, the statement of an individual atoned.

For Growth and Renewal: Recovery is a healing mix of mercy and honesty that gives us the fresh start we need to go on with the rest of our lives. Before the Holy Days, one asks for forgiveness from those we may have wronged. It's a beginning, a model for the year. So don't wait. Do it now. It's part of your Step Nine work.

> *When one forgets the essential nature of the soul,*
> *when one averts one's thought from the quality*
> *of introspection, everything becomes confused*
> *and in doubt. The principal of* teshuvah, *which*
> *illumines the dark places, is the return of the indi-*
> *vidual to the self, to the source of the soul, and*
> *immediately will return to God.*
>
> —*The Lights of Teshuvah*
> Rabbi Abraham Isaac Kook,
> early twentieth century rabbinic authority and thinker,
> first chief rabbi of Israel

You can't experience real joy in the dark. And darkness is the only place that addiction leads you, regardless of your chemical or compulsive behavior of choice. It may seem bright—even enjoyable—at first, but the artificial light of addiction will blind you, eventually leaving you in a darker place than you ever knew before. Left unchecked, without the benefit of recovery and renewal, addictions and compulsive behaviors prevent you from being able to see at all.

Rabbi Kook teaches us that, in *teshuvah*, we might regain that primordial light. It is *teshuvah* light which illumines the recesses of the soul and brings a beacon of hope into the dark places of our life. In this light, we are able to see ourselves once again. *Teshuvah* light pierces the darkness of addiction and compulsive behaviors, guiding us to the Source of all light.

For Growth and Renewal: Light up your life with *teshuvah.* Take a look deeply inside of yourself, in places where you had previously been unable (or afraid) to look.

> *Torah is not an empty thing for you.*
> *It is your life.*
>
> —Deuteronomy 32:47

This is explained by the rabbis in the Jerusalem Talmud (Ketubot 8:11) that if indeed Torah appears empty, it is because of you. Why? Because you have to work hard at Torah—to fill it up, so to speak. It can only be "your life" when you work hard at it. Sounds familiar, doesn't it? Don't we say similar things about working the program? Recovery and Torah do teach corollary wisdom. I guess good things in life don't just come at us from one place. We are surrounded by Torah insight. It just reaches out to us in different packages. Maybe if we keep listening to the message, we will eventually be able to *hear* it.

For those of us who don't live within the protective shelter of a distinctly Jewish community, the struggle to keep Torah ever present is our lives is a difficult one. Rest assured, you are not alone. Most of us face the same struggle. It is one of the many things that brings us together.

For Growth and Renewal: Do one thing today that adds Torah to your life. Then do something else, in addition, tomorrow. That's how you bring Torah into your life, one day at a time.

> *It's not your job to finish the work,*
> *but you are not free to walk away from it.*
>
> —*Pirke Avot* 2:16

So much to do to get back on the right track! Often it's paralyzing. We just don't know what to do, where to turn for help. We feel overwhelmed by the thought of it. We don't even know where or how to begin. As a result, we may not do anything. But we have to do something. Inaction leads us nowhere: we can't get anywhere if we are standing still. Or worse, it leaves us without control. And we learned that going the other way—through alcohol and drugs—got us worse than nowhere.

For Jews, *teshuvah*, the act of actually turning back to a life of the spirit, is a continual process, one that we work on throughout our entire lives. You are given the opportunity for a fresh start every day. Don't worry about how long it may take to get to the end of the road. We may never get there. The important thing is to find the road back, get on it, and stay on it. The joy is in the journey.

For Growth and Renewal: Identify what you do best—no matter how simple—and claim it as your own. It's your contribution to your recovery.

> *As a rose blooms with its heart turned upward,*
> *one should make* teshuvah *with one's heart*
> *turned toward heaven.*
>
> —Midrash Tehillim, 65

Teshuvah means a turning. It means an answer or response. And it means a return. *Teshuvah* is a turning of the personality, subtle but reorienting, not a radical refiguring of self but implying a friendliness to self, an acceptance of our limitations. Acceptance. This is who I am, the who I am requires only a turning to qualify as transformation. A turning toward God.

There is also the sense of *teshuvah* as response to the challenges of existence. What is our response to what life deals to us? We transform. We change. God hovers over us and demands, says the *midrash,* "Grow!" This is *our teshuvah, our* response: We grow. And *teshuvah* means a return, a coming home to who we rightfully are, our higher self. What we are required to do is to make space for the reality to arise, the wisdom and the good, the godliness that is already present, lurking within, in the non-local character of godliness which is shared by me and you and everyone.   —Rabbi James Stone Goodman

For Growth and Renewal: What opens that space for the real to rise? You begin by just showing up. Prayer and meditation, the Eleventh Step. Open that space inside and make room for the truth to arise.

Afterword

by Sir Jay M. Holder, D.C., M.D., Ph.D.
Founder/Medical Director
Exodus Treatment Center
Miami, Florida

The Jewish calendar is a blessing, as this inspirational and authentically Jewish book *100 Blessings* can readily attest. Its author has skillfully blended sound psychological insight with the spiritual resources of the Jewish calendar to provide an anchor in time for those who are adrift in this world, especially those in recovery from a chemical addiction or other compulsive behavior.

But as this volume masterfully demonstrates, the Jewish calendar, through its seasons and its holidays, provides all of us with a great deal of spiritual nourishment. As a blessing, the Jewish calendar provides us with a foundation on which to build a spiritual life that enriches the soul. Like recovery, the calendar provides us with the opportunity to move in a direction that fulfills the purpose of creation: Being here in the first place. Like the calendar, recovery is a process. Regardless of why you may be reading this book—whether Jew or non-Jew, addicted person or codependent other, or simply someone searching for more meaning in life—the Jewish calendar will move you forward, through the process of *teshuvah* (repentance), toward the repair of the soul. This is the unique genius of *teshuvah*, as seen through the lens of the calendar, as is felt so keenly in this sensitively written volume.

But why does the human soul need repair? How did it get broken in the first place? Each one of us has a spiritual component, as well as an animal component. Often difficult to keep separate, the spiritual component corresponds to what the rabbis call the *yetzer tov* (good inclination), and the animal component to the *yetzer hara* (evil inclination). Each of us has the inherent ability to make the separation, to access the spiritual and keep the animal at bay. This psychological notion is reflected in traditional Jewish thought, as well, and is often expressed in many traditional Jewish writings, most poignantly in the *Tanya*, a major Hasidic work. One of the best known teachers, Rabbi Nachman of Bratzlav, said it best: "If you believe you are capable of destruction, then believe you are capable of repair." In the human psyche, there is a constant battle between the animal and the spiritual. The spiritual is under constant attack by the animal within all of us. Addiction becomes our disease when the animal has overwhelmed the spiritual in us; as a result, we often hit bottom or come close to it. The resultant spiritual depravation is the hallmark of addiction and compulsive behaviors. When this happens, our choices are simple: Recovery or, as A.A. puts it, "jails, institutions or death."

In consultation with a therapist and a spiritual counselor, the Jewish calendar provides us with a therapeutic framework within which to work, to rebuild our lives, to grow, from the bottom up, so to speak. Reaching the bottom can motivate the addicted person positively by activating that person's free choice to make *teshuvah*. In traditional Jewish thinking, *teshuvah* begins by exercising one's free choice to not continue the acting out of that behavior, deed or thought which brought the negative behaviors (and their consequences) that motivated the *teshuvah* in the first place. Now that's Jewish psychology!

These concepts are only possible on a day-to-day basis, using the prism of the Jewish calendar. Jewish time is such that it relegates itself to calendar structure. Such structure governs the function of our lives. It gives us ultimate meaning and purpose which many of us sought through chemicals and compulsive behaviors—or simply by getting lost—but which none of us could find in these ways.

"Only today" and nothing more, allows the impossible to become possible. Guilt (often no more than anger turned inward), a "character defect" common to the chemically dependent, is a major stumbling block that halts recovery and provides the negative energy that makes relapse possible. However, guilt can be disposed of when one works at forgetting what has happened to oneself in the past, refuses to focus on the future, and deals with one's responsibilities of the day—marked on the Jewish calendar. For today, if one wants to embrace *teshuvah*, one has to feel that one is a totally new creation—born anew—each day! It is because of this notion that we say all of the blessings of the morning prayers each and every day, praising God again and again for everything God has given us today. In fact, God has given us this day.

For the many on the journey of recovery, the notion of God's presence in our lives may seem difficult to discover. Dr. Abraham Twerski, noted hasidic rabbi and psychiatrist, has suggested that "there is no person that does not believe in God; there are only those persons that think that they are God." In my own work at the Exodus Treatment Center, I have come to learn that one of the many "character defects" of those suffering from the disease of addiction is grandiosity. Yet, when a person humbles oneself or gives oneself over to a power that is greater than the self—as articulated in Step Three—that person begins to develop an ability to finally do something somebody else's way. From my perspective, this is the foundation of true spirituality and essential to recovery.

Traditional Torah, while it seems to be unlimited in its scope, can only be embraced in relation to time which is finite in nature, specifically a calendar. Therefore, Rabbi Olitzky's work is in keeping with such Torah tradition. If you will look only at today, you will realize that today you can deal with the worst of situations. What disturbs you the most, perhaps, is the fact that you remind yourself of what you dealt with yesterday or what you must deal with tomorrow. Therefore, do not look at your past or your future, look at only today. This will allow you to succeed. Today is the most beautiful blessing that the Creator bestows on a person.

According to a midrash, the day is like a large balloon. A person whose lungs are strong can easily blow it up and fill it completely. A person whose lungs are weak, who does not want to fill the balloon, will allow the balloon to remain small and empty. The same is true with today. The one who does not wish to fill the day will, in effect, constrict and shorten it. However, a person who wants to fill the day with good, will expand the day and cause it to be very precious.

Glossary of Important Words and Concepts

Adonai: God is known by various names in Jewish tradition. Adonai (literally "Lord") is used to refer to God since we do not know how to (and dare not) pronounce God's essential name.

cheshbon hanefesh: a probing inventory of the soul, taken by individuals throughout the year but most especially prior to the High Holy Days, corresponds to Steps Four and Ten

codependence: You may be a codependent person if you are in a relationship with an alcoholic or addicted person, someone who has an eating disorder, engages in compulsive gambling or sex, if you are addicted to a relationship or if you live in a dysfunctional family.

covenant: the agreement established some 3,200 years ago between God and the people of Israel at Sinai

Elul: the month prior to the High Holy Days (usually middle to late August to early to mid-September), which focuses on introspection, repentance, and renewal

emunah: faith, belief

kavannah: literally, the intention with which you do something; while technically the term is used to refer to all unfixed prayers, it also reflects those texts which when chanted repetitively prepare the individual for prayer

midbar: literally, "the desert;" a place of emotional emptiness

mishkan: the portable desert sanctuary

mitzvah (pl. mitzvot): divine commandments, holy instructions, given by God to the Jewish people. It also reflects the individual response to this Divine direction.

selichot: prayers of penitence, recited particularly prior to the High Holy Days

Shechinah: God's presence

shelemut (shalom): wholeness and completeness, serenity, epitomized by peace

teshuvah: literally, a turning toward God and to a righteous, religious way of life; in a broader sense, this represents returning and moving forward in recovery

tzedakah: generally translated as charity; from the Hebrew root for righteousness, perhaps "righteous giving"

yetzer hara: one's inner drives, the inclination to do evil

yetzer tov: the inner drive to do good

Yom Kippur: Day of Atonement; according to many the holiest day of the year, called the Sabbath of Sabbaths. More than any other time on the Jewish calendar, it epitomizes the focus on introspection, repentance, and personal renewal.

About the Authors

RABBI KERRY M. OLITZKY, D.H.L., is Director of the School of Education at Hebrew Union College-Jewish Institute of Religion in New York where he also directs its Doctor of Ministry Program. At the forefront of innovative religious education, he lectures widely on topics of chemical dependency and spiritual renewal.

Rabbi Olitzky is co-author of *Twelve Jewish Steps To Recovery: A Personal Guide To Turning From Alcoholism and Other Addictions* (Jewish Lights Publishing, 1991); *Renewed Each Day: Daily Twelve Step Recovery Meditations Based on the Bible* (Jewish Lights Publishing, 1992); and with Lawrence Kushner *Sparks Beneath the Surface: A Spiritual Commentary on the Torah* (Jason Aronson, 1993). He is also author of *Recovery from Codependence: A Jewish Twelve Steps Guide to Healing Your Soul* (Jewish Lights Publishing, 1993).

He is special issues editor on Aging and Judaism for the *Journal of Psychology and Judaism* and editor of *T'shuvah: Carrying the Message of Jewish Recovery* newsletter.

RABBI NEIL GILLMAN, Ph.D. is Associate Professor of Jewish Philosophy at The Jewish Theological Seminary of America. He is the author of *Sacred Fragments: Recovering Theology for the Modern Jew* (Jewish Publication Society of America, 1991) and *Conservative Judaism: The New Century* (Behrman House, 1993).

Rabbi James Stone Goodman is rabbi of Neve Shalom in St. Louis, Missouri and founder of S.L.I.C.H.A. (St. Louis Information Committee and Hotline on Addiction).

Sir Jay M. Holder, D.C., M.D., Ph.D. is Founder and Medical Director of the Exodus Treatment Center in Miami, Florida. Dr. Holder received the Albert Schweitzer Prize in Medicine in 1991 for his work in addiction.

Danny Siegel is an inspiring poet and writer who is also recognized for his creative *tzedakah* work in North America and in Israel. He is the author of books of poetry and inspirational essays, including the works *Where Heaven and Earth Touch* (Jason Aronson, 1989) and *The Lord is a Whisper at Midnight: Psalms and Prayers* (Town House Press, 1985). Danny Siegel is also the recipient of the 1993 Covenant Award for Exceptional Jewish Educators.

Rabbi Gordon Tucker is Assistant Professor of Jewish Philosophy at The Jewish Theological Seminary of America where he formerly served as dean of its rabbinical school.

About the Illustrations

Artist Maty Grünberg's illustrations of the gates of the Old City of Jerusalem open each chapter of *100 Blessings Every Day* as the reader is welcomed into another Jewish Twelve Steps experience. They were selected to emphasize the relationship between heavenly and earthly in all our lives through the prism of Jerusalem.

About JEWISH LIGHTS Publishing

People of all faiths and backgrounds yearn for books that attract, engage, educate and spiritually inspire.

Our principal goal is to stimulate thought and help all people learn about who the Jewish People are, where they come from, and what the future can be made to hold. While people of our diverse Jewish heritage are the primary audience, our books speak to the Christian world as well and will broaden their understanding of Judaism and the roots of their own faith.

We bring to you authors who are at the forefront of spiritual thought and experience. While each has something different to say, they all say it in a voice that you can hear.

Our books are designed to welcome you and then to engage, stimulate and inspire. We judge our success not only by whether or not our books are beautiful and commercially successful, but by whether or not they make a difference in your life.

We at Jewish Lights take great care to produce beautiful books that present meaningful spiritual content in a form that reflects the art of making high quality books. Therefore, we want to acknowledge those who contributed to the production of this book.

TEXT DESIGN AND PRODUCTION
Rachel Kahn

PROOFREADING
Sandra Korinchak

ART
Maty Grünberg, London & Jerusalem

TYPE
Set in Sabon, Optima and Mistral
Chelsea Dippel, Woodstock, Vermont

COVER PRINTING
New England Book Components

PRINTING AND BINDING
Book Press, Brattleboro, Vermont

The JEWISH LIGHTS TWELVE STEP RECOVERY SERIES

TWELVE JEWISH STEPS TO RECOVERY

A Personal Guide To Turning From Alcoholism & Other Addictions....Drugs, Food, Gambling, Sex

by *Rabbi Kerry M. Olitzky & Stuart A. Copans*, M.D.
Preface by *Abraham J. Twerski*, M.D.
Introduction by *Rabbi Sheldon Zimmerman*
Illustrations by *Maty Grünberg*
"Getting Help" by *JACS Foundation*

A Jewish perspective on the Twelve Steps of addiction recovery programs with consolation, inspiration and motivation for recovery. It draws from traditional sources, and quotes from what recovering Jewish people say about their experiences with addictions of all kinds. Inspiring illustrations of the twelve gates of the Old City of Jerusalem.

This book is not just for Jewish people. It's for all people who would gain strength to heal and insight from Jewish tradition.

- All people who are in trouble with alcohol and drugs and other addictions — food, gambling, sex
- Anyone seeking an understanding of the Twelve Steps from a Jewish perspective — regardless of religious background or affiliation
- Alcoholics and addicts in recovery
- Codependents
- Adult children of alcoholics
- Specialists in recovery and treatment

Experts Praise *Twelve Jewish Steps To Recovery*

"Recommended reading for people of all denominations."
— Rabbi Abraham J. Twerski, M.D.

"I read *Twelve Jewish Steps* with the eyes of a Christian and came away renewed in my heart. I felt like I had visited my Jewish roots. These authors have deep knowledge of recovery as viewed by Alcoholics Anonymous."
— Rock J. Stack, M.A., L.L.D.
Manager of Clinical/Pastoral Education,
Hazelden Foundation

6" x 9", 136 pp. Quality Paperback, ISBN 1-879045-09-5 **$12.95**

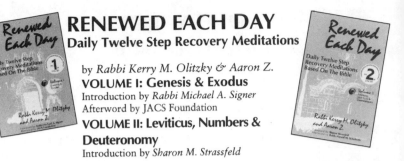

RENEWED EACH DAY
Daily Twelve Step Recovery Meditations

by *Rabbi Kerry M. Olitzky & Aaron Z.*
VOLUME I: Genesis & Exodus
Introduction by *Rabbi Michael A. Signer*
Afterword by JACS Foundation
VOLUME II: Leviticus, Numbers & Deuteronomy
Introduction by *Sharon M. Strassfeld*

Using a seven day/weekly guide format, a recovering person and a spiritual leader who is reaching out to addicted people reflect on the traditional weekly Bible reading. They bring strong spiritual support for daily living and recovery from addictions of all kinds: alcohol, drugs, eating, gambling and sex. A profound sense of the religious spirit soars through their words and brings all people in Twelve Step recovery programs home to a rich and spiritually enlightening tradition.

"Meets a vital need; it offers a chance for people turning from alcoholism and addiction to renew their spirits and draw upon the Jewish tradition to guide and enrich their lives."

> —Rabbi Irving (Yitz) Greenberg, President, CLAL,
> The National Jewish Center for Learning and Leadership

"Will benefit anyone familiar with a 'religion of the Book.' Jews, Christians, Muslims. . . ."

> —Ernest Kurtz, *author of* Not-God: A History of Alcoholics
> Anonymous & The Spirituality of Imperfection

"An enduring impact upon the faith community as it seeks to blend the wisdom of the ages represented in the tradition with the twelve steps to recovery and wholeness."

> —Robert H. Albers, Ph.D., Editor, Journal of Ministry in
> Addiction & Recovery

Beautiful Two-Volume Set
6"x 9", V. I, 224 pp. / V. II, 280 pp., Quality Paperback
ISBN 1-879045-21-4   **$27.90**

RECOVERY FROM CODEPENDENCE

by *Rabbi Kerry M. Olitzky*
Foreword by *Marc Galanter, M.D., Director,*
Division of Alcoholism & Drug Abuse, NYU Medical Center
Afterword by *Harriet Rosetto, Director,*
Gateways Beit T'shuvah

For the estimated 90% of America struggling with the addiction of a family member or loved one, or involved in a dysfunctional family or relationship. A follow-up to the ground-breaking *Twelve Jewish Steps to Recovery.*

"The disease of chemical dependency is also a family illness. Rabbi Olitzky offers spiritual hope and support." —*Jerry Spicer, President, Hazelden*

"Another major step forward in finding the sources and resources of healing, both physical and spiritual, in our tradition." —*Rabbi Sheldon Zimmerman, Temple Emanu-El, Dallas, TX; President, CCAR*

6" x 9", 160 pp. Hardcover, ISBN 1-879045-27-3 **$21.95**
6" x 9", 160 pp. Quality Paperback, ISBN 1-879045-32-X **$13.95**

CELEBRATE THE BEAUTY OF RECOVERY WITH THESE INSPIRING VISUAL REMINDERS OF COMMITMENT TO RECOVERY

THE JERUSALEM GATES PORTFOLIO

Any 3 Prints — $25
— Or Save 50% on the complete set of all 12
beautiful, frameable prints — Only $4.16 each

Illustrations from **Twelve Jewish Steps To Recovery**

Artist Maty Grünberg's striking illustrations of the gates of the Old City of Jerusalem emphasize the relationship between the heavenly and the earthly in all of our lives through the prism of this city, holy to people of all faiths.

• Beautiful 9"x 12" reproductions of twelve original pen and ink drawings by celebrated Israeli artist, Maty Grünberg. Commissioned by the publisher specially for *Twelve Jewish Steps To Recovery.*
• Printed on fine quality acid-free paper.
• Enhanced with key inspiration word printed in a second color.
• Presented as a portfolio of twelve separate prints, each suitable for framing

THE JERUSALEM GATES PORTFOLIO

1   Honesty

2   Hope

3   Faith

4   Courage

5   Integrity

6   Willingness

7   Humility

8   Love

9   Discipline

10   Perseverence

11   Illumination

12   Service

Any 3 Prints — $25.   All 12 Prints Only $49.95

100 Blessings Every Day

Daily Twelve Step Recovery Affirmations & Exercises for Personal Growth & Renewal Reflecting Seasons of the Jewish Year

Rabbi Kerry M. Olitzky

Foreword: Are The Twelve Steps Jewish?

Afterword: Spiritual Renewal in the Jewish Calendar

100 BLESSINGS EVERY DAY

Daily Twelve Step Recovery Affirmations & Exercises for Personal Growth & Renewal Reflecting Seasons of the Jewish Year

by Rabbi Kerry M. Olitzky

Foreword by Rabbi Neil Gillman, The Jewish Theological Society

Afterword by Sir Jay M. Holder, D.C., M.D., Ph.D.

Using a one-day-at-a-time monthly format, a spiritual leader who continues to reach out to addicted people, and all those seeking spiritual renewal, reflects on the rhythm of the Jewish calendar with recovering people and other teachers. Together they bring insight and experience to recovery from addictions and compulsive behaviors of all kinds. This sensitive volume soars with the spirit of the Jewish soul and the Jewish year. Its "exercises" help us move from *thinking* to *doing*.

"The quotations are extremely powerful and the commentary meaningful. It is one of the most moving documents I have ever read."

> —*Dr. David Ellenson, Professor of Religious Thought, Hebrew Union College–Jewish Institute of Religion*

4 1/2" x 6 1/2", 432 pp., Quality paperback
ISBN 1-879045-30-3 **$14.95**

Spiritual Inspiration for Family Life

GOD'S PAINTBRUSH by *Sandy Eisenberg Sasso*

Full color illustrations by *Annette Compton*

Multicultural, non-sectarian, non-denominational. Invites children of all faiths and backgrounds to encounter God openly in their own lives. Wonderfully interactive, provides questions adult and child can explore together at the end of each episode.

"The most exciting religious children's book I have seen in years."
—*Sylvia Avner, Children's Librarian, 92nd St. "Y," NYC*

"An excellent way to honor the imaginative breadth and depth of the spiritual life of the young."
—*Dr. Robert Coles, Harvard University*
For children K– 4 elementary

11"x 8½", 32 pp. Hardcover, Full color illustrations, ISBN 1-879045-22-2 **$15.95**

THE *NEW* JEWISH BABY BOOK A Guide For Today's Families

by *Anita Diamant*

A complete guide to the customs and rituals for welcoming a new child to the world and into the Jewish community, and for commemorating this joyous event in family life–whatever your family constellation. Updated, revised and expanded edition of the highly acclaimed *The Jewish Baby Book*. Includes new ceremonies for girls, celebrations in interfaith families. Also contains a unique directory of names that reflects the rich diversity of the Jewish experience.

6"x 9", 272 pp. Quality Paperback, ISBN 1-879045-28-1 **$15.95**

MOURNING *&* MITZVAH A Guided Journal for Walking the Mourner's Path Through Grief to Healing by *Anne Brener, L.C.S.W.*

"Fully engaging in mourning means you will be a different person than before you began."

For those who mourn a death, for those who would help them, for those who face a loss of any kind, Anne Brener teaches us the power and strength available to us in the fully experienced mourning process. Over 60 guided writing exercises help stimulate the processes of both conscious and unconscious healing.

"A stunning book! It offers an exploration in depth of the place where psychology and religious ritual intersect, and the name of that place is Truth."
—*Rabbi Harold Kushner, author of When Bad Things Happen to Good People*

"This book is marvelous. It is a work that I wish I had written. It is the best book on this subject that I have ever seen." —*Rabbi Levi Meier, Ph.D., Chaplain, Cedars Sinai Medical Center, Los Angeles, Orthodox Rabbi, Clinical Psychologist*

7 ½" x 9", 272 pp. Quality Paperback, ISBN 1-879045-23-0 **$19.95**

The Kushner Series by *Lawrence Kushner* . . .

GOD WAS IN THIS PLACE & I, i DID NOT KNOW
Finding Self, Spirituality & Ultimate Meaning

Who am I? Who is God? Kushner creates inspiring interpretations of Jacob's dream in Genesis, opening a window into Jewish spirituality for people of all faiths and backgrounds.

In a fascinating blend of scholarship, imagination, psychology and history, seven Jewish spiritual masters ask and answer fundamental questions of human experience.

"A brilliant fabric of classic rabbinic interpretations, Hasidic insights and literary criticism which warms us and sustains us."

—Dr. Norman J. Cohen, Dean, Hebrew Union College, NY

"Rich and intriguing." —M. Scott Peck, M.D., author of *The Road Less Traveled*

6"x 9", 192 pp. Hardcover, ISBN 1-879045-05-2 **$21.95**

6"x 9", 192 pp. Quality Paperback, ISBN 1-879045-33-8 **$16.95**

HONEY FROM THE ROCK
An Easy Introduction to Jewish Mysticism

An introduction to the ten gates of Jewish mysticism and how it applies to daily life.

"Quite simply the easiest introduction to Jewish mysticism you can read."

"Honey from the Rock captures the flavor and spark of Jewish mysticism. . . . Read it and be rewarded." —Elie Wiesel

"A work of love, lyrical beauty, and prophetic insight. "

—Father Malcolm Boyd, *The Christian Century*

6"x 9", 168 pp. Quality Paperback, ISBN 1-879045-02-8 **$14.95**

THE RIVER OF LIGHT Spirituality, Judaism, Consciousness

A "manual" for all spiritual travelers who would attempt a spiritual journey in our times. Taking us step by step, Kushner allows us to discover the meaning of our own quest: "to allow the river of light—the deepest currents of consciousness—to rise to the surface and animate our lives."

"Philosophy and mystical fantasy...exhilarating speculative flights launched from the Bible....Anybody—Jewish, Christian, or otherwise...will find this book an intriguing experience."—*The Kirkus Reviews*

"A very important book."—Rabbi Adin Steinsaltz

6"x 9", 180 pp. Quality Paperback, ISBN 1-879045-03-6 **$14.95**

... Spiritual Inspiration for Daily Living

THE BOOK OF WORDS
Talking Spiritual Life, Living Spiritual Talk

In the incomparable manner of his extraordinary *The Book of Letters: A Mystical Hebrew Alphabet*, Kushner now lifts up and shakes the dust off primary religious words we use to describe the spiritual dimension of life. The *Words* take on renewed spiritual significance, adding power and focus to the lives we live every day.

For each word Kushner offers us a startling, moving and insightful explication, and pointed readings from classical Jewish sources that further illuminate the concept. He concludes with a short exercise that helps unite the spirit of the word with our actions in the world.

6"x 9", 176 pp. Hardcover, two-color text ISBN 1-879045-35-4 **$21.95**

THE BOOK OF LETTERS
A Mystical Hebrew Alphabet

In calligraphy by the author. Folktales about and exploration of the mystical meanings of the Hebrew Alphabet. Open the old prayerbook-like pages of *The Book of Letters* and you will enter a special world of sacred tradition and religious feeling. More than just symbols, all twenty-two letters of the Hebrew alphabet overflow with meanings and personalities of their own.

Rabbi Kushner draws from ancient Judaic sources, weaving Talmudic commentary, Hasidic folktales, and Kabbalistic mysteries around the letters.

"A book which is in love with Jewish letters." — Isaac Bashevis Singer

• Popular Hardcover Edition
6"x 9", 80 pp. Hardcover, two colors, inspiring new Foreword.
ISBN 1-879045-00-1 **$24.95**

• Deluxe Gift Edition
9"x 12", 80 pp. Hardcover, four-color text, ornamentation, in a beautiful slipcase.
ISBN 1-879045-01-X **$79.95**

• Collector's Limited Edition
9"x 12", 80 pp. Hardcover, gold embossed pages, hand assembled slipcase. With silkscreened print.

Limited to 500 signed and numbered copies.

ISBN 1-879045-04-4 **$349.00**

JEWISH LIGHTS Classic Reprints 🔥

TORMENTED MASTER The Life and Spiritual Quest of Rabbi Nahman of Bratslav by *Arthur Green*

Explores the personality and religious quest of Nahman of Bratslav (1772–1810), one of Hasidism's major figures. It unlocks the great themes of spiritual searching that make him a figure of universal religious importance.

"A model of clarity and percipience....Utterly relevant to our time."
—*New York Times Book Review*

6"x 9", 408 pp. Quality Paperback, ISBN 1-879045-11-7 **$17.95**

THE LAST TRIAL On the Legends and Lore of the Command to Abraham to Offer Isaac as a Sacrifice — The Akedah by *Shalom Spiegel*

New Introduction by *Judah Goldin, Emeritus Professor, University of Pennsylvania*

A classic. An eminent Jewish scholar examines the total body of texts, legends, and traditions referring to the Binding of Isaac and weaves them all together into a definitive study of the *Akedah* as one of the central events in all of human history.

"A model in the history of biblical interpretation, and a centerpiece for Jewish-Christian discussion."—*Dr. Michael Fishbane, Nathan Cummings Professor of Jewish Studies, University of Chicago*

6"x 9", 208 pp. Quality Paperback, ISBN 1-879045-29-X **$17.95**

ASPECTS OF RABBINIC THEOLOGY by *Solomon Schechter*

Including the original Preface from the 1909 edition & *Louis Finkelstein's* Introduction to the 1961 edition with an important new Introduction by *Dr. Neil Gillman, Chair, Department of Jewish Philosophy, JTS*

Learned yet highly accessible classic statement of the ideas that form the religious consciousness of the Jewish people at large, by one of the great minds of Jewish scholarship of our century.

"This is the only book on the theology of Judaism written 100 years ago that anyone can read today with profit." — *Jacob Neusner, Distinguished Research Professor of Religious Studies, University of South Florida*

6" x 9", 440 pp., Quality Paperback, ISBN 1-879045-24-9 **$18.95**

YOUR WORD IS FIRE The Hasidic Masters on Contemplative Prayer

Edited and translated with a new Introduction by *Arthur Green* and *Barry W. Holtz*

The power of prayer for spiritual renewal and personal transformation is at the core of all religious traditions. From the teachings of the Hasidic Masters the editors have gleaned "hints as to the various rungs of inner prayer and how they are attained." These parables and aphorisms of the Hasidic masters pierce to the heart of the modern reader's search for God.

6"x 9", 160 pp. Quality Paperback, ISBN 1-879045-25-7 **$14.95**

Add Greater Understanding to Your Life

THE SPIRIT OF RENEWAL Crisis & Response in Jewish Life by *Edward Feld*

"Boldly redefines the landscape of Jewish religious thought after the Holocaust."
— Rabbi Lawrence Kushner

Trying to understand the Holocaust and addressing the question of faith after the Holocaust, Rabbi Feld explores three key cycles of destruction and recovery in Jewish history, each of which radically reshaped Jewish understanding of God, people, and the world.

"Undoubtedly the most moving book I have read....'Must' reading."
— Rabbi Howard A. Addison, *Conservative Judaism*

"...a profound meditation on Jewish history [and the Holocaust]....Christians, as well as many others, need to share in this story." —The Rt. Rev. Frederick H. Borsch, Ph.D., Episcopal Bishop of L.A.

6"x 9", 216 pp. Hardcover, ISBN 1-879045-06-0 **$22.95**

SEEKING THE PATH TO LIFE Theological Meditations On God and the Nature of People, Love, Life and Death by *Rabbi Ira F. Stone*

For people who never thought they would read a book of theology—let alone understand it, enjoy it, savor it and have it affect the way they think about their lives.

In 45 intense meditations, each a page or two in length, Stone takes us on explorations of the most basic human struggles: life and death, love and anger, peace and war, covenant and exile.

"Exhilarating—unlike any other reading that I have done in years."
—Rabbi Neil Gillman, The Jewish Theological Seminary

"A bold book....The reader of any faith will be inspired, challenged and led more deeply into their own encounter with God."
— The Rev. Carla Berkedal, Episcopal Priest, Executive Director of Earth Ministry

6"x 9", 144 pp. Hardcover, ISBN 1-879045 17-6 **$19.95**

SO THAT YOUR VALUES LIVE ON Ethical Wills & How To Prepare Them Edited by *Rabbi Jack Riemer & Professor Nathaniel Stampfer*

A cherished Jewish tradition, ethical wills, parents writing to children or grandparents to grandchildren, sum up what people have learned and express what they want most for, and from, their loved ones. Includes an intensive guide, "How to Write Your Own Ethical Will," and a topical index. A marvelous treasury of wills: Herzl, Sholom Aleichem, Israelis, Holocaust victims, contemporary American Jews.

6"x 9", 272 pp. Hardcover, ISBN 1-879045-07-9 **$23.95**

6"x 9", 272 pp. Quality Paperback, ISBN 1-879045-34-6 **$16.95**

Order Information

$ Amount

• Motivation & Inspiration for Recovery •

_____ One Hundred Blessings, (pb) $14.95
_____ Recovery From Codependence, (hc) $21.95; (pb) $13.95   _____
_____ Renewed Each Day, 2-Volume Set, (pb) $27.90   _____
_____ Twelve Jewish Steps To Recovery, (pb) $12.95   _____
_____ The Jerusalem Gates Portfolio (all 12 prints), $49.95 *50% SAVINGS*   _____
_____ The Jerusalem Gates Portfolio, Any 3 prints $25.00   _____
         List numbers here: _____ _____ _____

• The Kushner Series •

The Book of Letters
_____ • Popular Hardcover Edition, $24.95*   _____
_____ • Deluxe Presentation Edition w/ slipcase, $79.95, *plus* $5.95 s/h   _____
_____ • Collector's Limited Edition, $349.00, *plus* $12.95 s/h   _____
_____ The Book of Words, (hc) $21.95*   _____
_____ God Was In This Place And I, i Did Not Know, (hc) $21.95; (pb) $16.95*   _____
_____ Honey From The Rock, (pb) $14.95*   _____
_____ The River Of Light, (pb) $14.95*   _____
_____ The Kushner Series - All 5 Books - *marked with an asterisk above*- $93.75   _____

• Other Inspiring Books •

_____ Aspects Of Rabbinic Theology, (pb) $18.95   _____
_____ God's Paintbrush, (hc) $15.95   _____
_____ The Last Trial, (pb) $17.95   _____
_____ Mourning & Mitzvah, (pb) $19.95   _____
_____ The *NEW* Jewish Baby Book (pb) $15.95   _____
_____ Putting God On The Guest List, (hc) $21.95; (pb) $14.95   _____
_____ Seeking The Path To Life, (hc) $19.95   _____
_____ So That Your Values Live On, (hc) $23.95; (pb) $16.95   _____
_____ Spirit Of Renewal, (hc) $22.95   _____
_____ Tormented Master, (pb) $17.95   _____
_____ Your Word Is Fire, (pb) $14.95   _____

For s/h, add $2.95 for the first book, $1 each for each add'l book.   _____

                                              Total $ _____

Check enclosed for $ _____ *payable to:* JEWISH LIGHTS Publishing
Charge my credit card: ❏ MasterCard   ❏ Visa   ❏ Discover   ❏ AMEX
Credit Card # _____ | Expires _____
Name _____ | Phone (___) _____
Street _____ | Name on card _____
City / State / Zip _____ | Signature _____

Phone, fax, or mail to: JEWISH LIGHTS Publishing
Box 237, Sunset Farm Offices, Route 4, Woodstock, Vermont 05091
Tel (802) 457-4000   *Fax* (802) 457-4004
Toll free credit card orders (800) 962-4544 (9AM–5PM EST Monday–Friday)
Generous discounts on quantity orders. SATISFACTION GUARANTEED. Prices subject to change.
AVAILABLE FROM BETTER BOOKSTORES. TRY YOUR BOOKSTORE FIRST.